Spoof on Titan

1

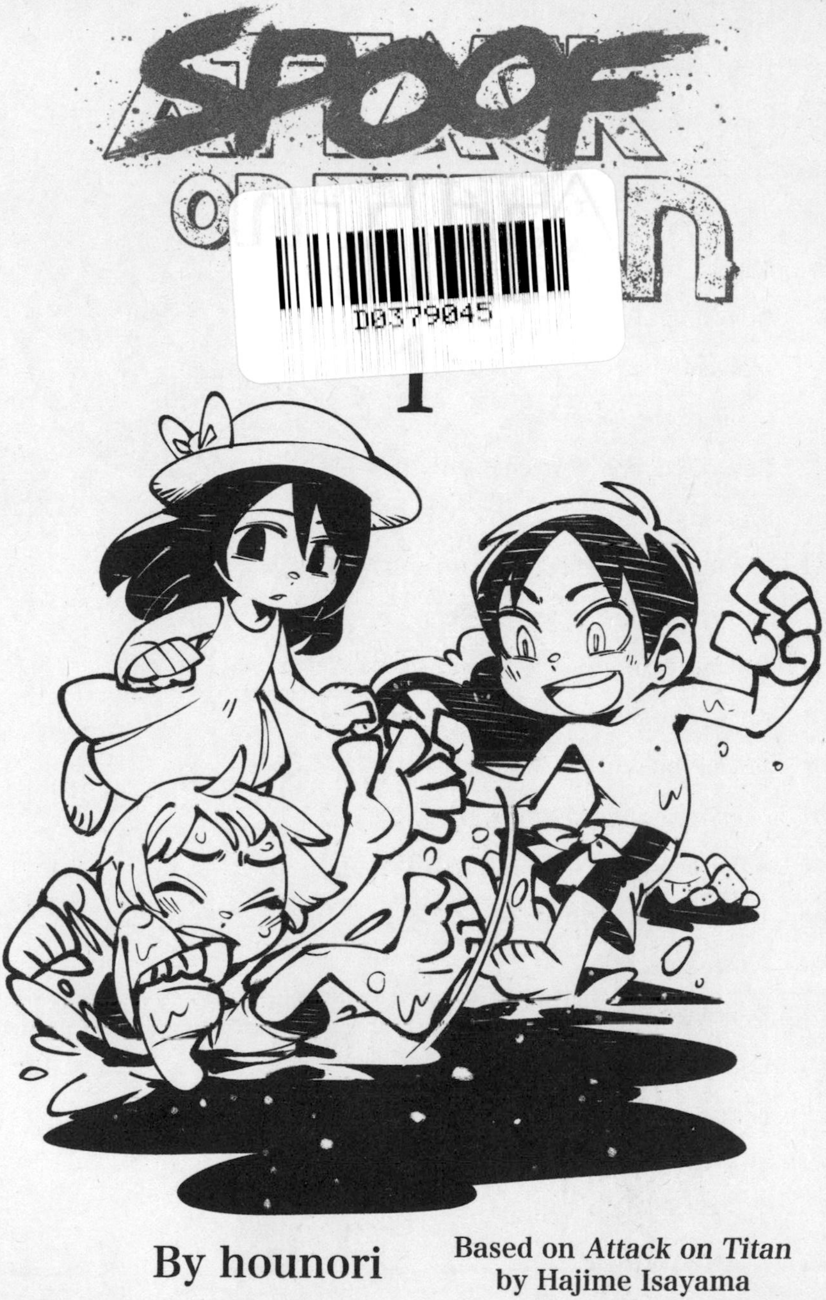

By hounori

Based on *Attack on Titan*
by Hajime Isayama

CONTENTS

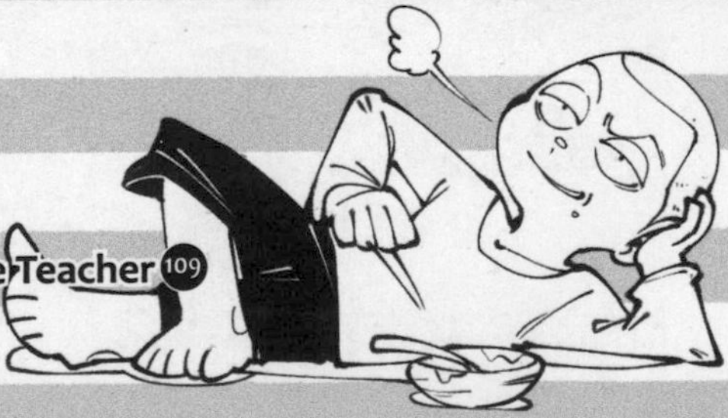

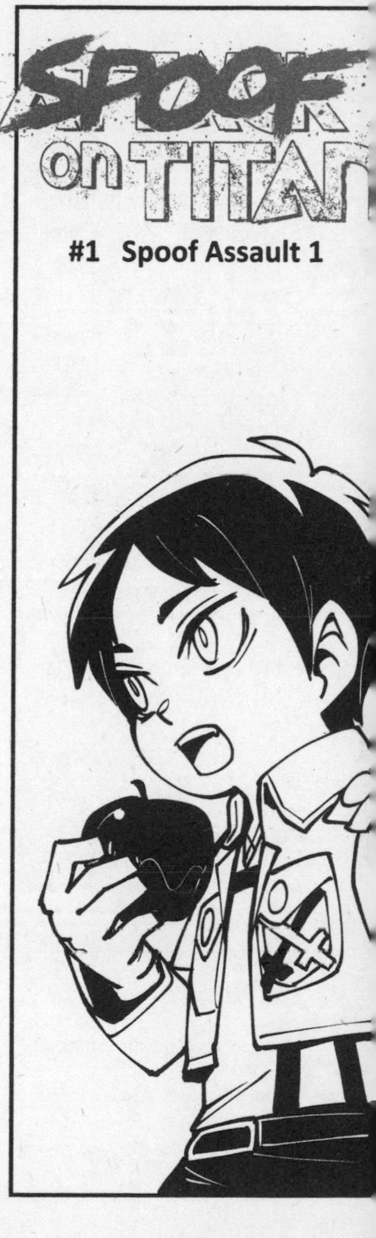
SPOOF on TITAN
#1 Spoof Assault 1

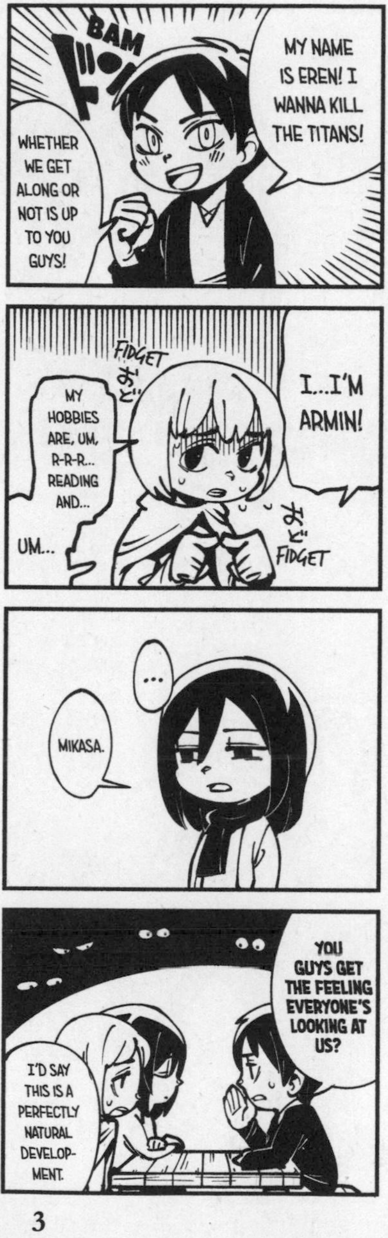
MY NAME IS EREN! I WANNA KILL THE TITANS!
BAM
WHETHER WE GET ALONG OR NOT IS UP TO YOU GUYS!
I...I'M ARMIN!
FIDGET おど
MY HOBBIES ARE, UM, R-R-R... READING AND...
おど FIDGET
UM...
...
MIKASA.
YOU GUYS GET THE FEELING EVERYONE'S LOOKING AT US?
I'D SAY THIS IS A PERFECTLY NATURAL DEVELOPMENT.

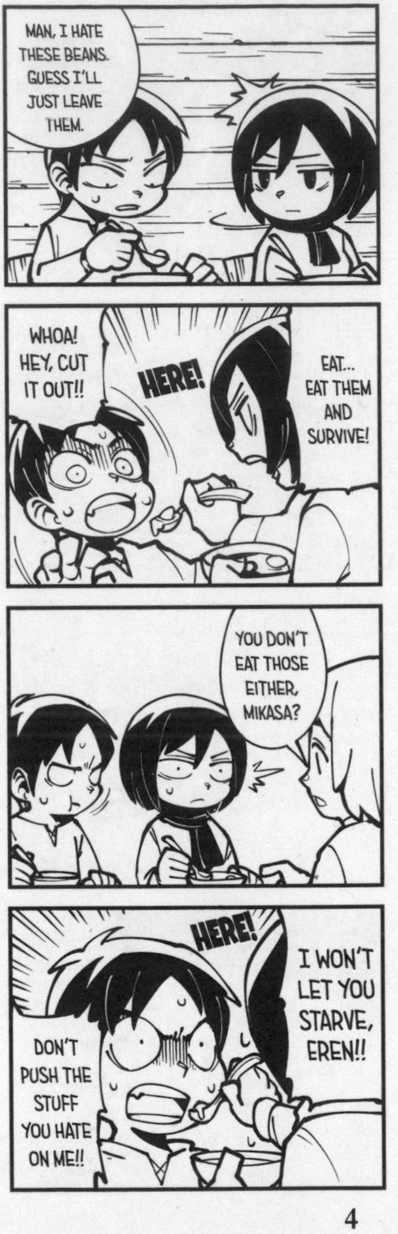
MAN, I HATE THESE BEANS. GUESS I'LL JUST LEAVE THEM.
EAT... EAT THEM AND SURVIVE!
HERE!
WHOA! HEY, CUT IT OUT!!
YOU DON'T EAT THOSE EITHER, MIKASA?
I WON'T LET YOU STARVE, EREN!!
HERE!
DON'T PUSH THE STUFF YOU HATE ON ME!!

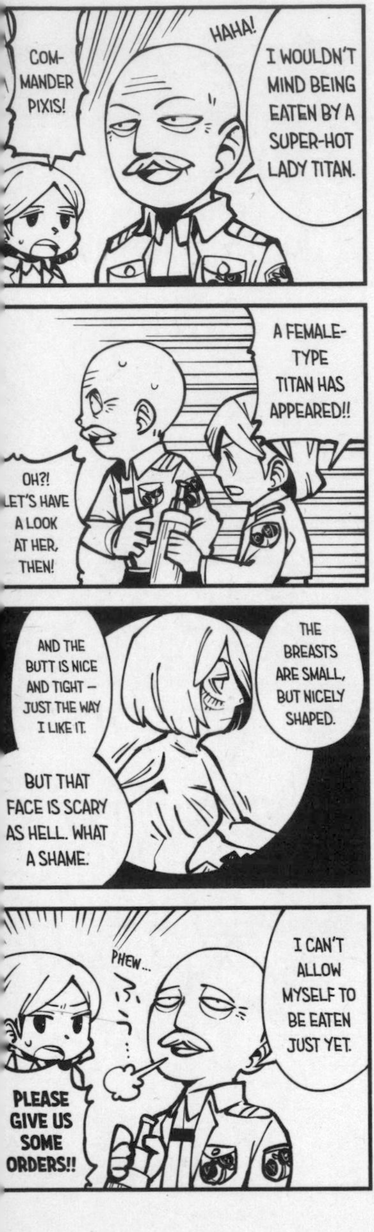
I WOULDN'T MIND BEING EATEN BY A SUPER-HOT LADY TITAN.
HAHA!
COM-MANDER PIXIS!
A FEMALE-TYPE TITAN HAS APPEARED!!
OH?! LET'S HAVE A LOOK AT HER, THEN!
THE BREASTS ARE SMALL, BUT NICELY SHAPED.
AND THE BUTT IS NICE AND TIGHT — JUST THE WAY I LIKE IT.
BUT THAT FACE IS SCARY AS HELL. WHAT A SHAME.
I CAN'T ALLOW MYSELF TO BE EATEN JUST YET.
PHEW...
PLEASE GIVE US SOME ORDERS!!

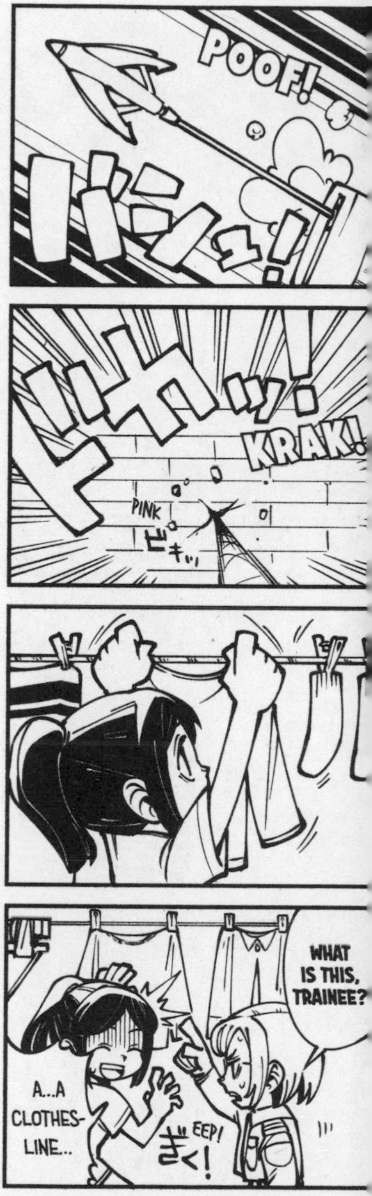
POOF!
KRAK!
PINK
WHAT IS THIS, TRAINEE?
A...A CLOTHES-LINE...
EEP!
ぎく!

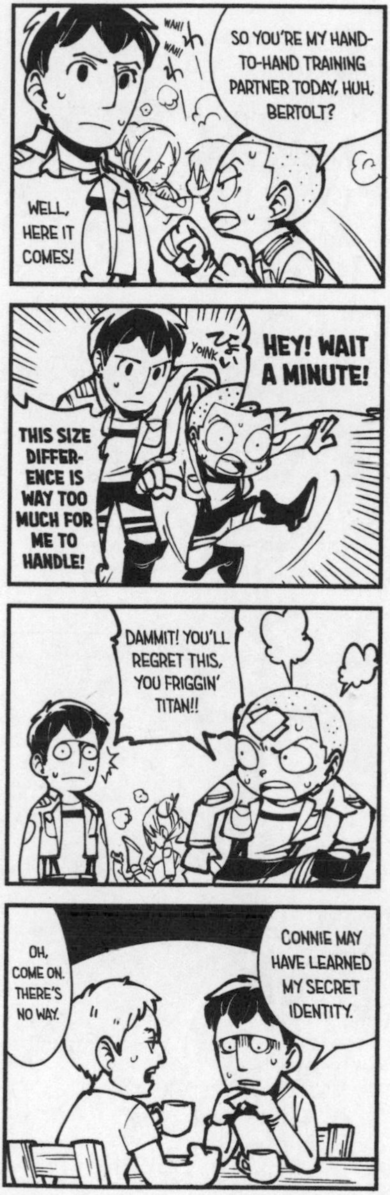
SO YOU'RE MY HAND-TO-HAND TRAINING PARTNER TODAY, HUH, BERTOLT?
WAH! WAH!
WELL, HERE IT COMES!
HEY! WAIT A MINUTE!
YOINK
THIS SIZE DIFFERENCE IS WAY TOO MUCH FOR ME TO HANDLE!
DAMMIT! YOU'LL REGRET THIS, YOU FRIGGIN' TITAN!!
CONNIE MAY HAVE LEARNED MY SECRET IDENTITY.
OH, COME ON. THERE'S NO WAY.

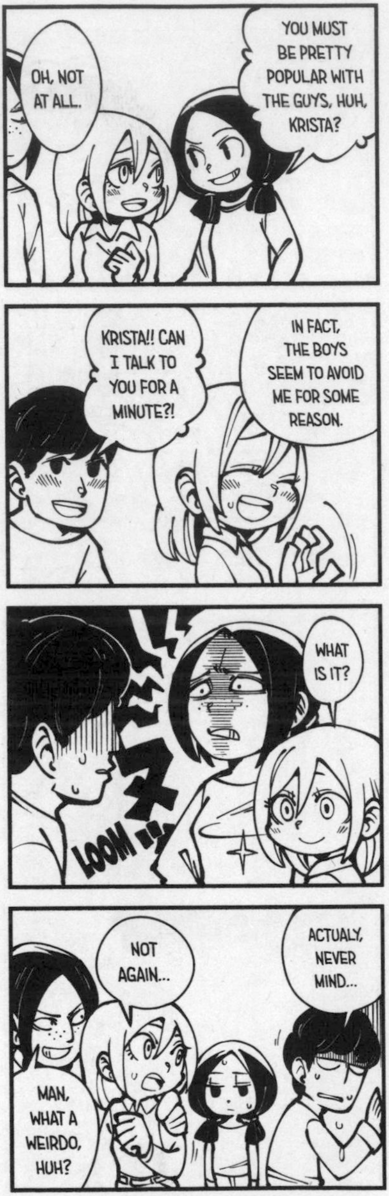
YOU MUST BE PRETTY POPULAR WITH THE GUYS, HUH, KRISTA?
OH, NOT AT ALL.
IN FACT, THE BOYS SEEM TO AVOID ME FOR SOME REASON.
KRISTA!! CAN I TALK TO YOU FOR A MINUTE?!
WHAT IS IT?
LOOM
ACTUALY, NEVER MIND...
NOT AGAIN...
MAN, WHAT A WEIRDO, HUH?

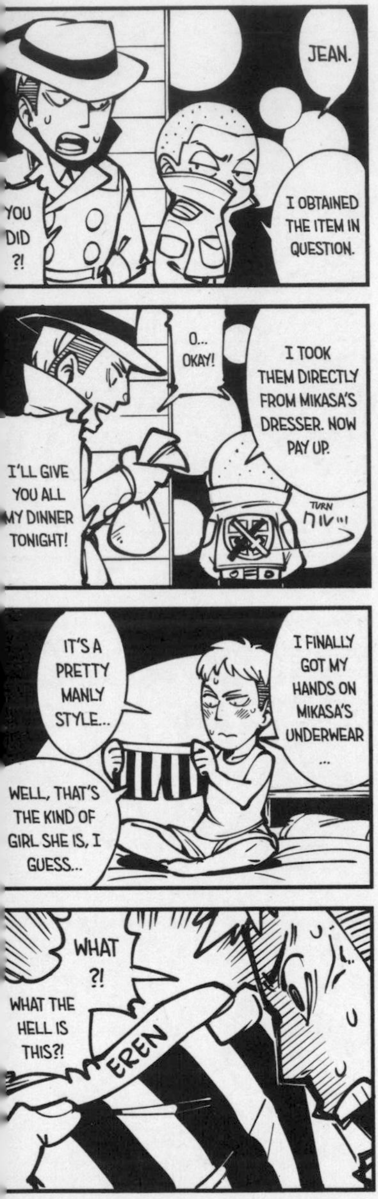
JEAN.
I OBTAINED THE ITEM IN QUESTION.
YOU DID ?!
I TOOK THEM DIRECTLY FROM MIKASA'S DRESSER. NOW PAY UP.
O... OKAY!
TURN
I'LL GIVE YOU ALL MY DINNER TONIGHT!
I FINALLY GOT MY HANDS ON MIKASA'S UNDERWEAR ...
IT'S A PRETTY MANLY STYLE...
WELL, THAT'S THE KIND OF GIRL SHE IS, I GUESS...
WHAT ?!
WHAT THE HELL IS THIS?!
EREN

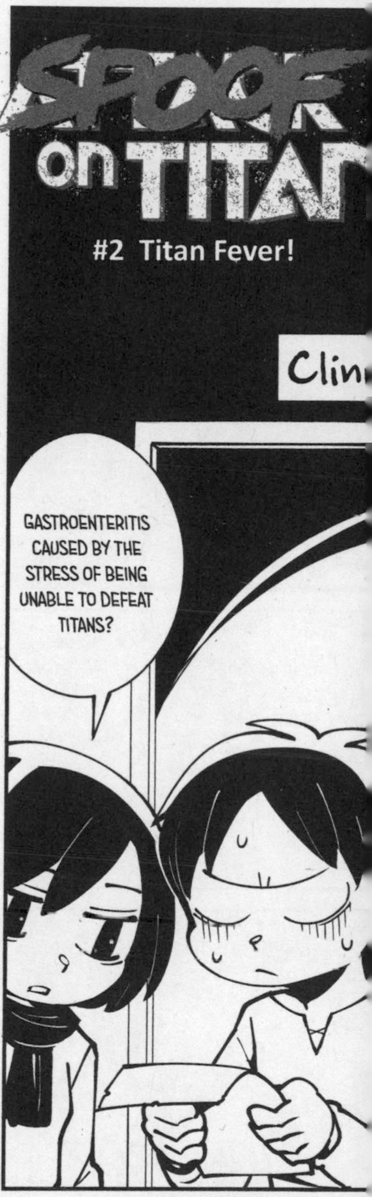
#2 Titan Fever!
GASTROENTERITIS CAUSED BY THE STRESS OF BEING UNABLE TO DEFEAT TITANS?

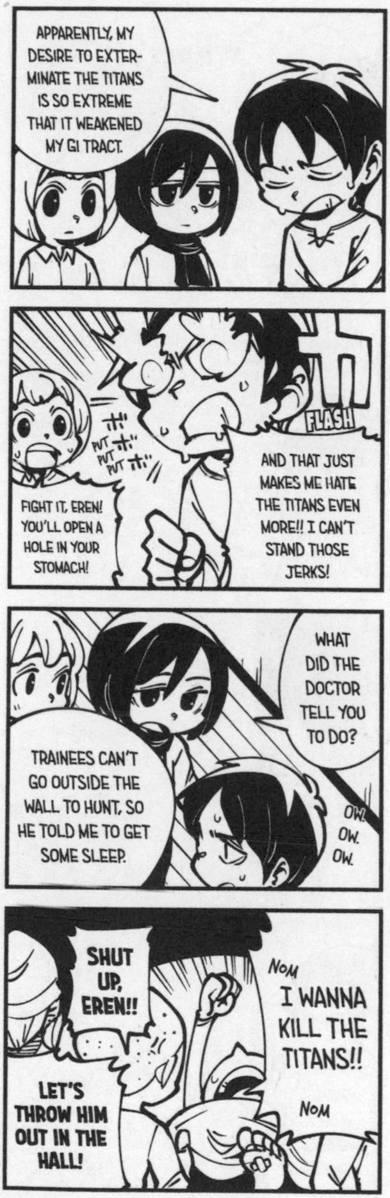
APPARENTLY, MY DESIRE TO EXTER-MINATE THE TITANS IS SO EXTREME THAT IT WEAKENED MY GI TRACT.
FLASH
AND THAT JUST MAKES ME HATE THE TITANS EVEN MORE!! I CAN'T STAND THOSE JERKS!
ボ PUT ボ PUT ボ PUT ボ
FIGHT IT, EREN! YOU'LL OPEN A HOLE IN YOUR STOMACH!
WHAT DID THE DOCTOR TELL YOU TO DO?
OW. OW. OW.
TRAINEES CAN'T GO OUTSIDE THE WALL TO HUNT, SO HE TOLD ME TO GET SOME SLEEP.
NOM
I WANNA KILL THE TITANS!!
NOM
SHUT UP, EREN!!
LET'S THROW HIM OUT IN THE HALL!

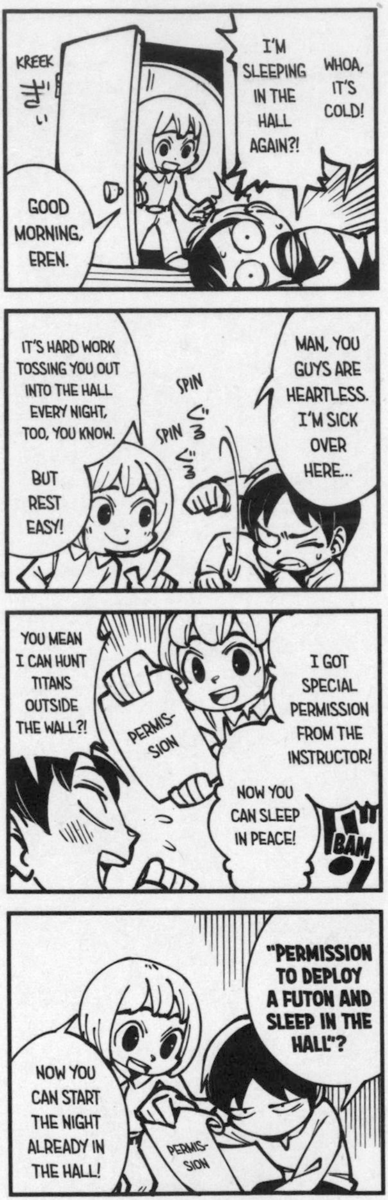
WHOA, IT'S COLD!
I'M SLEEPING IN THE HALL AGAIN?!
KREEK ぎい
GOOD MORNING, EREN.
MAN, YOU GUYS ARE HEARTLESS. I'M SICK OVER HERE...
SPIN ぐる SPIN ぐる
IT'S HARD WORK TOSSING YOU OUT INTO THE HALL EVERY NIGHT, TOO, YOU KNOW.
BUT REST EASY!
I GOT SPECIAL PERMISSION FROM THE INSTRUCTOR!
YOU MEAN I CAN HUNT TITANS OUTSIDE THE WALL?!
PERMISSION
NOW YOU CAN SLEEP IN PEACE!
BAM!
"PERMISSION TO DEPLOY A FUTON AND SLEEP IN THE HALL"?
NOW YOU CAN START THE NIGHT ALREADY IN THE HALL!
PERMISSION

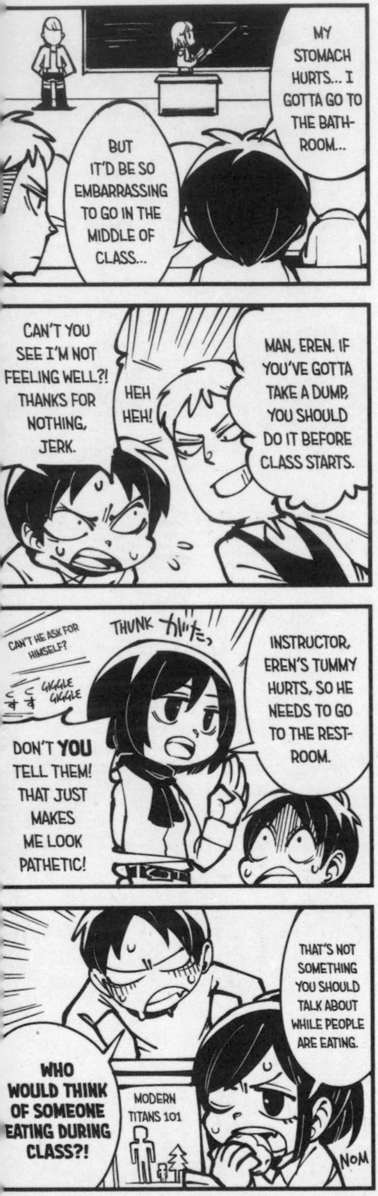
MY STOMACH HURTS... I GOTTA GO TO THE BATHROOM...
BUT IT'D BE SO EMBARRASSING TO GO IN THE MIDDLE OF CLASS...
MAN, EREN. IF YOU'VE GOTTA TAKE A DUMP, YOU SHOULD DO IT BEFORE CLASS STARTS.
HEH HEH!
CAN'T YOU SEE I'M NOT FEELING WELL?! THANKS FOR NOTHING, JERK.
INSTRUCTOR, EREN'S TUMMY HURTS, SO HE NEEDS TO GO TO THE RESTROOM.
THUNK
CAN'T HE ASK FOR HIMSELF?
GIGGLE GIGGLE くすくす
DON'T YOU TELL THEM! THAT JUST MAKES ME LOOK PATHETIC!
THAT'S NOT SOMETHING YOU SHOULD TALK ABOUT WHILE PEOPLE ARE EATING.
MODERN TITANS 101
NOM
WHO WOULD THINK OF SOMEONE EATING DURING CLASS?!

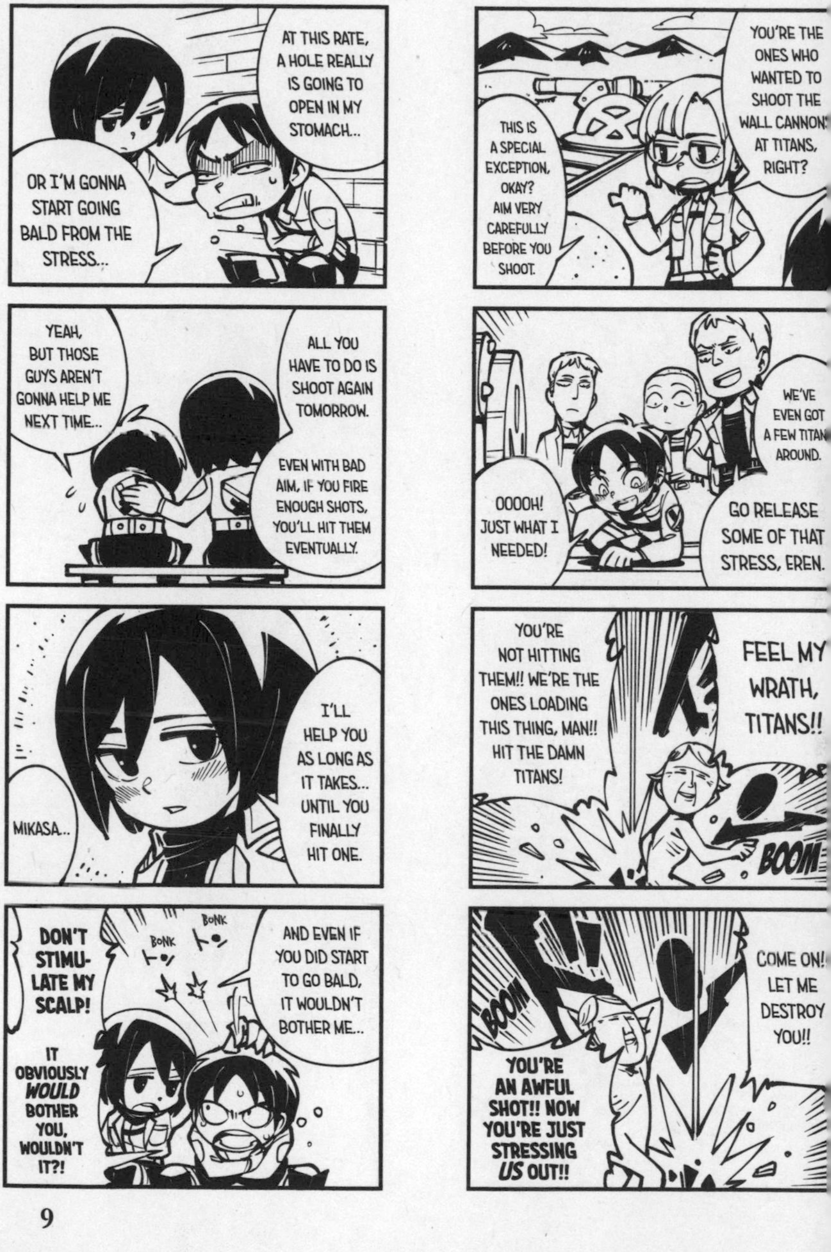
YOU'RE THE ONES WHO WANTED TO SHOOT THE WALL CANNON AT TITANS, RIGHT?
THIS IS A SPECIAL EXCEPTION, OKAY? AIM VERY CAREFULLY BEFORE YOU SHOOT.
WE'VE EVEN GOT A FEW TITAN AROUND.
GO RELEASE SOME OF THAT STRESS, EREN.
OOOOH! JUST WHAT I NEEDED!
FEEL MY WRATH, TITANS!!
YOU'RE NOT HITTING THEM!! WE'RE THE ONES LOADING THIS THING, MAN!! HIT THE DAMN TITANS!
BOOM
COME ON! LET ME DESTROY YOU!!
BOOM
YOU'RE AN AWFUL SHOT!! NOW YOU'RE JUST STRESSING *US* OUT!!
AT THIS RATE, A HOLE REALLY IS GOING TO OPEN IN MY STOMACH...
OR I'M GONNA START GOING BALD FROM THE STRESS...
ALL YOU HAVE TO DO IS SHOOT AGAIN TOMORROW.
EVEN WITH BAD AIM, IF YOU FIRE ENOUGH SHOTS, YOU'LL HIT THEM EVENTUALLY.
YEAH, BUT THOSE GUYS AREN'T GONNA HELP ME NEXT TIME...
I'LL HELP YOU AS LONG AS IT TAKES... UNTIL YOU FINALLY HIT ONE.
MIKASA...
AND EVEN IF YOU DID START TO GO BALD, IT WOULDN'T BOTHER ME...
BONK
BONK
DON'T STIMULATE MY SCALP!
IT OBVIOUSLY *WOULD* BOTHER YOU, WOULDN'T IT?!

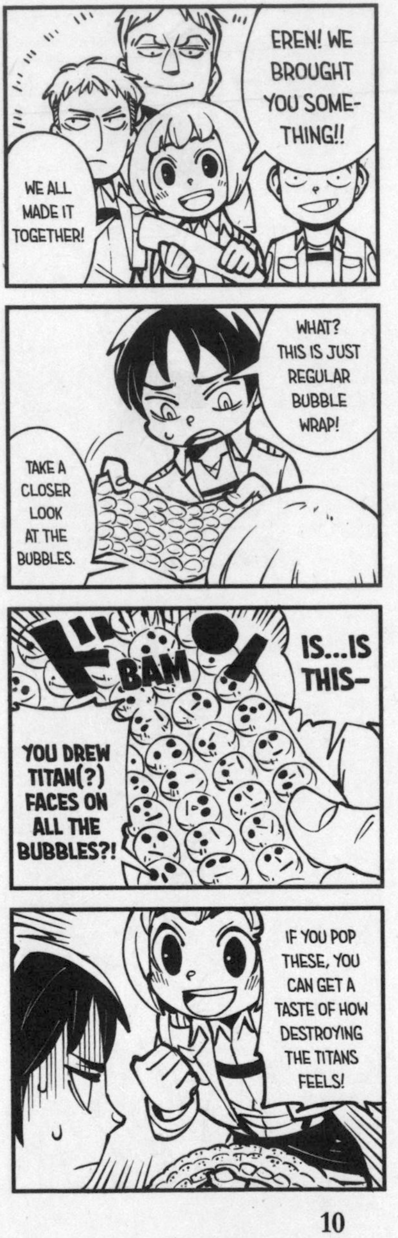
EREN! WE BROUGHT YOU SOME-THING!!
WE ALL MADE IT TOGETHER!
WHAT? THIS IS JUST REGULAR BUBBLE WRAP!
TAKE A CLOSER LOOK AT THE BUBBLES.
BAM
IS...IS THIS–
YOU DREW TITAN(?) FACES ON ALL THE BUBBLES?!
IF YOU POP THESE, YOU CAN GET A TASTE OF HOW DESTROYING THE TITANS FEELS!

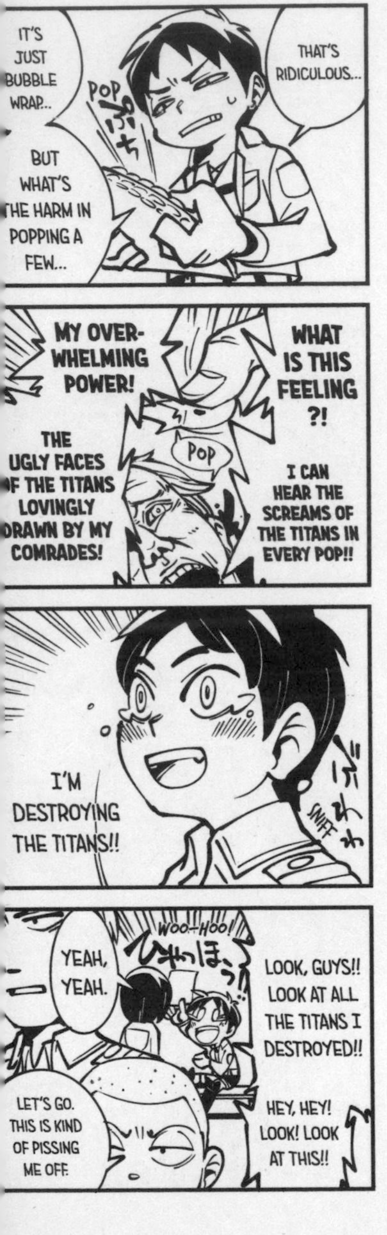
THAT'S RIDICULOUS...
POP
IT'S JUST BUBBLE WRAP...
BUT WHAT'S THE HARM IN POPPING A FEW...
WHAT IS THIS FEELING ?!
MY OVER-WHELMING POWER!
POP
I CAN HEAR THE SCREAMS OF THE TITANS IN EVERY POP!!
THE UGLY FACES OF THE TITANS LOVINGLY DRAWN BY MY COMRADES!
SNIFF
I'M DESTROYING THE TITANS!!
WOO-HOO!
LOOK, GUYS!! LOOK AT ALL THE TITANS I DESTROYED!!
HEY, HEY! LOOK! LOOK AT THIS!!
YEAH, YEAH.
LET'S GO. THIS IS KIND OF PISSING ME OFF.

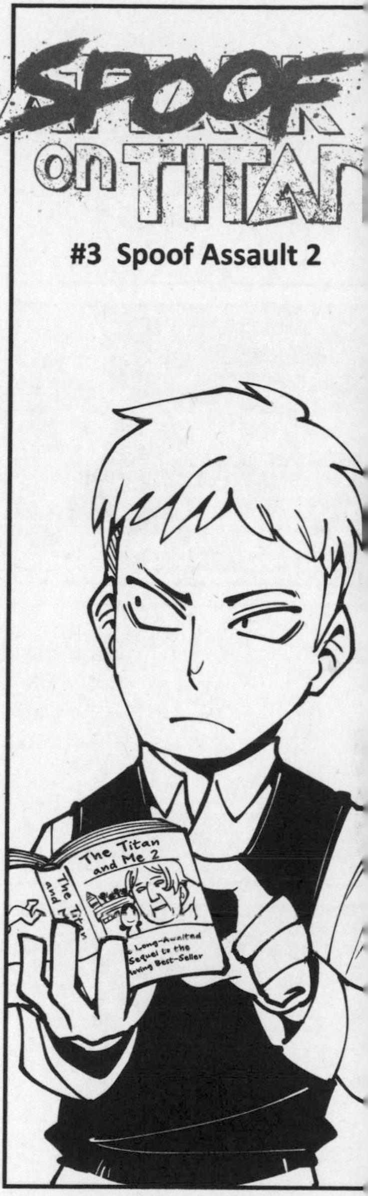
SPOOF on TITAN
#3 Spoof Assault 2
The Titan and Me 2

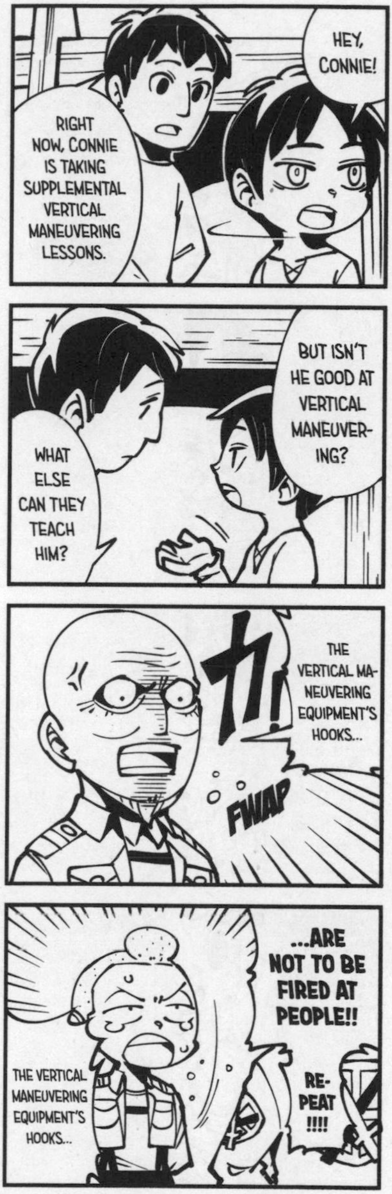
HEY, CONNIE!
RIGHT NOW, CONNIE IS TAKING SUPPLEMENTAL VERTICAL MANEUVERING LESSONS.
BUT ISN'T HE GOOD AT VERTICAL MANEUVER-ING?
WHAT ELSE CAN THEY TEACH HIM?
THE VERTICAL MA-NEUVERING EQUIPMENT'S HOOKS...
FWAP
...ARE NOT TO BE FIRED AT PEOPLE!!
RE-PEAT !!!!
THE VERTICAL MANEUVERING EQUIPMENT'S HOOKS...

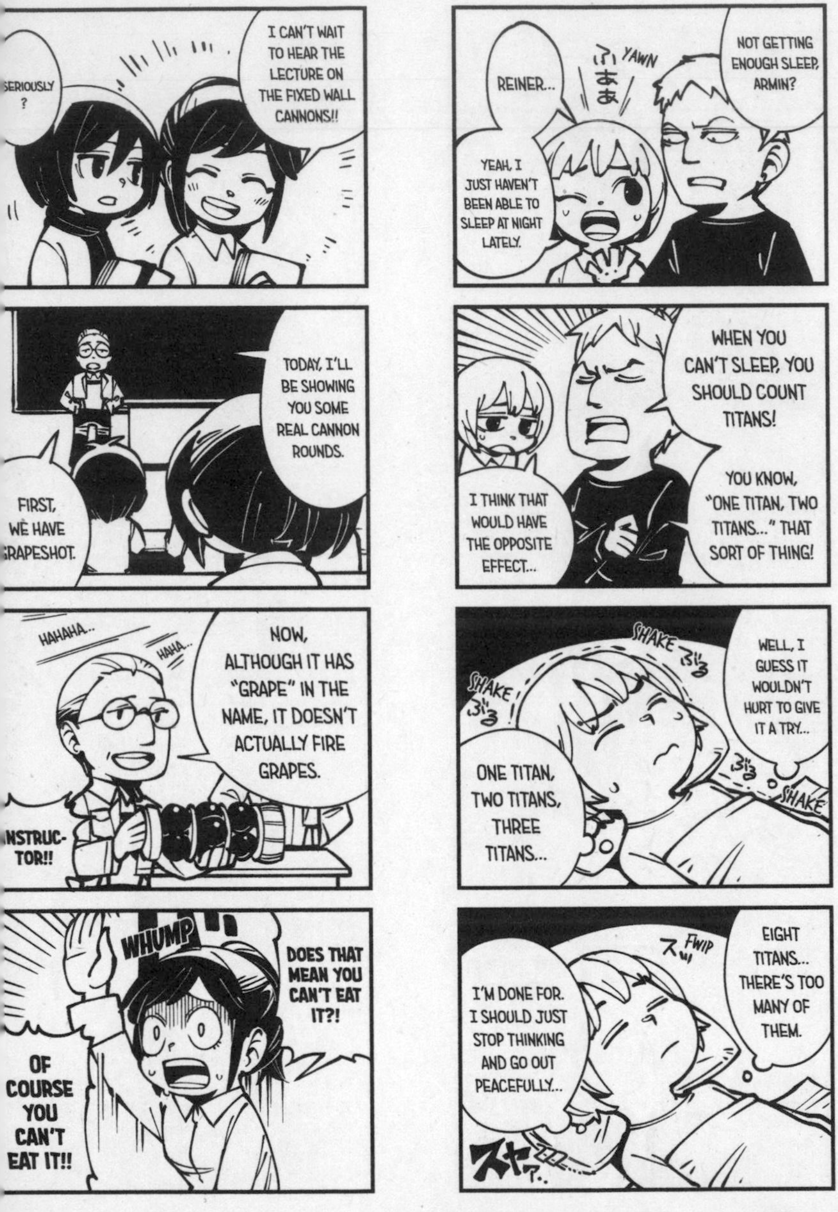
NOT GETTING ENOUGH SLEEP, ARMIN?
YAWN ふぁあ
REINER...
YEAH, I JUST HAVEN'T BEEN ABLE TO SLEEP AT NIGHT LATELY.
WHEN YOU CAN'T SLEEP, YOU SHOULD COUNT TITANS!
YOU KNOW, "ONE TITAN, TWO TITANS..." THAT SORT OF THING!
I THINK THAT WOULD HAVE THE OPPOSITE EFFECT...
WELL, I GUESS IT WOULDN'T HURT TO GIVE IT A TRY...
SHAKE ぶる
SHAKE ぶる
ぶる SHAKE
ONE TITAN, TWO TITANS, THREE TITANS...
EIGHT TITANS... THERE'S TOO MANY OF THEM.
FWIP スッ
I'M DONE FOR. I SHOULD JUST STOP THINKING AND GO OUT PEACEFULLY...
スヤァ.. ZZZ...
I CAN'T WAIT TO HEAR THE LECTURE ON THE FIXED WALL CANNONS!!
SERIOUSLY?
TODAY, I'LL BE SHOWING YOU SOME REAL CANNON ROUNDS.
FIRST, WE HAVE GRAPESHOT.
NOW, ALTHOUGH IT HAS "GRAPE" IN THE NAME, IT DOESN'T ACTUALLY FIRE GRAPES.
HAHA...
HAHAHA...
INSTRUCTOR!!
DOES THAT MEAN YOU CAN'T EAT IT?!
WHUMP
OF COURSE YOU CAN'T EAT IT!!

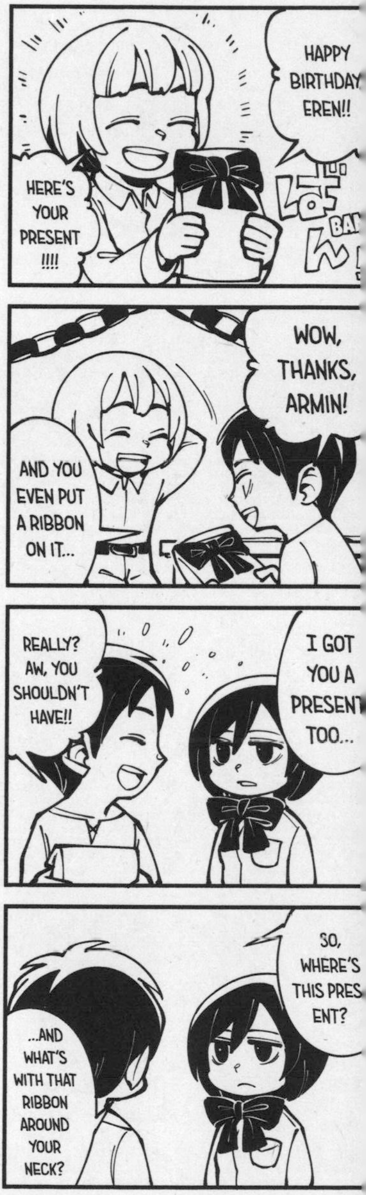
HAPPY BIRTHDAY, EREN!!
HERE'S YOUR PRESENT !!!!
WOW, THANKS, ARMIN!
AND YOU EVEN PUT A RIBBON ON IT...
I GOT YOU A PRESENT TOO...
REALLY? AW, YOU SHOULDN'T HAVE!!
SO, WHERE'S THIS PRES-ENT?
...AND WHAT'S WITH THAT RIBBON AROUND YOUR NECK?
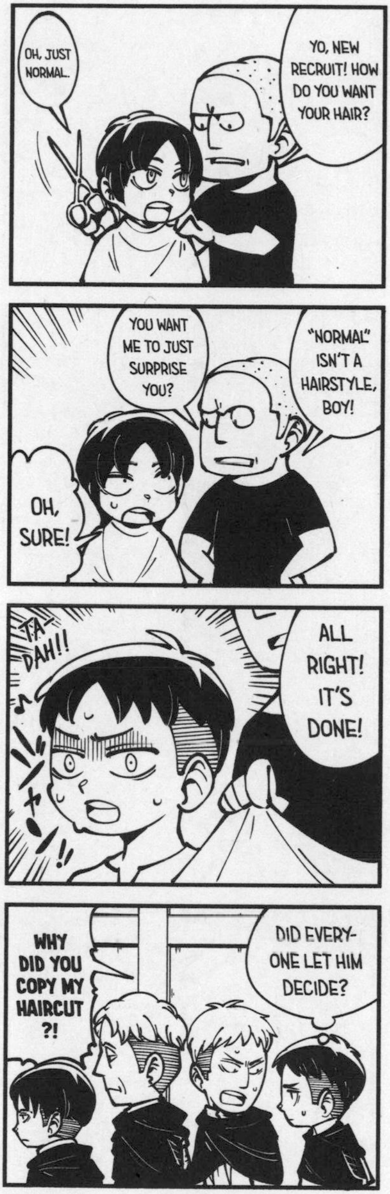
YO, NEW RECRUIT! HOW DO YOU WANT YOUR HAIR?
OH, JUST NORMAL.
"NORMAL" ISN'T A HAIRSTYLE, BOY!
YOU WANT ME TO JUST SURPRISE YOU?
OH, SURE!
ALL RIGHT! IT'S DONE!
TA-DAH!!
DID EVERY-ONE LET HIM DECIDE?
WHY DID YOU COPY MY HAIRCUT ?!

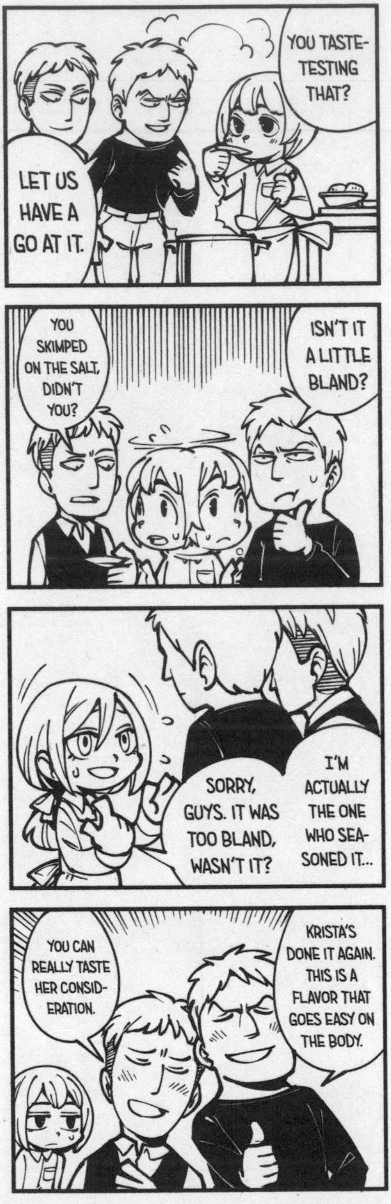
YOU TASTE-TESTING THAT?
LET US HAVE A GO AT IT.
ISN'T IT A LITTLE BLAND?
YOU SKIMPED ON THE SALT, DIDN'T YOU?
I'M ACTUALLY THE ONE WHO SEA-SONED IT...
SORRY, GUYS. IT WAS TOO BLAND, WASN'T IT?
KRISTA'S DONE IT AGAIN. THIS IS A FLAVOR THAT GOES EASY ON THE BODY.
YOU CAN REALLY TASTE HER CONSID-ERATION.

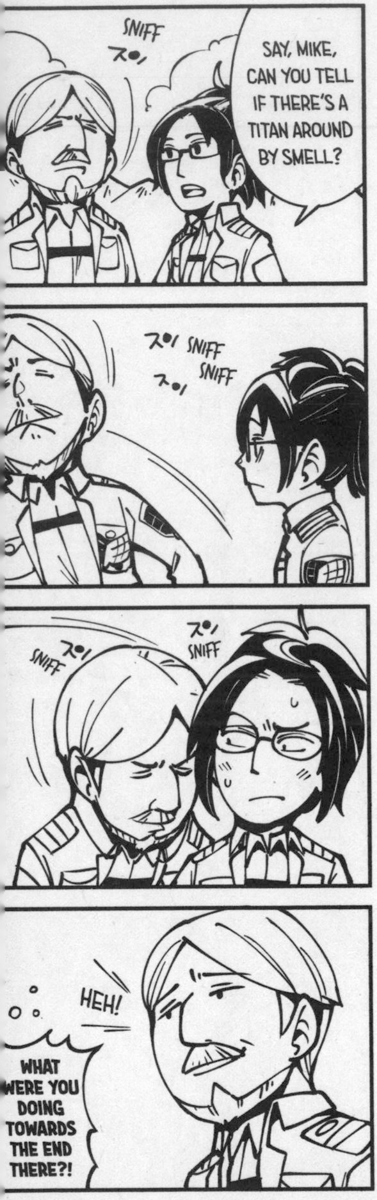
SAY, MIKE, CAN YOU TELL IF THERE'S A TITAN AROUND BY SMELL?
SNIFF
SNIFF
SNIFF
SNIFF
SNIFF
HEH!
WHAT WERE YOU DOING TOWARDS THE END THERE?!

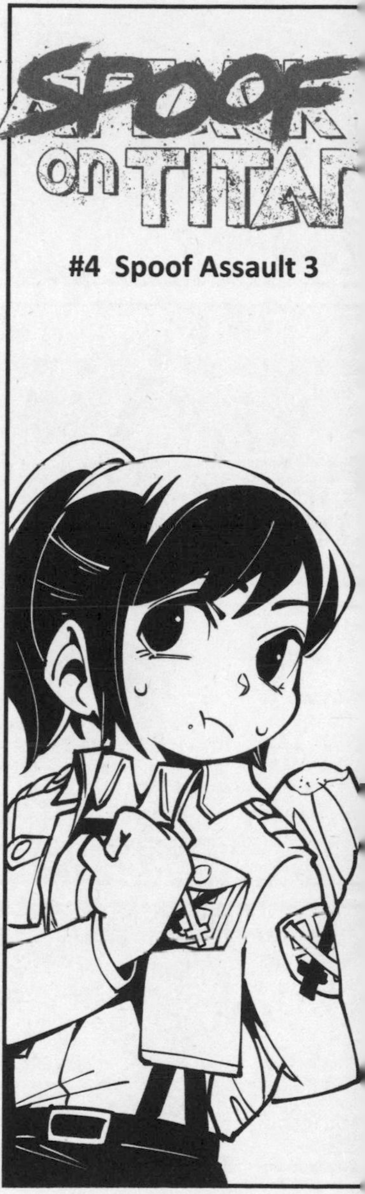
SPOOF on TITAN
#4 Spoof Assault 3

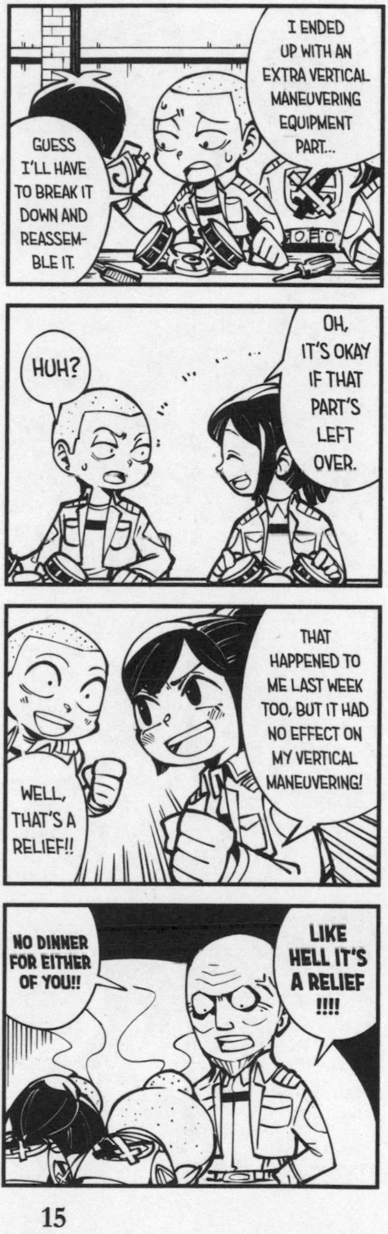
I ENDED UP WITH AN EXTRA VERTICAL MANEUVERING EQUIPMENT PART...
GUESS I'LL HAVE TO BREAK IT DOWN AND REASSEM-BLE IT.
OH, IT'S OKAY IF THAT PART'S LEFT OVER.
HUH?
THAT HAPPENED TO ME LAST WEEK TOO, BUT IT HAD NO EFFECT ON MY VERTICAL MANEUVERING!
WELL, THAT'S A RELIEF!!
LIKE HELL IT'S A RELIEF !!!!
NO DINNER FOR EITHER OF YOU!!

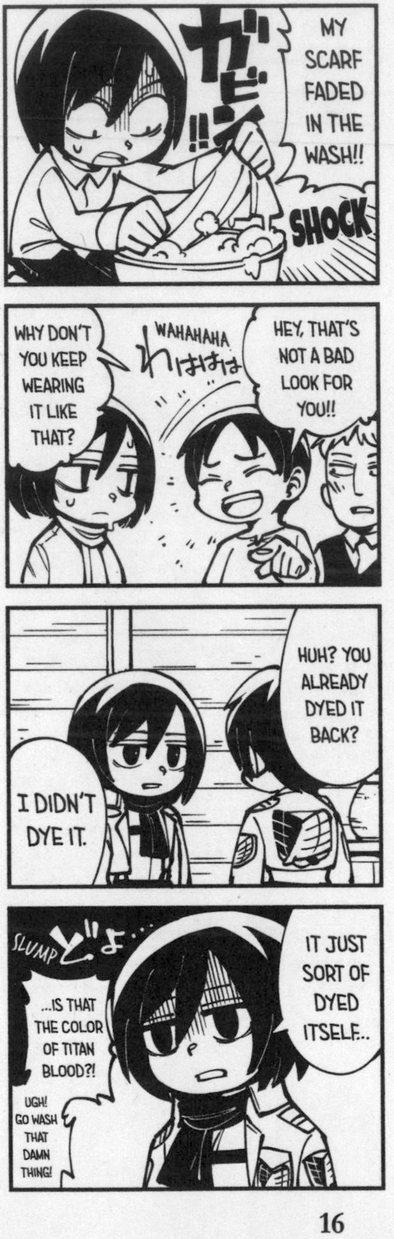
MY SCARF FADED IN THE WASH!!
ガビーン!!
SHOCK
HEY, THAT'S NOT A BAD LOOK FOR YOU!!
WAHAHAHA
WHY DON'T YOU KEEP WEARING IT LIKE THAT?
HUH? YOU ALREADY DYED IT BACK?
I DIDN'T DYE IT.
IT JUST SORT OF DYED ITSELF...
SLUMP
...IS THAT THE COLOR OF TITAN BLOOD?!
UGH! GO WASH THAT DAMN THING!

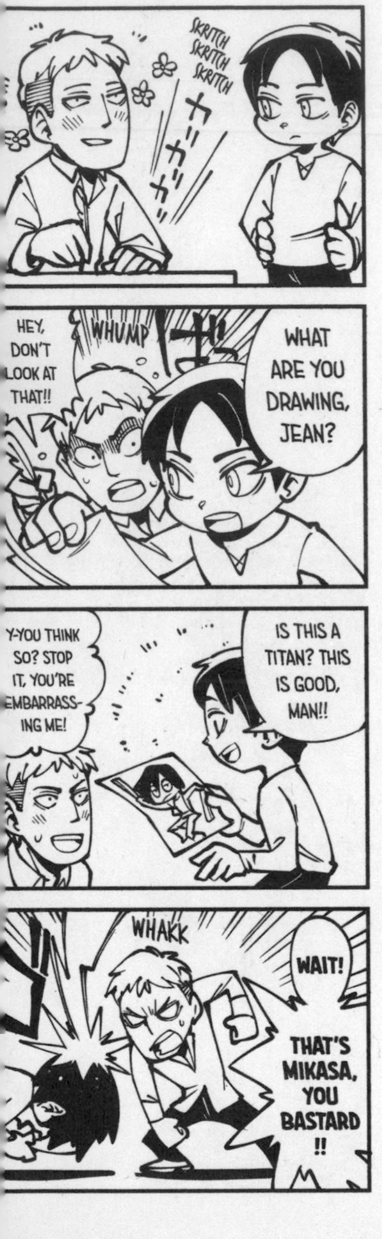
SKRITCH SKRITCH SKRITCH
WHAT ARE YOU DRAWING, JEAN?
WHUMP
HEY, DON'T LOOK AT THAT!!
IS THIS A TITAN? THIS IS GOOD, MAN!!
Y-YOU THINK SO? STOP IT, YOU'RE EMBARRASSING ME!
WAIT!
WHAKK
THAT'S MIKASA, YOU BASTARD!!

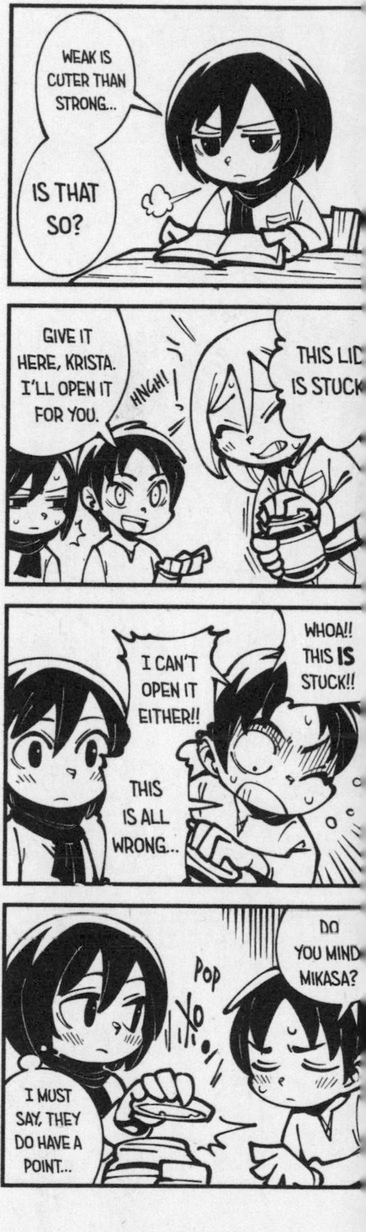
WEAK IS CUTER THAN STRONG...
IS THAT SO?
THIS LID IS STUCK
HNGH!
GIVE IT HERE, KRISTA. I'LL OPEN IT FOR YOU.
WHOA!! THIS **IS** STUCK!!
I CAN'T OPEN IT EITHER!!
THIS IS ALL WRONG...
DO YOU MIND MIKASA?
POP
I MUST SAY, THEY DO HAVE A POINT...

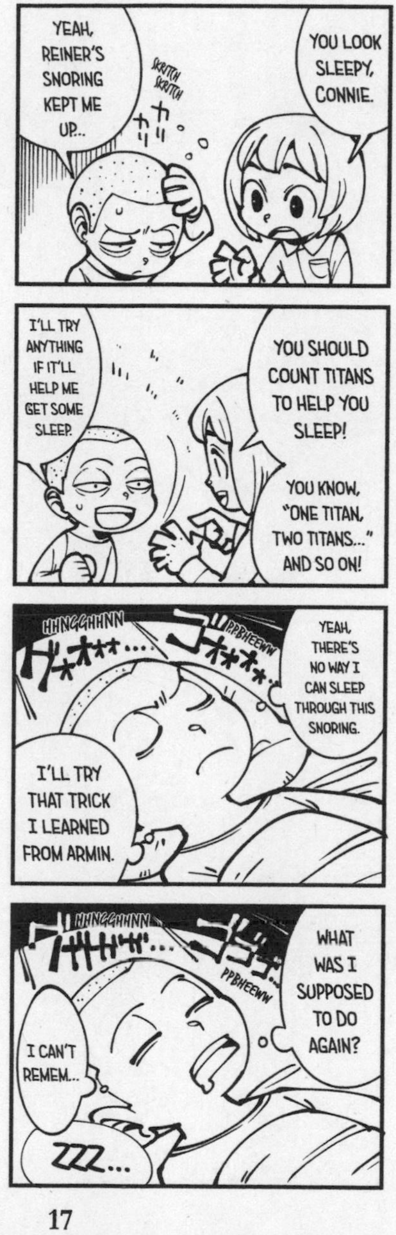
YOU LOOK SLEEPY, CONNIE.
SKRITCH SKRITCH
YEAH, REINER'S SNORING KEPT ME UP...
YOU SHOULD COUNT TITANS TO HELP YOU SLEEP!
YOU KNOW, "ONE TITAN, TWO TITANS..." AND SO ON!
I'LL TRY ANYTHING IF IT'LL HELP ME GET SOME SLEEP.
YEAH, THERE'S NO WAY I CAN SLEEP THROUGH THIS SNORING.
PPBHEEWW
HHNGGHHNN
I'LL TRY THAT TRICK I LEARNED FROM ARMIN.
WHAT WAS I SUPPOSED TO DO AGAIN?
PPBHEEWW
HHNGGHHNN
I CAN'T REMEM...
ZZZ...

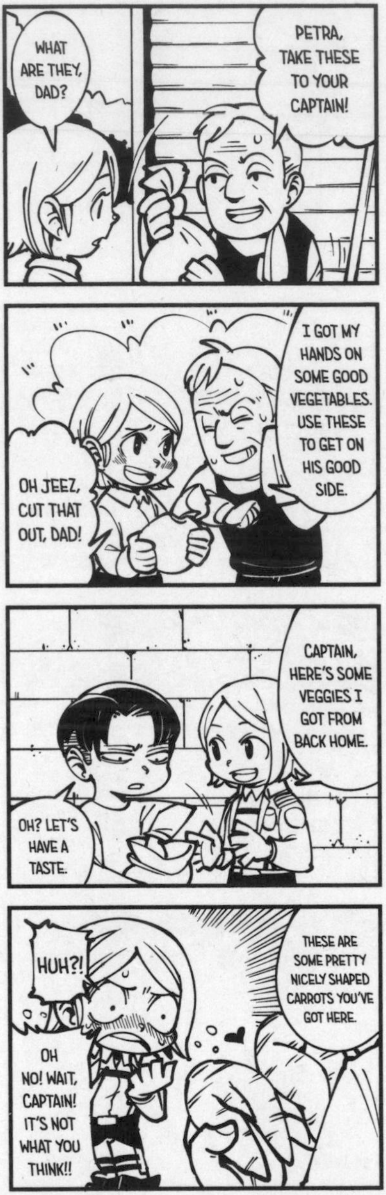
PETRA, TAKE THESE TO YOUR CAPTAIN!
WHAT ARE THEY, DAD?
I GOT MY HANDS ON SOME GOOD VEGETABLES. USE THESE TO GET ON HIS GOOD SIDE.
OH JEEZ, CUT THAT OUT, DAD!
CAPTAIN, HERE'S SOME VEGGIES I GOT FROM BACK HOME.
OH? LET'S HAVE A TASTE.
THESE ARE SOME PRETTY NICELY SHAPED CARROTS YOU'VE GOT HERE.
HUH?!
OH NO! WAIT, CAPTAIN! IT'S NOT WHAT YOU THINK!!

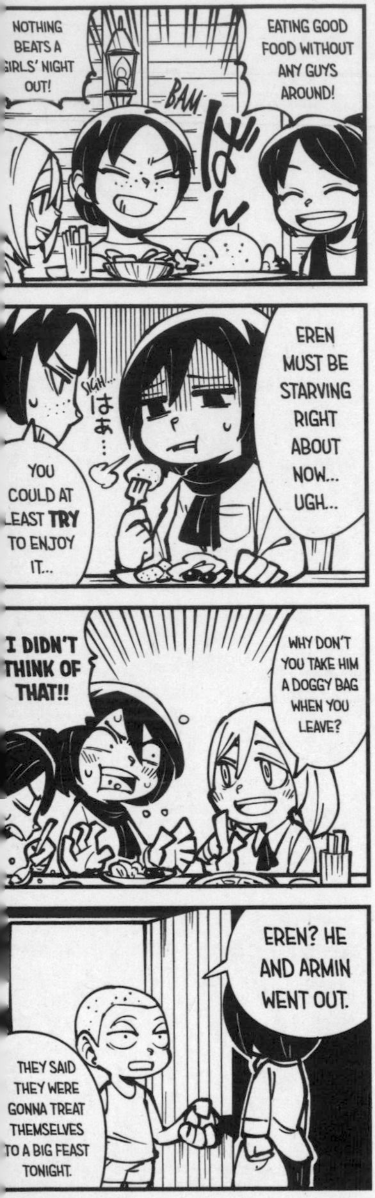
EATING GOOD FOOD WITHOUT ANY GUYS AROUND!
NOTHING BEATS A GIRLS' NIGHT OUT!
BAM
ばん
EREN MUST BE STARVING RIGHT ABOUT NOW... UGH...
SIGH...
はぁ…
YOU COULD AT LEAST **TRY** TO ENJOY IT...
WHY DON'T YOU TAKE HIM A DOGGY BAG WHEN YOU LEAVE?
I DIDN'T THINK OF THAT!!
EREN? HE AND ARMIN WENT OUT.
THEY SAID THEY WERE GONNA TREAT THEMSELVES TO A BIG FEAST TONIGHT.

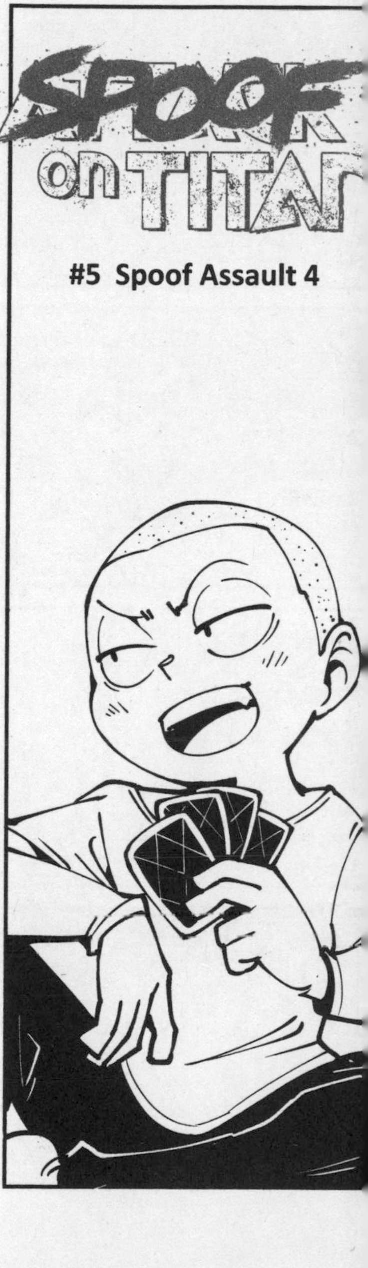
SPOOF
on TITAN
#5 Spoof Assault 4

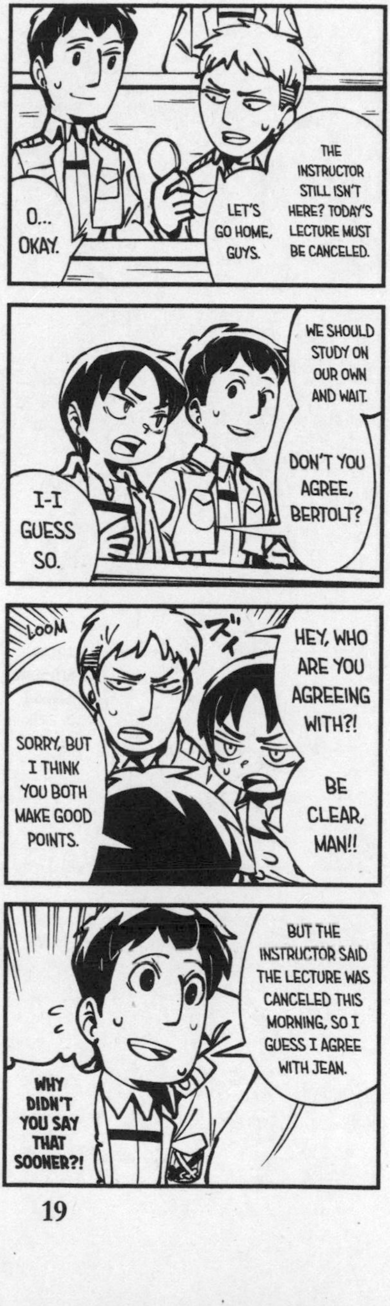
THE INSTRUCTOR STILL ISN'T HERE? TODAY'S LECTURE MUST BE CANCELED.
LET'S GO HOME, GUYS.
O... OKAY.
WE SHOULD STUDY ON OUR OWN AND WAIT.
DON'T YOU AGREE, BERTOLT?
I-I GUESS SO.
HEY, WHO ARE YOU AGREEING WITH?!
ズイ
BE CLEAR, MAN!!
LOOM
SORRY, BUT I THINK YOU BOTH MAKE GOOD POINTS.
BUT THE INSTRUCTOR SAID THE LECTURE WAS CANCELED THIS MORNING, SO I GUESS I AGREE WITH JEAN.
WHY DIDN'T YOU SAY THAT SOONER?!

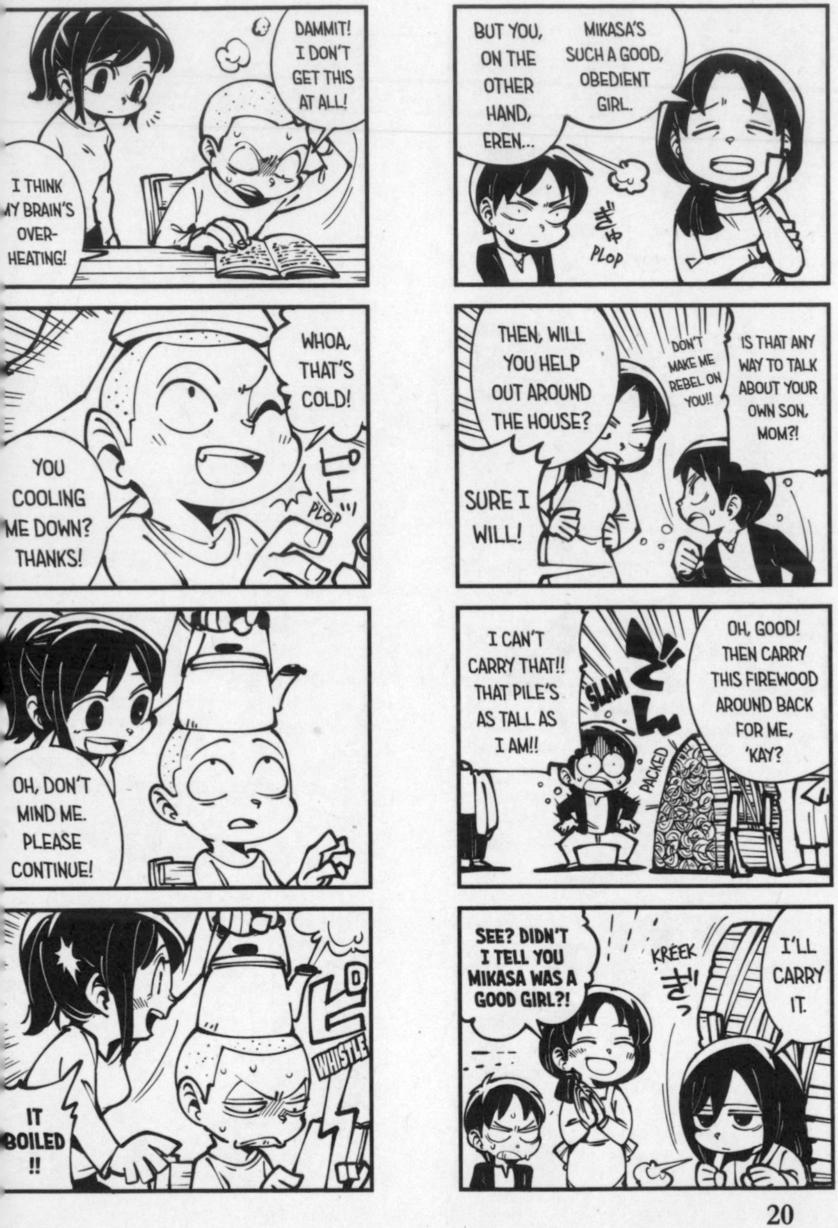
MIKASA'S SUCH A GOOD, OBEDIENT GIRL.
BUT YOU, ON THE OTHER HAND, EREN...
PLOP
IS THAT ANY WAY TO TALK ABOUT YOUR OWN SON, MOM?!
DON'T MAKE ME REBEL ON YOU!!
THEN, WILL YOU HELP OUT AROUND THE HOUSE?
SURE I WILL!
OH, GOOD! THEN CARRY THIS FIREWOOD AROUND BACK FOR ME, 'KAY?
PACKED
SLAM
I CAN'T CARRY THAT!! THAT PILE'S AS TALL AS I AM!!
I'LL CARRY IT.
KREEK
SEE? DIDN'T I TELL YOU MIKASA WAS A GOOD GIRL?!
DAMMIT! I DON'T GET THIS AT ALL!
I THINK MY BRAIN'S OVER-HEATING!
WHOA, THAT'S COLD!
PLOP
YOU COOLING ME DOWN? THANKS!
OH, DON'T MIND ME. PLEASE CONTINUE!
WHISTLE
IT BOILED!!

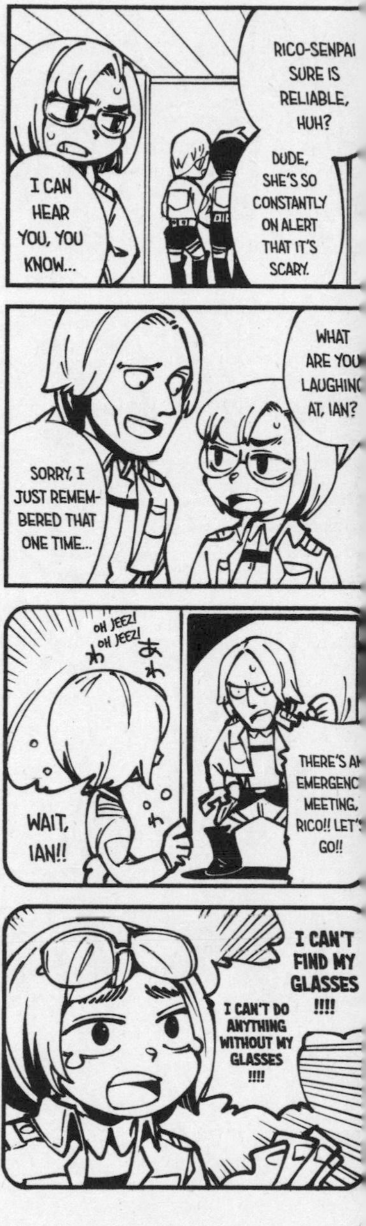
RICO-SENPAI SURE IS RELIABLE, HUH?
DUDE, SHE'S SO CONSTANTLY ON ALERT THAT IT'S SCARY.
I CAN HEAR YOU, YOU KNOW...
WHAT ARE YOU LAUGHIN AT, IAN?
SORRY, I JUST REMEMBERED THAT ONE TIME...
THERE'S A EMERGENC MEETING, RICO!! LET' GO!!
OH JEEZ! OH JEEZ!
WAIT, IAN!!
I CAN'T FIND MY GLASSES!!!!
I CAN'T DO ANYTHING WITHOUT MY GLASSES!!!!

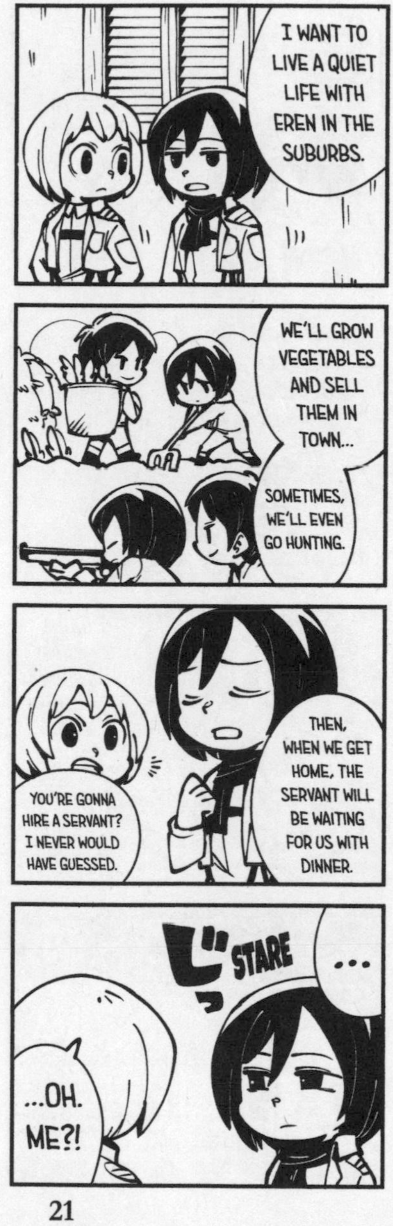
I WANT TO LIVE A QUIET LIFE WITH EREN IN THE SUBURBS.
WE'LL GROW VEGETABLES AND SELL THEM IN TOWN...
SOMETIMES, WE'LL EVEN GO HUNTING.
THEN, WHEN WE GET HOME, THE SERVANT WILL BE WAITING FOR US WITH DINNER.
YOU'RE GONNA HIRE A SERVANT? I NEVER WOULD HAVE GUESSED.
STARE
...
...OH. ME?!

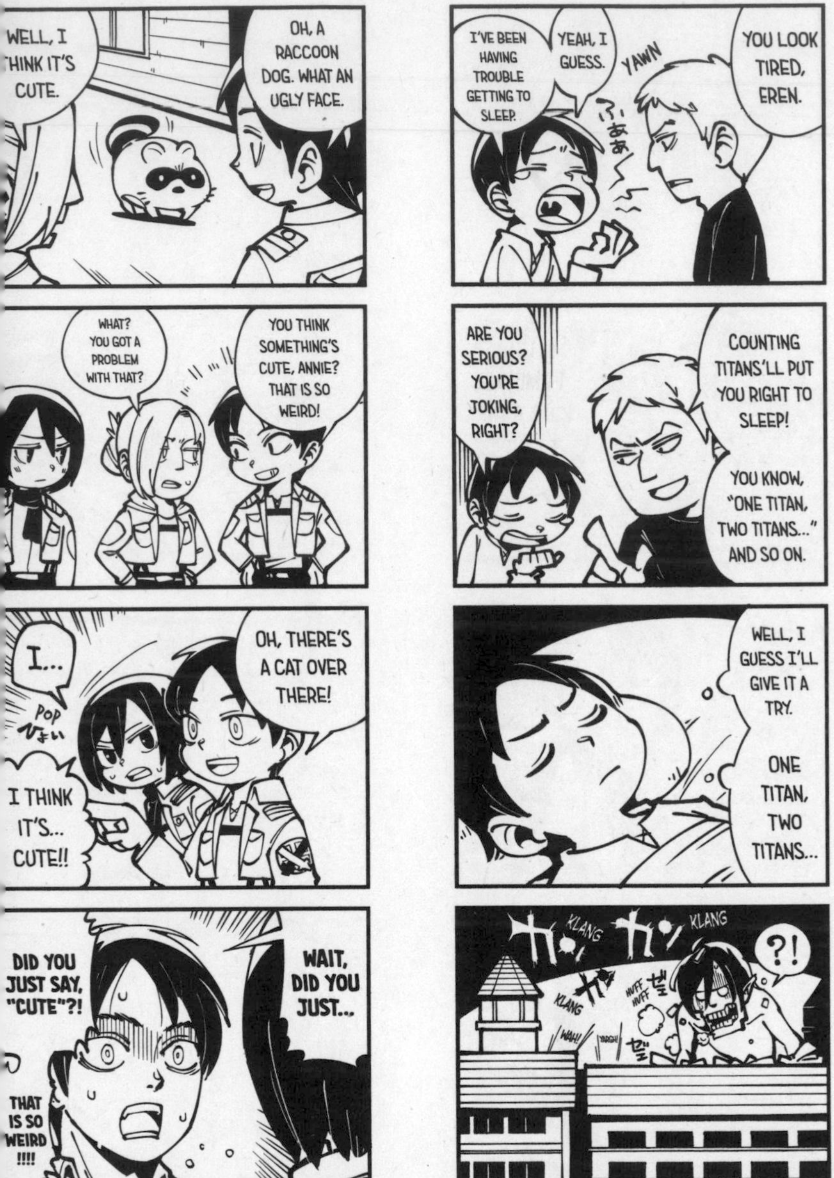

YOU LOOK TIRED, EREN.
YAWN
ふあぁ
YEAH, I GUESS.
I'VE BEEN HAVING TROUBLE GETTING TO SLEEP.
COUNTING TITANS'LL PUT YOU RIGHT TO SLEEP!
YOU KNOW, "ONE TITAN, TWO TITANS..." AND SO ON.
ARE YOU SERIOUS? YOU'RE JOKING, RIGHT?
WELL, I GUESS I'LL GIVE IT A TRY.
ONE TITAN, TWO TITANS...
?!
KLANG
カン
KLANG
カン
KLANG
HUFF HUFF
WAH!!
YARGH!
OH, A RACCOON DOG. WHAT AN UGLY FACE.
WELL, I THINK IT'S CUTE.
YOU THINK SOMETHING'S CUTE, ANNIE? THAT IS SO WEIRD!
WHAT? YOU GOT A PROBLEM WITH THAT?
OH, THERE'S A CAT OVER THERE!
I...
POP
ぴょい
I THINK IT'S... CUTE!!
WAIT, DID YOU JUST...
DID YOU JUST SAY, "CUTE"?!
THAT IS SO WEIRD!!!!

#6 Mikasa, the Queen of Style

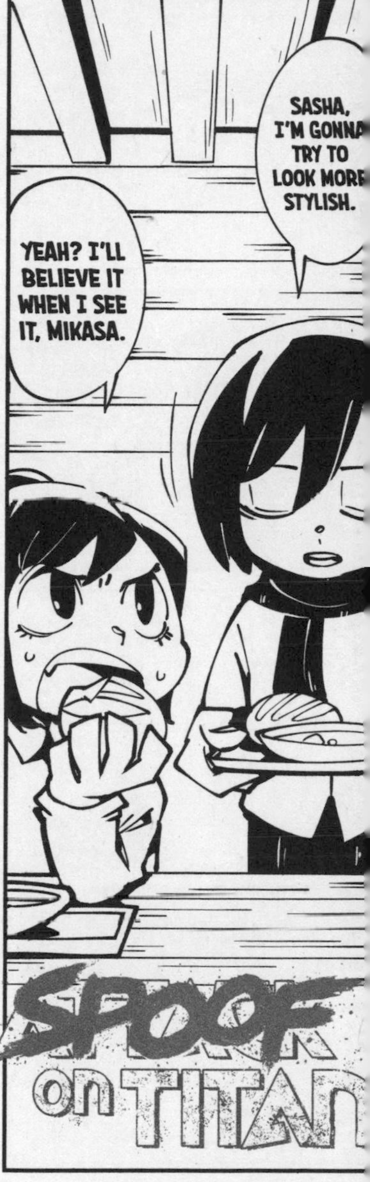
SASHA, I'M GONNA TRY TO LOOK MORE STYLISH.
YEAH? I'LL BELIEVE IT WHEN I SEE IT, MIKASA.
SPOOF on TITAN

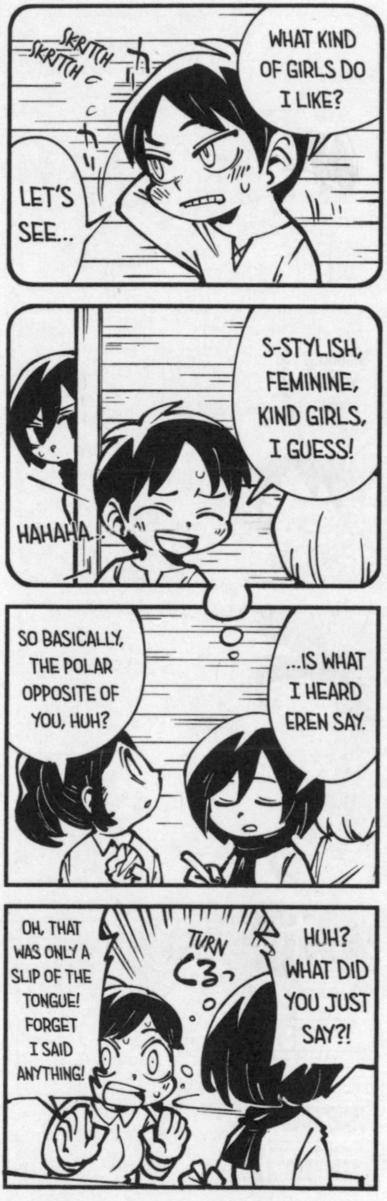
WHAT KIND OF GIRLS DO I LIKE?
SKRITCH SKRITCH
LET'S SEE...
S-STYLISH, FEMININE, KIND GIRLS, I GUESS!
HAHAHA...
...IS WHAT I HEARD EREN SAY.
SO BASICALLY, THE POLAR OPPOSITE OF YOU, HUH?
HUH? WHAT DID YOU JUST SAY?!
TURN
OH, THAT WAS ONLY A SLIP OF THE TONGUE! FORGET I SAID ANYTHING!

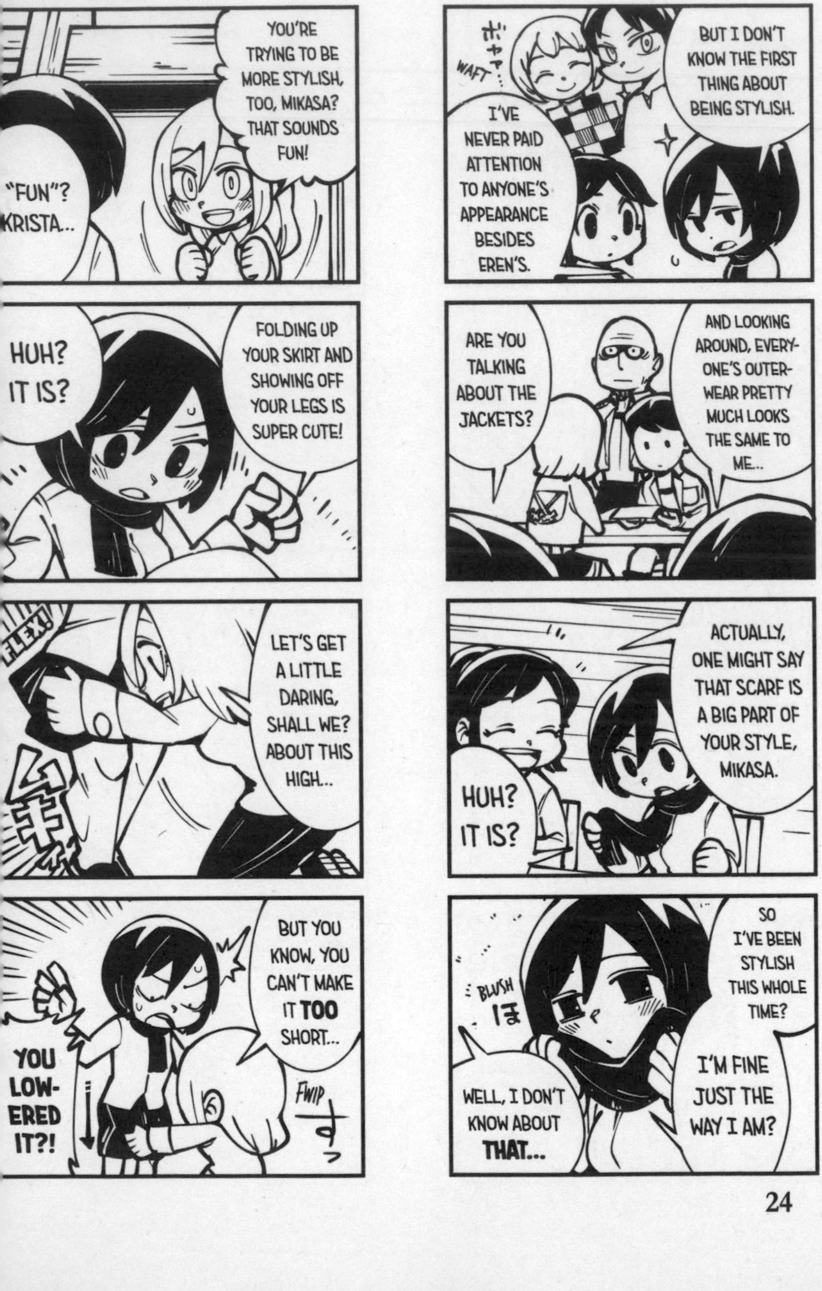
BUT I DON'T KNOW THE FIRST THING ABOUT BEING STYLISH.
ポヤァ WAFT
I'VE NEVER PAID ATTENTION TO ANYONE'S APPEARANCE BESIDES EREN'S.
AND LOOKING AROUND, EVERYONE'S OUTERWEAR PRETTY MUCH LOOKS THE SAME TO ME...
ARE YOU TALKING ABOUT THE JACKETS?
ACTUALLY, ONE MIGHT SAY THAT SCARF IS A BIG PART OF YOUR STYLE, MIKASA.
HUH? IT IS?
SO I'VE BEEN STYLISH THIS WHOLE TIME?
BLUSH ほ
I'M FINE JUST THE WAY I AM?
WELL, I DON'T KNOW ABOUT **THAT...**
YOU'RE TRYING TO BE MORE STYLISH, TOO, MIKASA? THAT SOUNDS FUN!
"FUN"? KRISTA...
FOLDING UP YOUR SKIRT AND SHOWING OFF YOUR LEGS IS SUPER CUTE!
HUH? IT IS?
LET'S GET A LITTLE DARING, SHALL WE? ABOUT THIS HIGH...
FLEX!
ムキ
BUT YOU KNOW, YOU CAN'T MAKE IT **TOO** SHORT...
FWIP すっ
YOU LOWERED IT?!

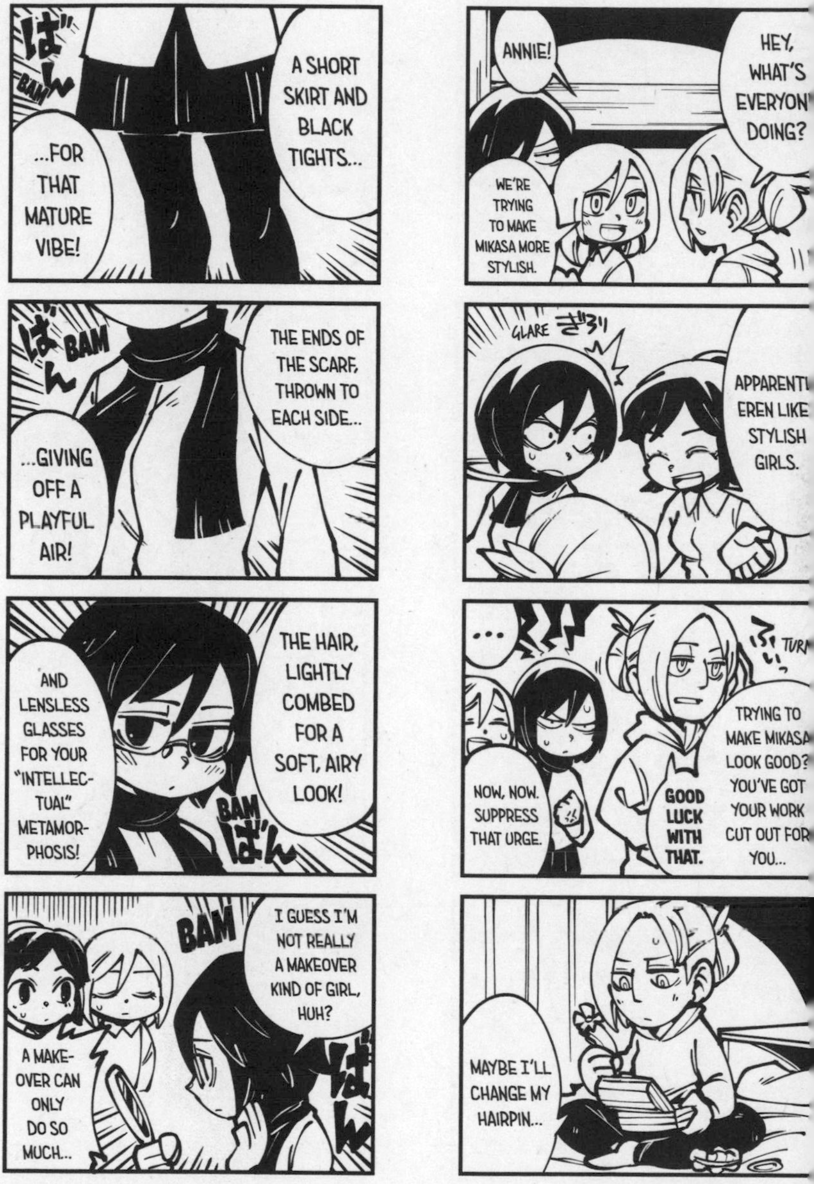
HEY, WHAT'S EVERYON DOING?
ANNIE!
WE'RE TRYING TO MAKE MIKASA MORE STYLISH.
GLARE ぎろり
APPARENTL EREN LIKE STYLISH GIRLS.
TURN ふい
TRYING TO MAKE MIKASA LOOK GOOD? YOU'VE GOT YOUR WORK CUT OUT FOR YOU...
...
GOOD LUCK WITH THAT.
NOW, NOW. SUPPRESS THAT URGE.
MAYBE I'LL CHANGE MY HAIRPIN...
A SHORT SKIRT AND BLACK TIGHTS...
ばーん BAM
...FOR THAT MATURE VIBE!
THE ENDS OF THE SCARF, THROWN TO EACH SIDE...
ばん BAM
...GIVING OFF A PLAYFUL AIR!
THE HAIR, LIGHTLY COMBED FOR A SOFT, AIRY LOOK!
BAM ばん
AND LENSLESS GLASSES FOR YOUR "INTELLECTUAL" METAMORPHOSIS!
BAM
I GUESS I'M NOT REALLY A MAKEOVER KIND OF GIRL, HUH?
ばん
A MAKEOVER CAN ONLY DO SO MUCH...

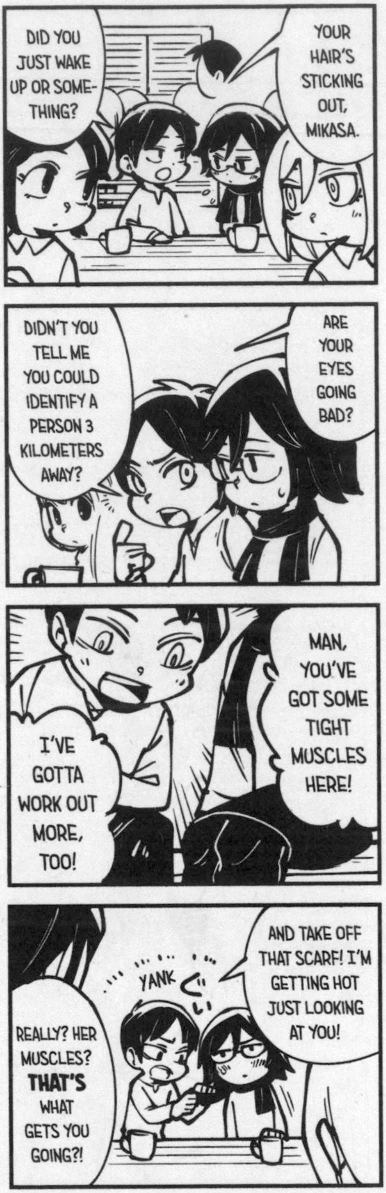
YOUR HAIR'S STICKING OUT, MIKASA.
DID YOU JUST WAKE UP OR SOME-THING?
ARE YOUR EYES GOING BAD?
DIDN'T YOU TELL ME YOU COULD IDENTIFY A PERSON 3 KILOMETERS AWAY?
MAN, YOU'VE GOT SOME TIGHT MUSCLES HERE!
I'VE GOTTA WORK OUT MORE, TOO!
AND TAKE OFF THAT SCARF! I'M GETTING HOT JUST LOOKING AT YOU!
ぐい
YANK
REALLY? HER MUSCLES? **THAT'S** WHAT GETS YOU GOING?!

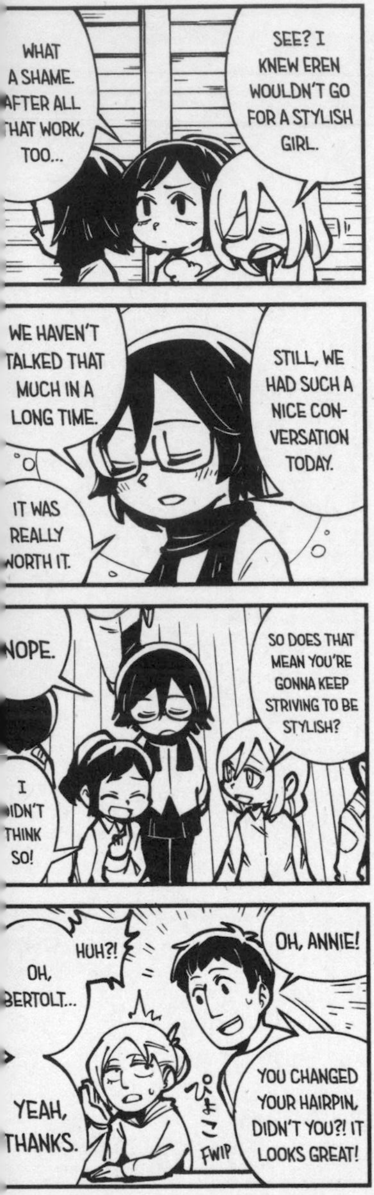
SEE? I KNEW EREN WOULDN'T GO FOR A STYLISH GIRL.
WHAT A SHAME. AFTER ALL THAT WORK, TOO...
STILL, WE HAD SUCH A NICE CON-VERSATION TODAY.
WE HAVEN'T TALKED THAT MUCH IN A LONG TIME.
IT WAS REALLY WORTH IT.
SO DOES THAT MEAN YOU'RE GONNA KEEP STRIVING TO BE STYLISH?
NOPE.
I DIDN'T THINK SO!
OH, ANNIE!
HUH?!
OH, BERTOLT...
YOU CHANGED YOUR HAIRPIN, DIDN'T YOU?! IT LOOKS GREAT!
ぴょこ
FWIP
YEAH, THANKS.

SPOOF on TITAN

SPOOF on TITAN

#7 Oluo's Demise

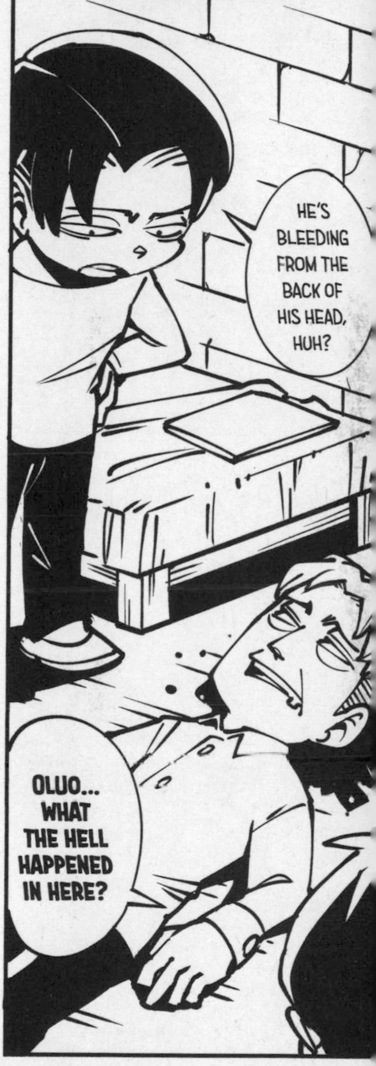
HE'S BLEEDING FROM THE BACK OF HIS HEAD, HUH?
OLUO... WHAT THE HELL HAPPENED IN HERE?

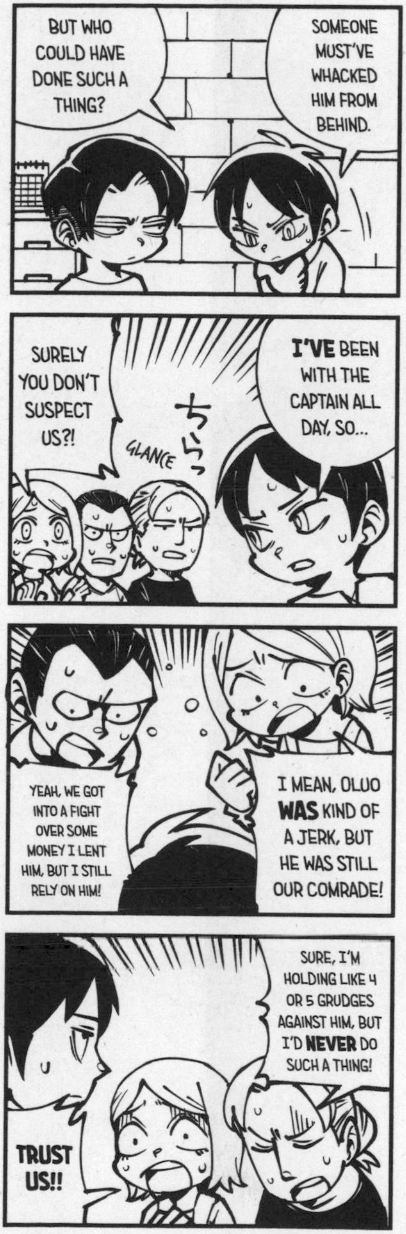
SOMEONE MUST'VE WHACKED HIM FROM BEHIND.
BUT WHO COULD HAVE DONE SUCH A THING?
I'VE BEEN WITH THE CAPTAIN ALL DAY, SO...
ちらっ
GLANCE
SURELY YOU DON'T SUSPECT US?!
I MEAN, OLUO WAS KIND OF A JERK, BUT HE WAS STILL OUR COMRADE!
YEAH, WE GOT INTO A FIGHT OVER SOME MONEY I LENT HIM, BUT I STILL RELY ON HIM!
SURE, I'M HOLDING LIKE 4 OR 5 GRUDGES AGAINST HIM, BUT I'D NEVER DO SUCH A THING!
TRUST US!!

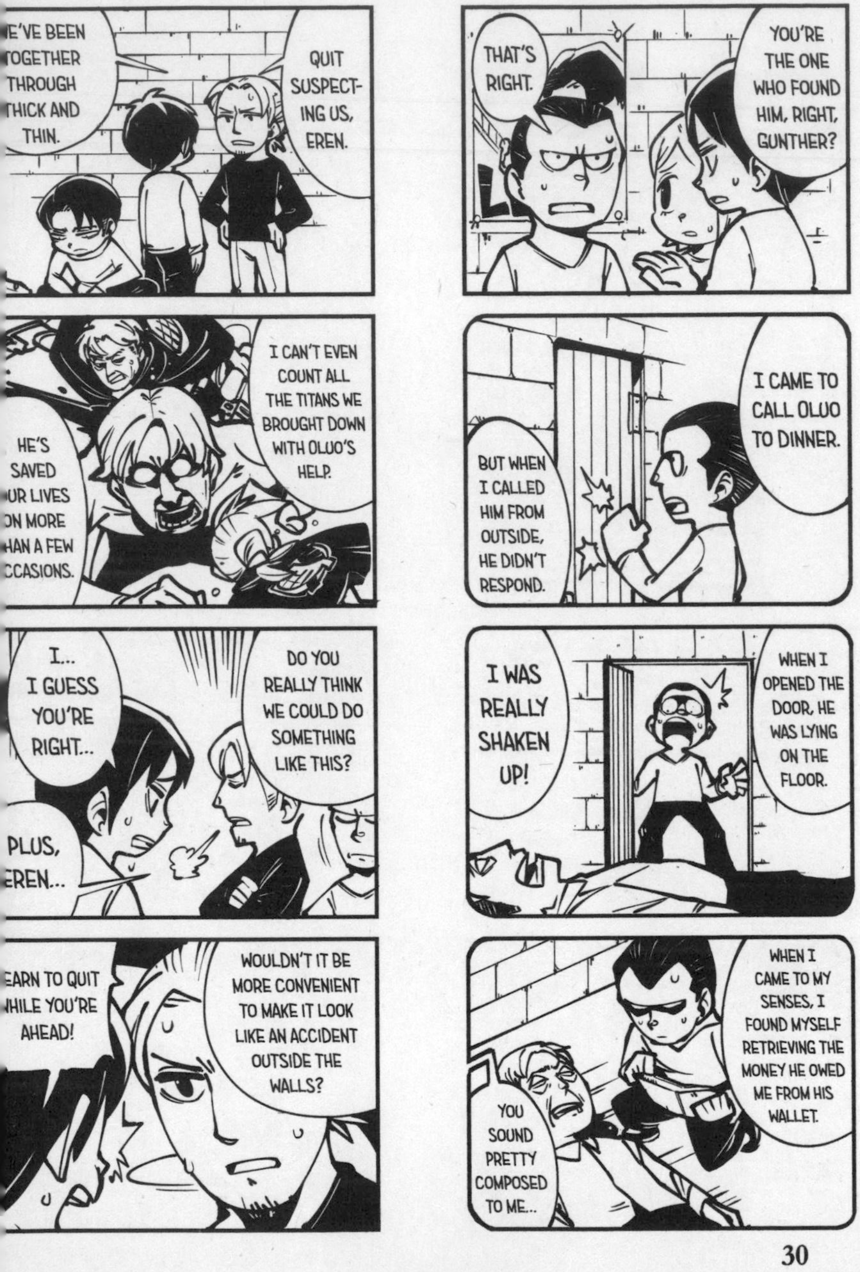
YOU'RE THE ONE WHO FOUND HIM, RIGHT, GUNTHER?
THAT'S RIGHT.
I CAME TO CALL OLUO TO DINNER.
BUT WHEN I CALLED HIM FROM OUTSIDE, HE DIDN'T RESPOND.
WHEN I OPENED THE DOOR, HE WAS LYING ON THE FLOOR.
I WAS REALLY SHAKEN UP!
WHEN I CAME TO MY SENSES, I FOUND MYSELF RETRIEVING THE MONEY HE OWED ME FROM HIS WALLET.
YOU SOUND PRETTY COMPOSED TO ME...
QUIT SUSPECT-ING US, EREN.
E'VE BEEN TOGETHER THROUGH THICK AND THIN.
I CAN'T EVEN COUNT ALL THE TITANS WE BROUGHT DOWN WITH OLUO'S HELP.
HE'S SAVED UR LIVES ON MORE HAN A FEW CCASIONS.
DO YOU REALLY THINK WE COULD DO SOMETHING LIKE THIS?
I... I GUESS YOU'RE RIGHT...
PLUS, EREN...
WOULDN'T IT BE MORE CONVENIENT TO MAKE IT LOOK LIKE AN ACCIDENT OUTSIDE THE WALLS?
EARN TO QUIT HILE YOU'RE AHEAD!

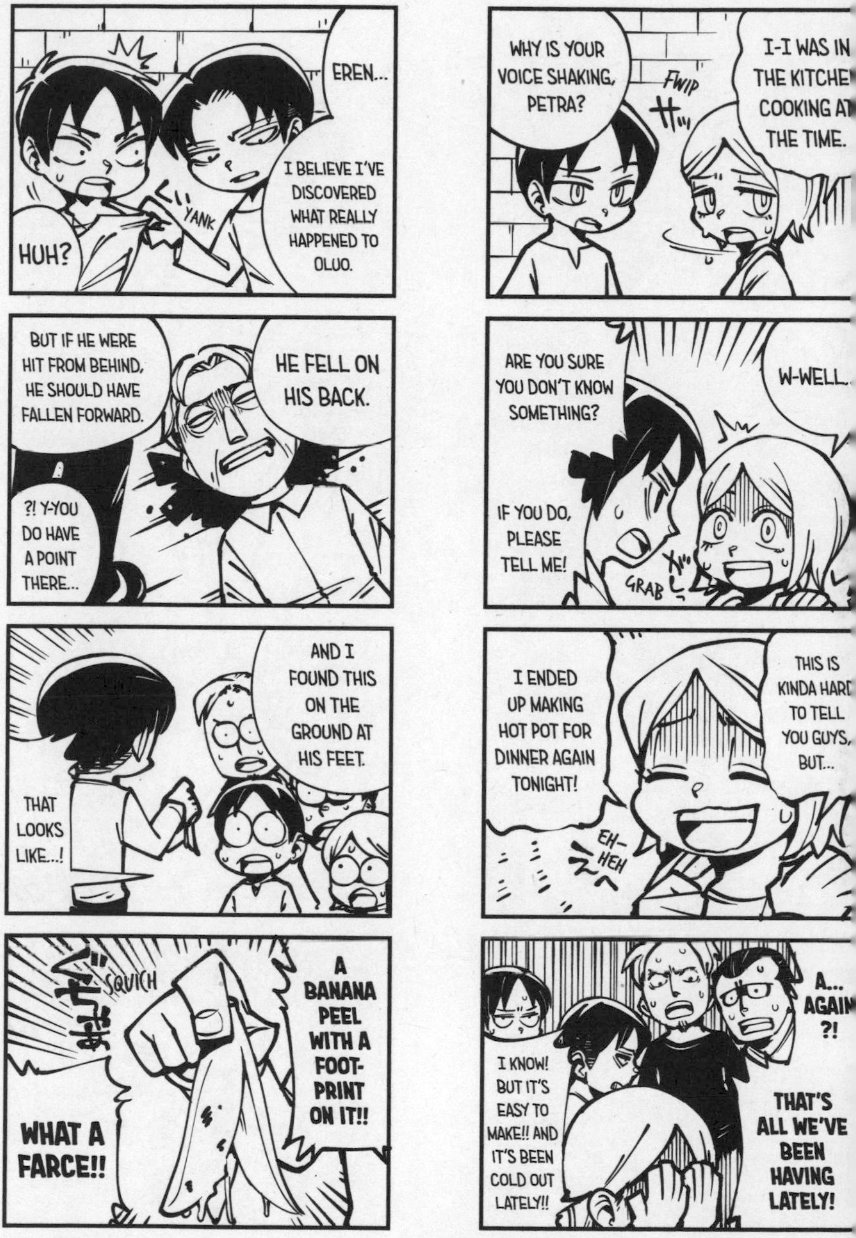
I-I WAS IN THE KITCHE COOKING AT THE TIME.
FWIP
WHY IS YOUR VOICE SHAKING, PETRA?
W-WELL.
ARE YOU SURE YOU DON'T KNOW SOMETHING?
IF YOU DO, PLEASE TELL ME!
GRAB
THIS IS KINDA HAR TO TELL YOU GUYS, BUT...
I ENDED UP MAKING HOT POT FOR DINNER AGAIN TONIGHT!
EH-HEH
A... AGAI ?!
THAT'S ALL WE'VE BEEN HAVING LATELY!
I KNOW! BUT IT'S EASY TO MAKE!! AND IT'S BEEN COLD OUT LATELY!!
EREN...
I BELIEVE I'VE DISCOVERED WHAT REALLY HAPPENED TO OLUO.
YANK
HUH?
HE FELL ON HIS BACK.
BUT IF HE WERE HIT FROM BEHIND, HE SHOULD HAVE FALLEN FORWARD.
?! Y-YOU DO HAVE A POINT THERE...
AND I FOUND THIS ON THE GROUND AT HIS FEET.
THAT LOOKS LIKE...!
A BANANA PEEL WITH A FOOT-PRINT ON IT!!
SQUICH
WHAT A FARCE!!

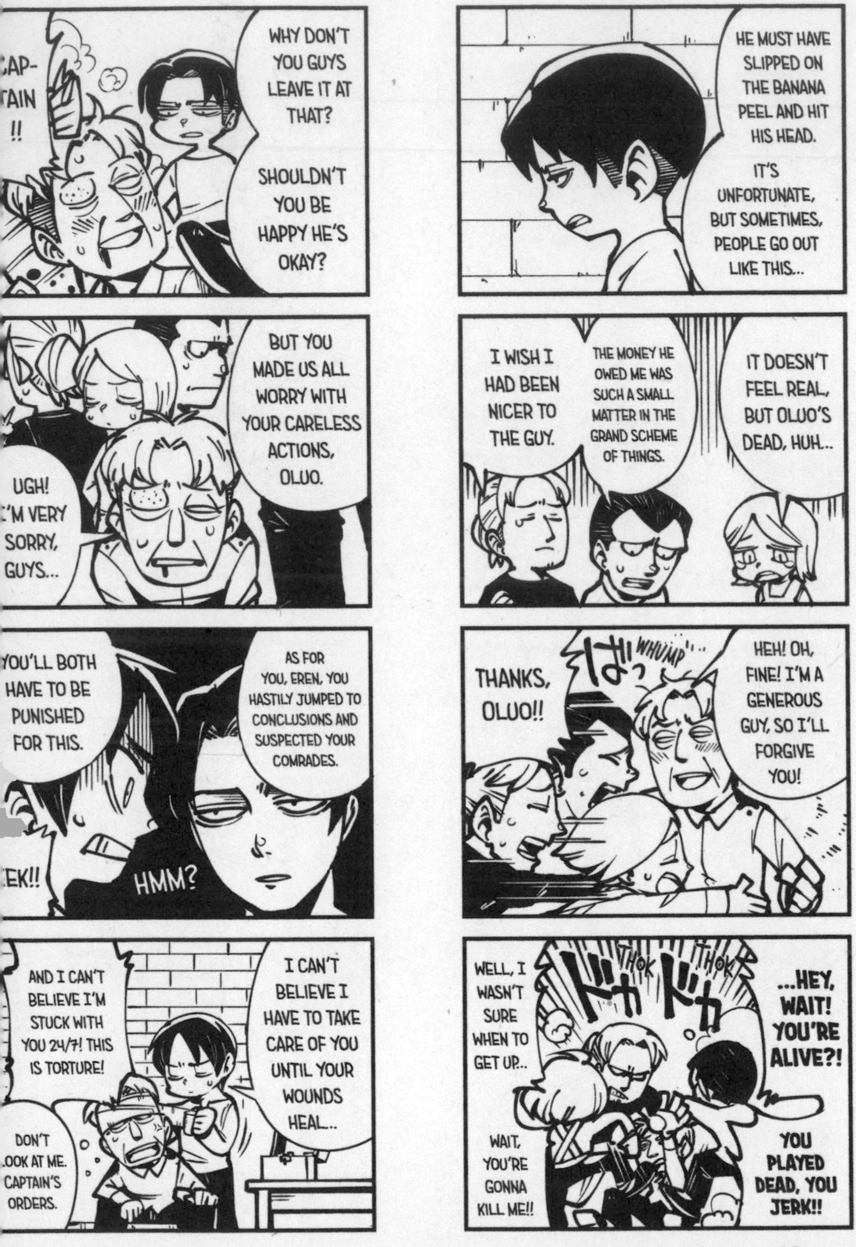
HE MUST HAVE SLIPPED ON THE BANANA PEEL AND HIT HIS HEAD.
IT'S UNFORTUNATE, BUT SOMETIMES, PEOPLE GO OUT LIKE THIS...
IT DOESN'T FEEL REAL, BUT OLUO'S DEAD, HUH...
THE MONEY HE OWED ME WAS SUCH A SMALL MATTER IN THE GRAND SCHEME OF THINGS.
I WISH I HAD BEEN NICER TO THE GUY.
HEH! OH, FINE! I'M A GENEROUS GUY, SO I'LL FORGIVE YOU!
WHUMP
THANKS, OLUO!!
...HEY, WAIT! YOU'RE ALIVE?!
THOK THOK
WELL, I WASN'T SURE WHEN TO GET UP...
YOU PLAYED DEAD, YOU JERK!!
WAIT, YOU'RE GONNA KILL ME!!
WHY DON'T YOU GUYS LEAVE IT AT THAT?
SHOULDN'T YOU BE HAPPY HE'S OKAY?
AP- AIN !!
BUT YOU MADE US ALL WORRY WITH YOUR CARELESS ACTIONS, OLUO.
UGH! 'M VERY SORRY, GUYS...
AS FOR YOU, EREN, YOU HASTILY JUMPED TO CONCLUSIONS AND SUSPECTED YOUR COMRADES.
YOU'LL BOTH HAVE TO BE PUNISHED FOR THIS.
HMM?
EK!!
I CAN'T BELIEVE I HAVE TO TAKE CARE OF YOU UNTIL YOUR WOUNDS HEAL...
AND I CAN'T BELIEVE I'M STUCK WITH YOU 24/7! THIS IS TORTURE!
DON'T OOK AT ME. CAPTAIN'S ORDERS.

SPOOF on TITAN

#8 Jean and the Love Umbrellas

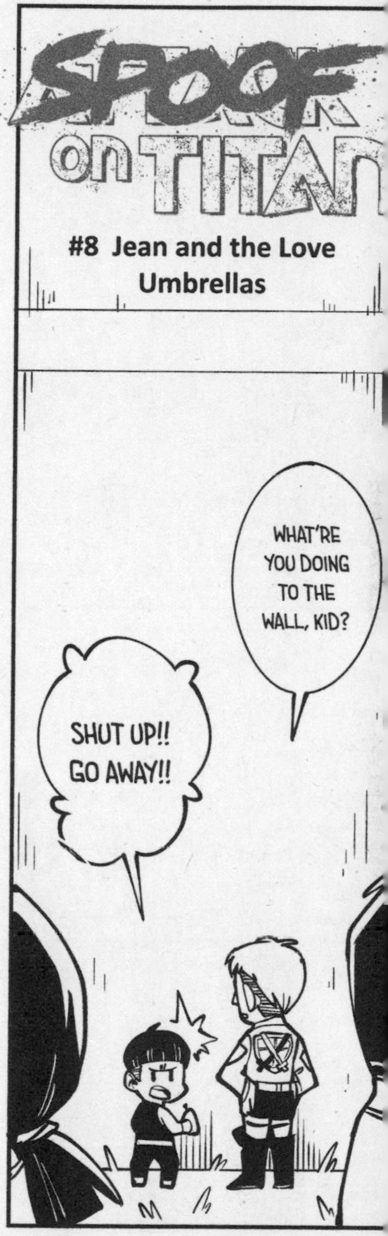
WHAT'RE YOU DOING TO THE WALL, KID?
SHUT UP!! GO AWAY!!

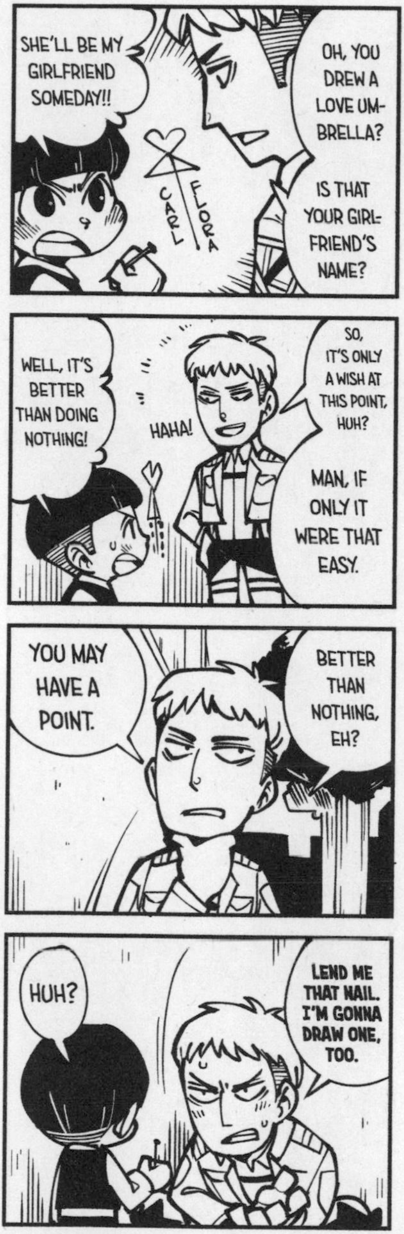
OH, YOU DREW A LOVE UM-BRELLA?
IS THAT YOUR GIRL-FRIEND'S NAME?
SHE'LL BE MY GIRLFRIEND SOMEDAY!!
FLORA
CARL
SO, IT'S ONLY A WISH AT THIS POINT, HUH?
WELL, IT'S BETTER THAN DOING NOTHING!
HAHA!
MAN, IF ONLY IT WERE THAT EASY.
BETTER THAN NOTHING, EH?
YOU MAY HAVE A POINT.
LEND ME THAT NAIL. I'M GONNA DRAW ONE, TOO.
HUH?

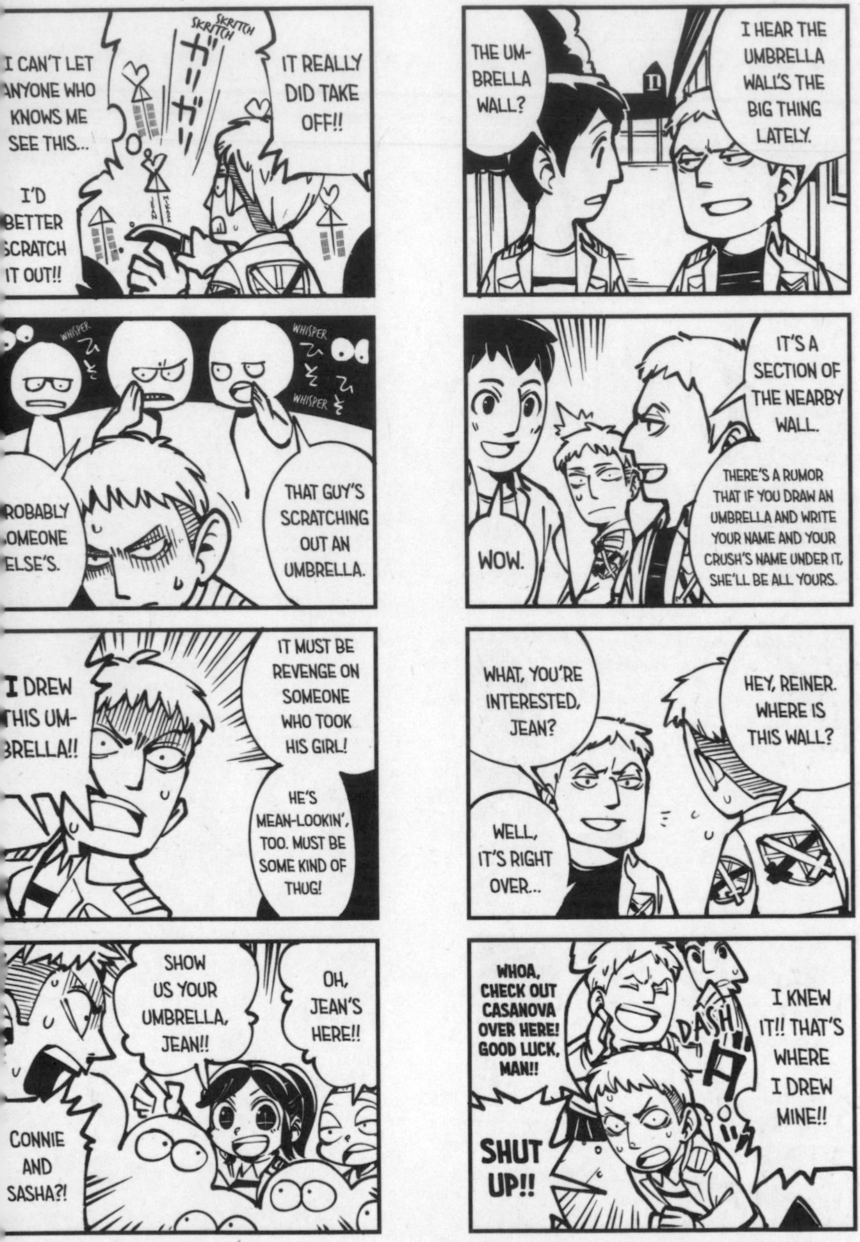

I HEAR THE UMBRELLA WALL'S THE BIG THING LATELY.
THE UM-BRELLA WALL?
IT'S A SECTION OF THE NEARBY WALL.
THERE'S A RUMOR THAT IF YOU DRAW AN UMBRELLA AND WRITE YOUR NAME AND YOUR CRUSH'S NAME UNDER IT, SHE'LL BE ALL YOURS.
WOW.
HEY, REINER. WHERE IS THIS WALL?
WHAT, YOU'RE INTERESTED, JEAN?
WELL, IT'S RIGHT OVER...
I KNEW IT!! THAT'S WHERE I DREW MINE!!
DASH
WHOA, CHECK OUT CASANOVA OVER HERE! GOOD LUCK, MAN!!
SHUT UP!!
IT REALLY DID TAKE OFF!!
SKRITCH SKRITCH
ガリガリ
I CAN'T LET ANYONE WHO KNOWS ME SEE THIS...
I'D BETTER SCRATCH IT OUT!!
WHISPER WHISPER
THAT GUY'S SCRATCHING OUT AN UMBRELLA.
ROBABLY OMEONE ELSE'S.
IT MUST BE REVENGE ON SOMEONE WHO TOOK HIS GIRL!
HE'S MEAN-LOOKIN', TOO. MUST BE SOME KIND OF THUG!
I DREW THIS UM-BRELLA!!
OH, JEAN'S HERE!!
SHOW US YOUR UMBRELLA, JEAN!!
CONNIE AND SASHA?!

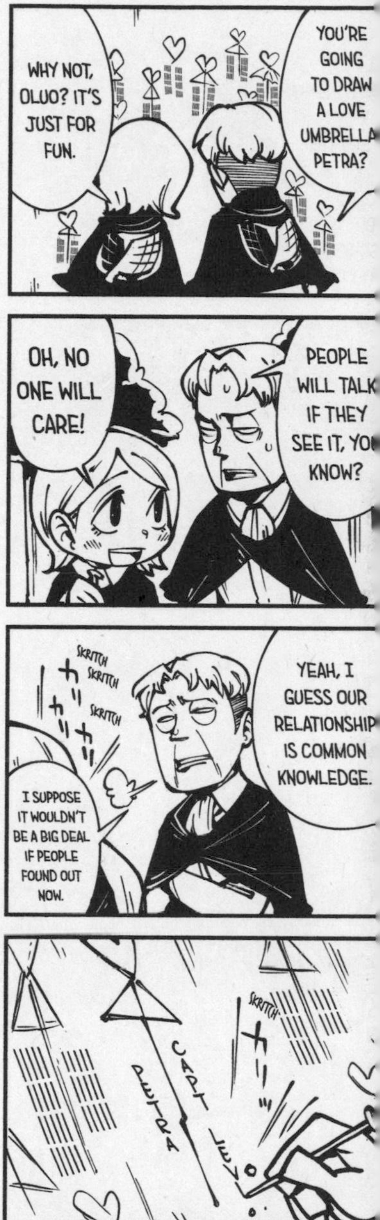
YOU'RE GOING TO DRAW A LOVE UMBRELLA PETRA?
WHY NOT, OLUO? IT'S JUST FOR FUN.
PEOPLE WILL TALK IF THEY SEE IT, YOU KNOW?
OH, NO ONE WILL CARE!
YEAH, I GUESS OUR RELATIONSHIP IS COMMON KNOWLEDGE.
SKRITCH SKRITCH
SKRITCH
I SUPPOSE IT WOULDN'T BE A BIG DEAL IF PEOPLE FOUND OUT NOW.
SKRITCH
CAPT
LEV
PETRA

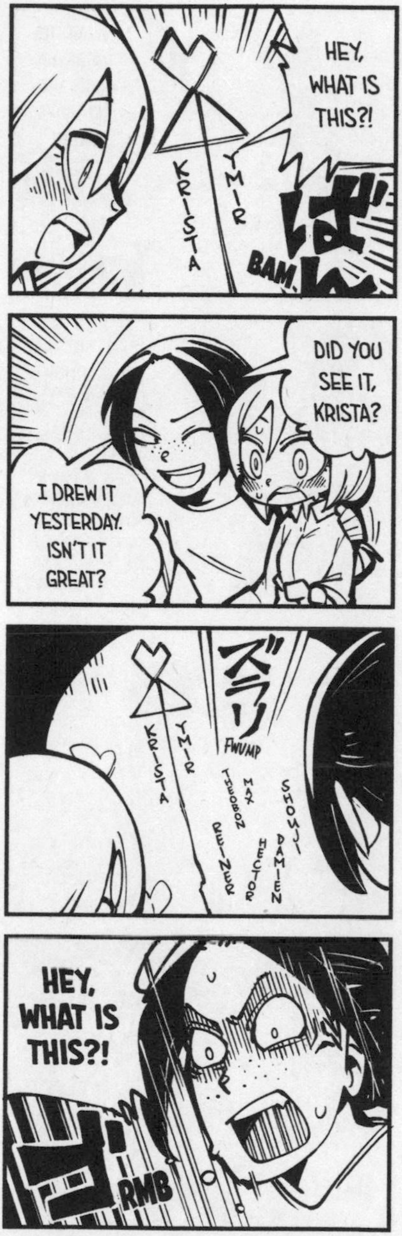
HEY, WHAT IS THIS?!
YMIR
KRISTA
ばん
BAM
DID YOU SEE IT, KRISTA?
I DREW IT YESTERDAY. ISN'T IT GREAT?
ズラリ
FWUMP
SHOUJI
DAMIEN
HECTOR
MAX
THEOBON
REINER
YMIR
KRISTA
HEY, WHAT IS THIS?!
RMB

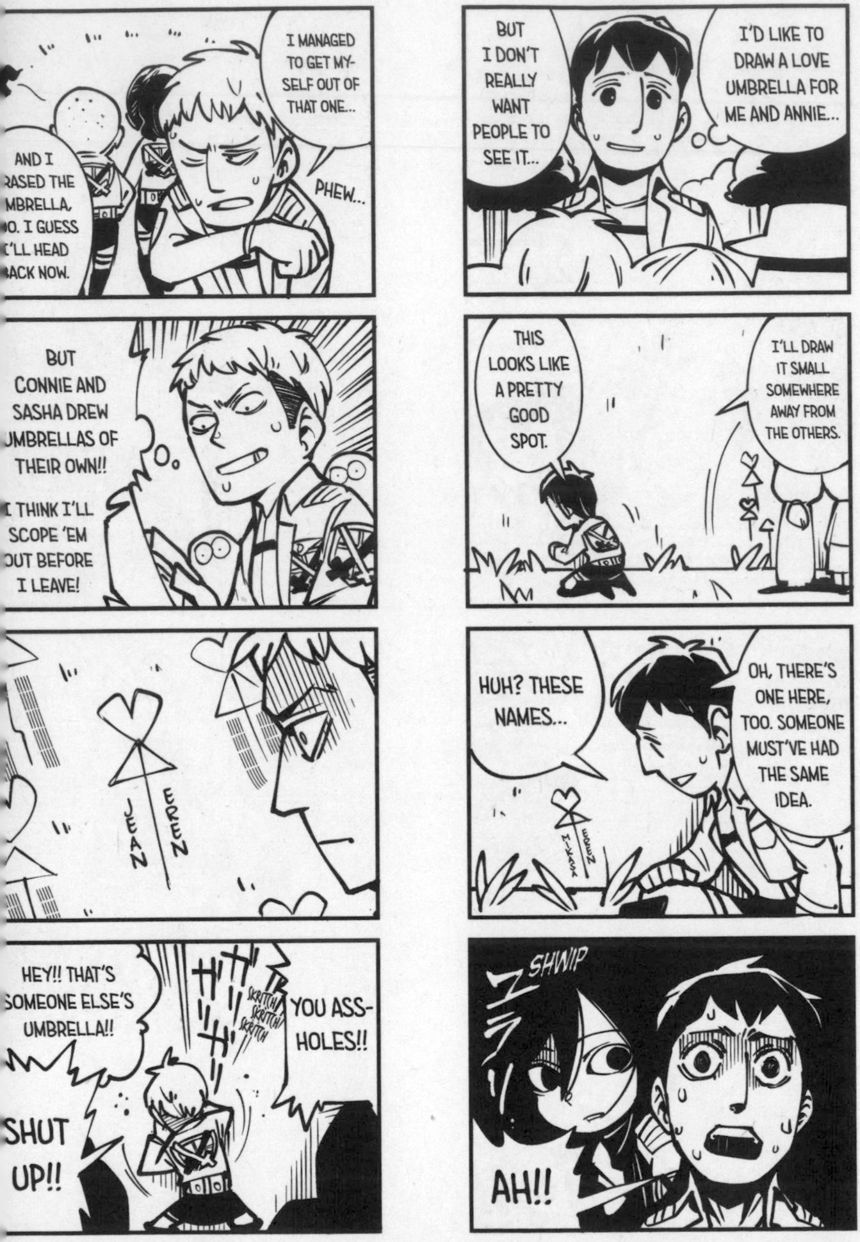

I'D LIKE TO DRAW A LOVE UMBRELLA FOR ME AND ANNIE...
BUT I DON'T REALLY WANT PEOPLE TO SEE IT...
I'LL DRAW IT SMALL SOMEWHERE AWAY FROM THE OTHERS.
THIS LOOKS LIKE A PRETTY GOOD SPOT.
OH, THERE'S ONE HERE, TOO. SOMEONE MUST'VE HAD THE SAME IDEA.
HUH? THESE NAMES...
EREN
MIKASA
SHWIP
AH!!
I MANAGED TO GET MY-SELF OUT OF THAT ONE...
PHEW...
AND I RASED THE MBRELLA, O. I GUESS 'LL HEAD ACK NOW.
BUT CONNIE AND SASHA DREW MBRELLAS OF THEIR OWN!!
THINK I'LL SCOPE 'EM UT BEFORE I LEAVE!
EREN
JEAN
YOU ASS-HOLES!!
SKRITCH SKRITCH SKRITCH
HEY!! THAT'S OMEONE ELSE'S UMBRELLA!!
SHUT UP!!

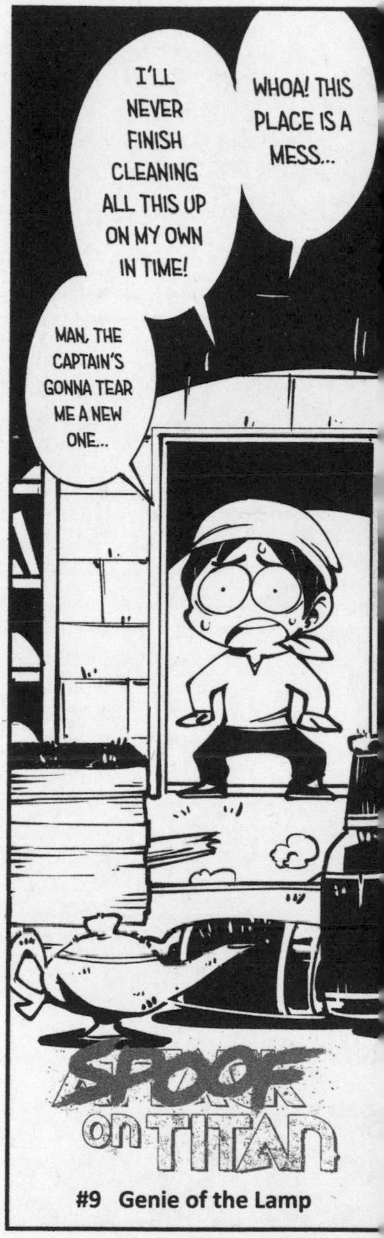
WHOA! THIS PLACE IS A MESS...
I'LL NEVER FINISH CLEANING ALL THIS UP ON MY OWN IN TIME!
MAN, THE CAPTAIN'S GONNA TEAR ME A NEW ONE...
SPOOF on TITAN
#9 Genie of the Lamp

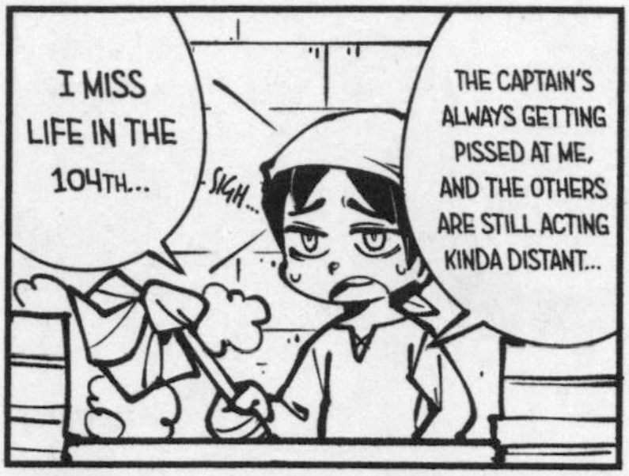
THE CAPTAIN'S ALWAYS GETTING PISSED AT ME, AND THE OTHERS ARE STILL ACTING KINDA DISTANT...
SIGH...
I MISS LIFE IN THE 104TH...

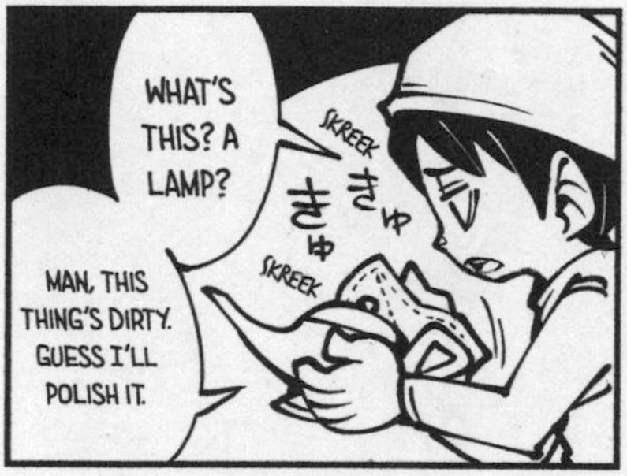
きゅ
SKREEK
きゅ
SKREEK
WHAT'S THIS? A LAMP?
MAN, THIS THING'S DIRTY. GUESS I'LL POLISH IT.

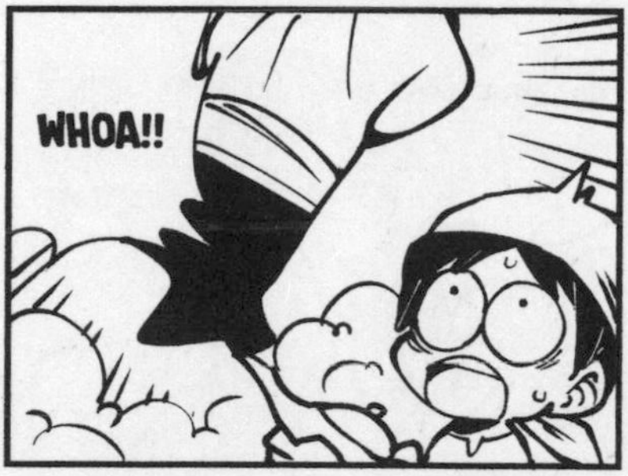
WHOA!!

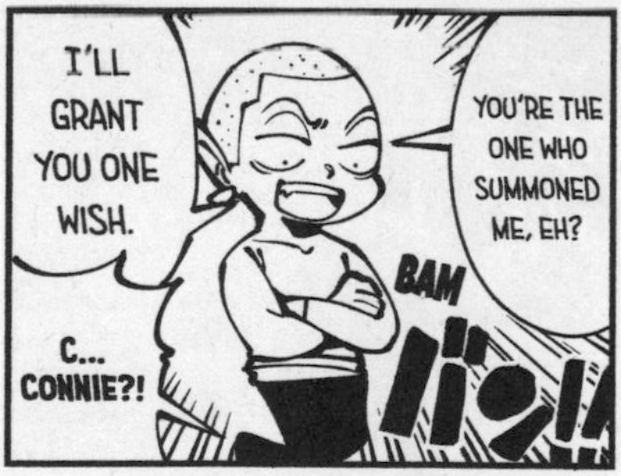
YOU'RE THE ONE WHO SUMMONED ME, EH?
BAM
I'LL GRANT YOU ONE WISH.
C... CONNIE?!

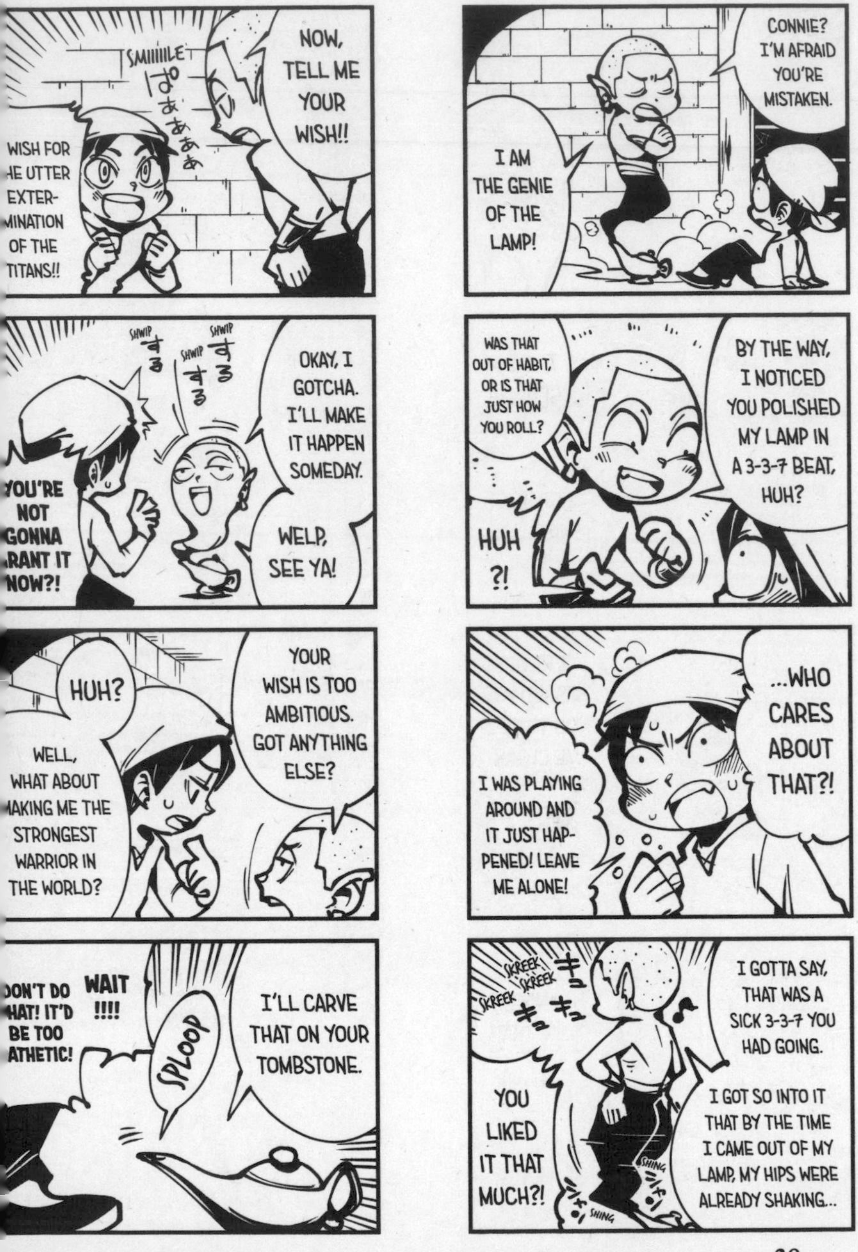
CONNIE? I'M AFRAID YOU'RE MISTAKEN.
I AM THE GENIE OF THE LAMP!
BY THE WAY, I NOTICED YOU POLISHED MY LAMP IN A 3-3-7 BEAT, HUH?
WAS THAT OUT OF HABIT, OR IS THAT JUST HOW YOU ROLL?
HUH ?!
...WHO CARES ABOUT THAT?!
I WAS PLAYING AROUND AND IT JUST HAPPENED! LEAVE ME ALONE!
SKREEK キュ SKREEK キュ SKREEK キュ
I GOTTA SAY, THAT WAS A SICK 3-3-7 YOU HAD GOING.
I GOT SO INTO IT THAT BY THE TIME I CAME OUT OF MY LAMP, MY HIPS WERE ALREADY SHAKING...
YOU LIKED IT THAT MUCH?!
SHING シャ! SHING シャ!
NOW, TELL ME YOUR WISH!!
SMIIIIILE ぱぁぁぁぁ
WISH FOR HE UTTER EXTER-MINATION OF THE TITANS!!
OKAY, I GOTCHA. I'LL MAKE IT HAPPEN SOMEDAY.
SHWIP する SHWIP する SHWIP する
WELP, SEE YA!
YOU'RE NOT GONNA RANT IT NOW?!
YOUR WISH IS TOO AMBITIOUS. GOT ANYTHING ELSE?
HUH?
WELL, WHAT ABOUT AKING ME THE STRONGEST WARRIOR IN THE WORLD?
I'LL CARVE THAT ON YOUR TOMBSTONE.
SPLOOP
WAIT !!!!
ON'T DO HAT! IT'D BE TOO ATHETIC!

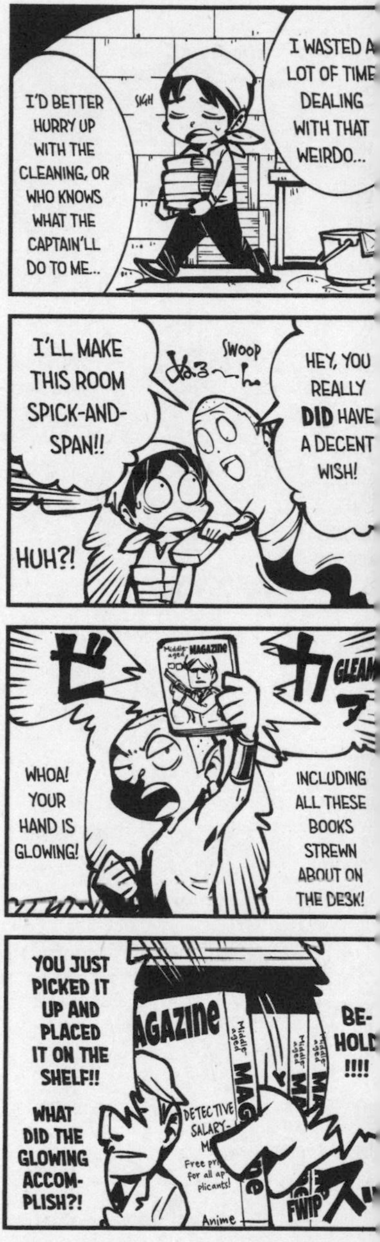
I WASTED A LOT OF TIME DEALING WITH THAT WEIRDO...
SIGH
I'D BETTER HURRY UP WITH THE CLEANING, OR WHO KNOWS WHAT THE CAPTAIN'LL DO TO ME..
HEY, YOU REALLY DID HAVE A DECENT WISH!
SWOOP
I'LL MAKE THIS ROOM SPICK-AND-SPAN!!
HUH?!
GLEAM
INCLUDING ALL THESE BOOKS STREWN ABOUT ON THE DESK!
Middle-aged MAGAZINE
WHOA! YOUR HAND IS GLOWING!
BE-HOLD!!!!
MAGAZINE
YOU JUST PICKED IT UP AND PLACED IT ON THE SHELF!!
WHAT DID THE GLOWING ACCOMPLISH?!
FWIP

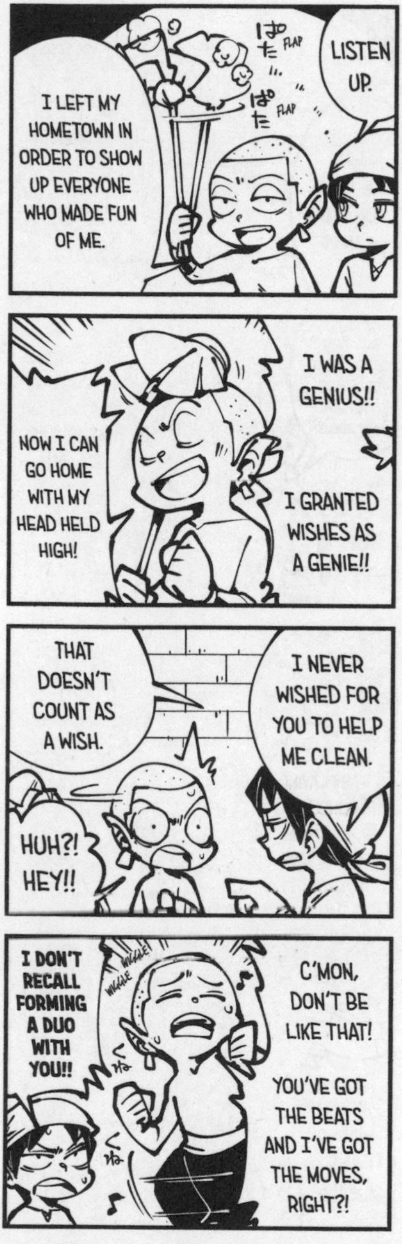
LISTEN UP.
FLAP
FLAP
I LEFT MY HOMETOWN IN ORDER TO SHOW UP EVERYONE WHO MADE FUN OF ME.
I WAS A GENIUS!!
I GRANTED WISHES AS A GENIE!!
NOW I CAN GO HOME WITH MY HEAD HELD HIGH!
I NEVER WISHED FOR YOU TO HELP ME CLEAN.
THAT DOESN'T COUNT AS A WISH.
HUH?! HEY!!
C'MON, DON'T BE LIKE THAT!
YOU'VE GOT THE BEATS AND I'VE GOT THE MOVES, RIGHT?!
WIGGLE
WIGGLE
I DON'T RECALL FORMING A DUO WITH YOU!!

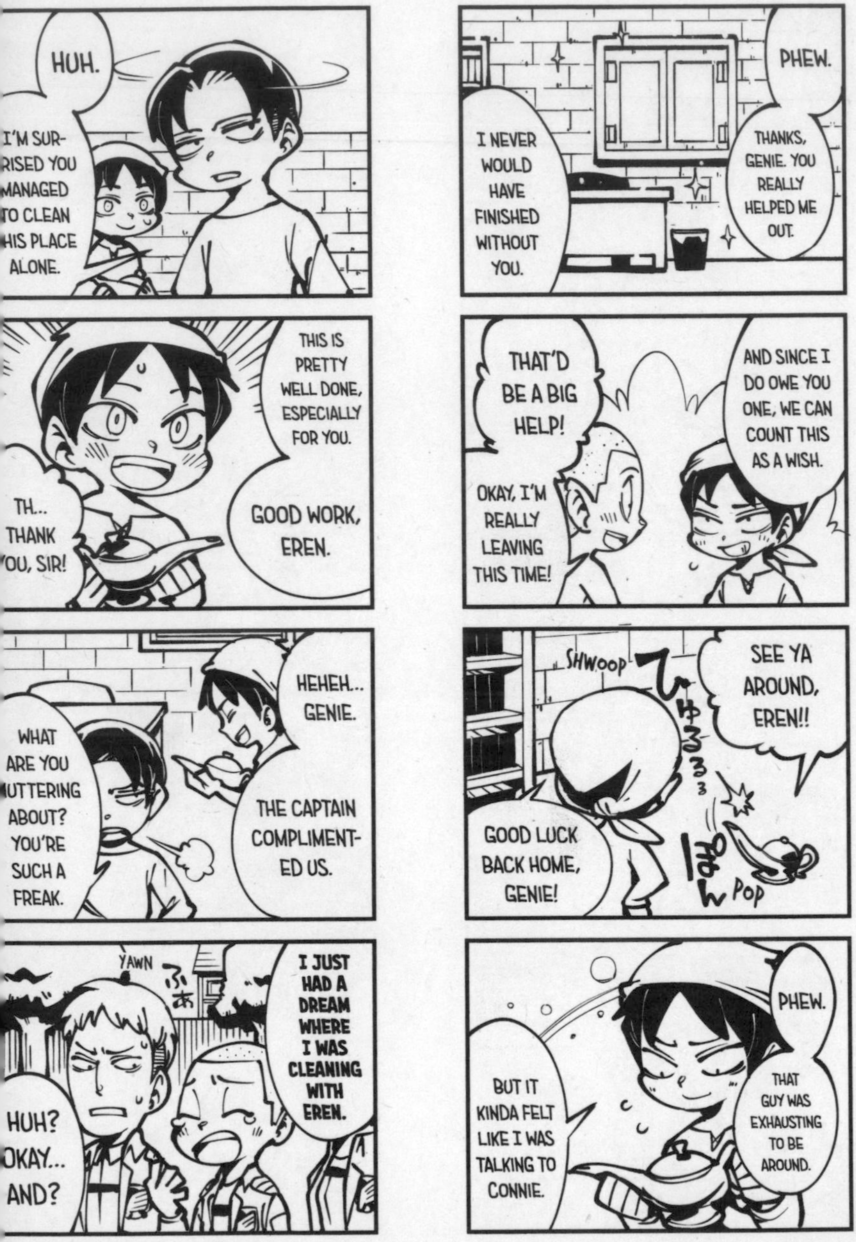
PHEW.
THANKS, GENIE. YOU REALLY HELPED ME OUT.
I NEVER WOULD HAVE FINISHED WITHOUT YOU.
AND SINCE I DO OWE YOU ONE, WE CAN COUNT THIS AS A WISH.
THAT'D BE A BIG HELP!
OKAY, I'M REALLY LEAVING THIS TIME!
SEE YA AROUND, EREN!!
ひゅるるる
SHWOOP
ぽん
POP
GOOD LUCK BACK HOME, GENIE!
PHEW.
THAT GUY WAS EXHAUSTING TO BE AROUND.
BUT IT KINDA FELT LIKE I WAS TALKING TO CONNIE.
HUH.
I'M SUR- RISED YOU MANAGED TO CLEAN HIS PLACE ALONE.
THIS IS PRETTY WELL DONE, ESPECIALLY FOR YOU.
GOOD WORK, EREN.
TH... THANK OU, SIR!
HEHEH... GENIE.
THE CAPTAIN COMPLIMENT- ED US.
WHAT ARE YOU UTTERING ABOUT? YOU'RE SUCH A FREAK.
I JUST HAD A DREAM WHERE I WAS CLEANING WITH EREN.
YAWN
ふあ
HUH? OKAY... AND?

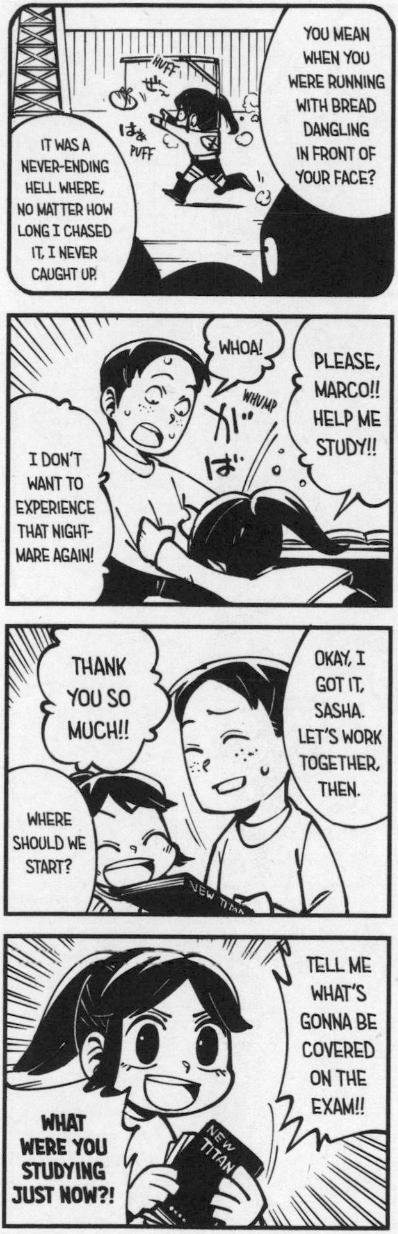
YOU MEAN WHEN YOU WERE RUNNING WITH BREAD DANGLING IN FRONT OF YOUR FACE?
HUFF
ぜぇ
はぁ
PUFF
IT WAS A NEVER-ENDING HELL WHERE, NO MATTER HOW LONG I CHASED IT, I NEVER CAUGHT UP.
PLEASE, MARCO!! HELP ME STUDY!!
WHOA!
WHUMP
がば
I DON'T WANT TO EXPERIENCE THAT NIGHT-MARE AGAIN!
OKAY, I GOT IT, SASHA. LET'S WORK TOGETHER, THEN.
THANK YOU SO MUCH!!
WHERE SHOULD WE START?
NEW TITAN
TELL ME WHAT'S GONNA BE COVERED ON THE EXAM!!
NEW TITAN
WHAT WERE YOU STUDYING JUST NOW?!

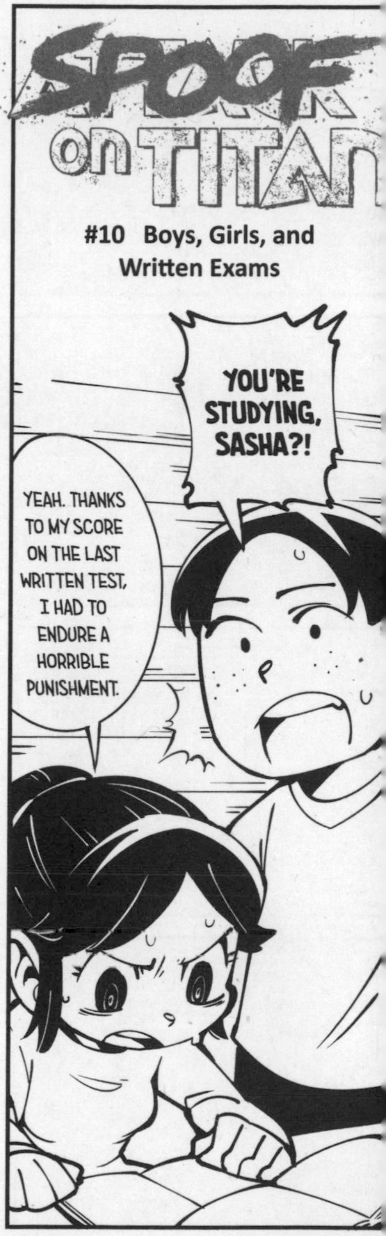
SPOOF on TITAN
#10 Boys, Girls, and Written Exams
YOU'RE STUDYING, SASHA?!
YEAH. THANKS TO MY SCORE ON THE LAST WRITTEN TEST, I HAD TO ENDURE A HORRIBLE PUNISHMENT.

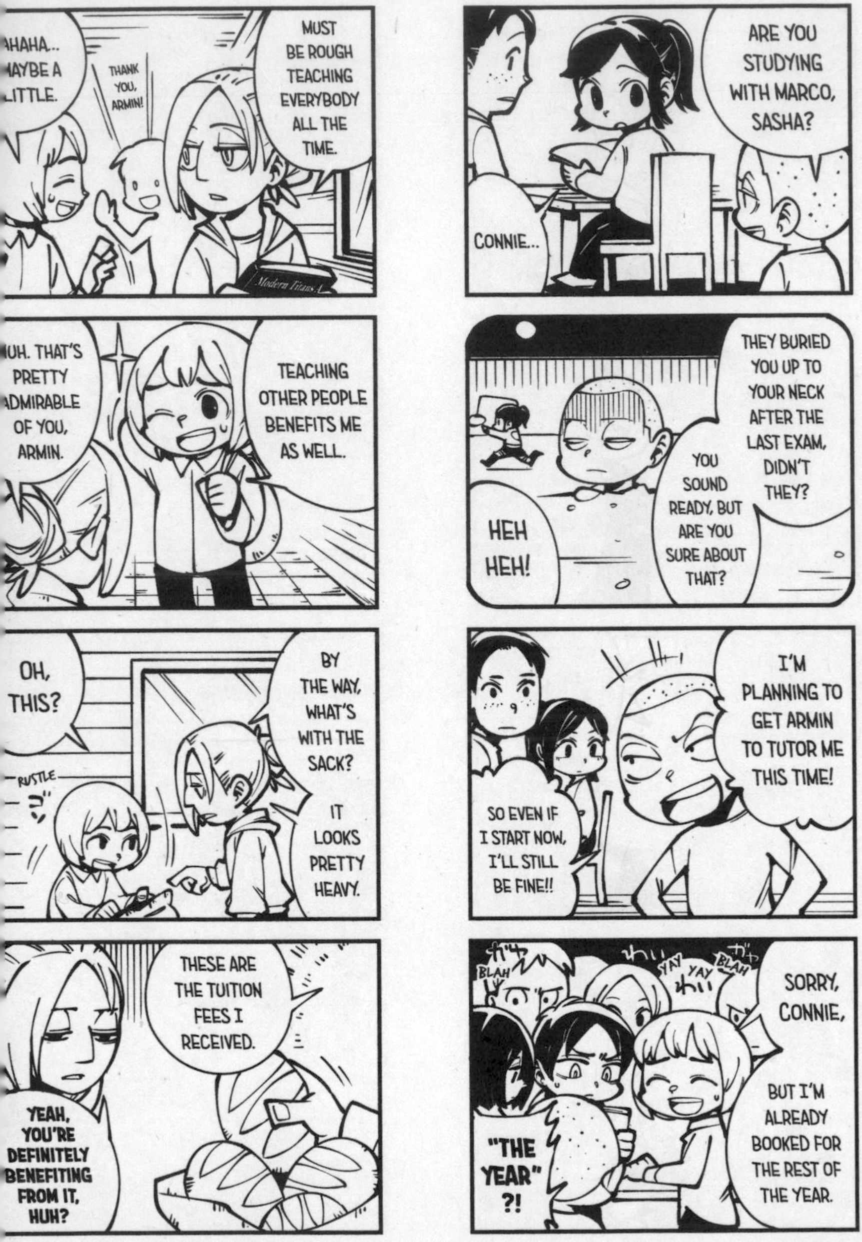
ARE YOU STUDYING WITH MARCO, SASHA?
CONNIE...
THEY BURIED YOU UP TO YOUR NECK AFTER THE LAST EXAM, DIDN'T THEY?
YOU SOUND READY, BUT ARE YOU SURE ABOUT THAT?
HEH HEH!
I'M PLANNING TO GET ARMIN TO TUTOR ME THIS TIME!
SO EVEN IF I START NOW, I'LL STILL BE FINE!!
BLAH
YAY
YAY
BLAH
SORRY, CONNIE,
BUT I'M ALREADY BOOKED FOR THE REST OF THE YEAR.
"THE YEAR"?!
MUST BE ROUGH TEACHING EVERYBODY ALL THE TIME.
THANK YOU, ARMIN!
AHAHA... MAYBE A LITTLE.
Modern Titans
TEACHING OTHER PEOPLE BENEFITS ME AS WELL.
HUH. THAT'S PRETTY ADMIRABLE OF YOU, ARMIN.
BY THE WAY, WHAT'S WITH THE SACK?
IT LOOKS PRETTY HEAVY.
OH, THIS?
RUSTLE
THESE ARE THE TUITION FEES I RECEIVED.
YEAH, YOU'RE DEFINITELY BENEFITING FROM IT, HUH?

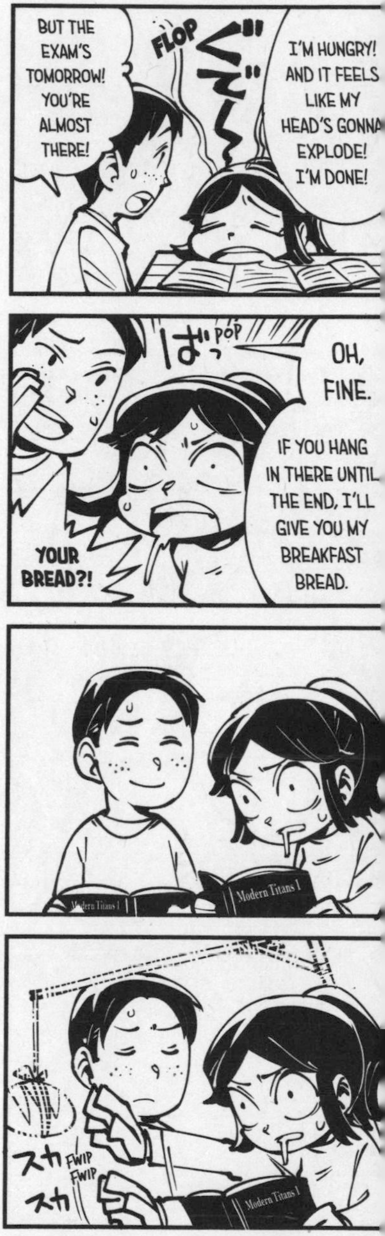
I'M HUNGRY! AND IT FEELS LIKE MY HEAD'S GONNA EXPLODE! I'M DONE!
FLOP
BUT THE EXAM'S TOMORROW! YOU'RE ALMOST THERE!
OH, FINE.
IF YOU HANG IN THERE UNTIL THE END, I'LL GIVE YOU MY BREAKFAST BREAD.
ばっ POP
YOUR BREAD?!
Modern Titans I
Modern Titans I
スカ FWIP
FWIP スカ
Modern Titans I

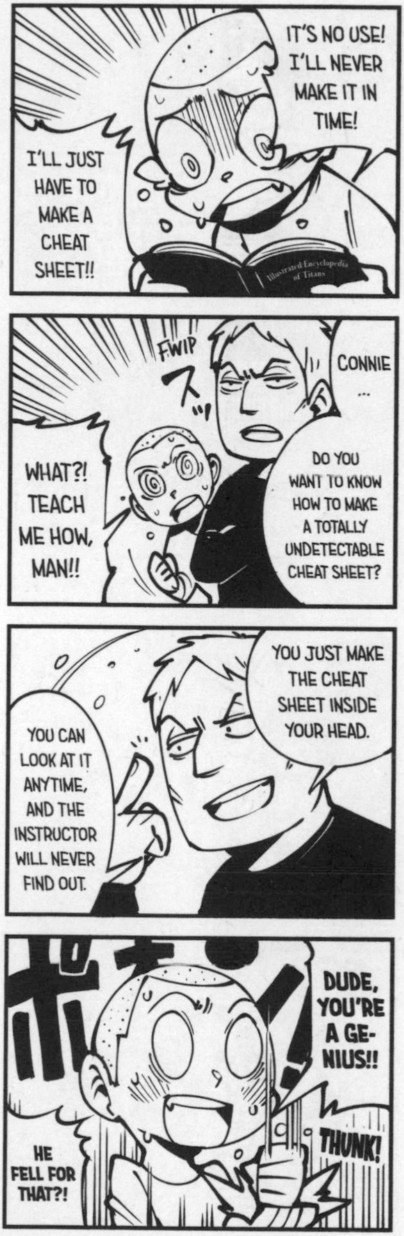
IT'S NO USE! I'LL NEVER MAKE IT IN TIME!
I'LL JUST HAVE TO MAKE A CHEAT SHEET!!
Illustrated Encyclopedia of Titans
CONNIE ...
FWIP ス
DO YOU WANT TO KNOW HOW TO MAKE A TOTALLY UNDETECTABLE CHEAT SHEET?
WHAT?! TEACH ME HOW, MAN!!
YOU JUST MAKE THE CHEAT SHEET INSIDE YOUR HEAD.
YOU CAN LOOK AT IT ANYTIME, AND THE INSTRUCTOR WILL NEVER FIND OUT.
DUDE, YOU'RE A GE- NIUS!!
THUNK!
HE FELL FOR THAT?!

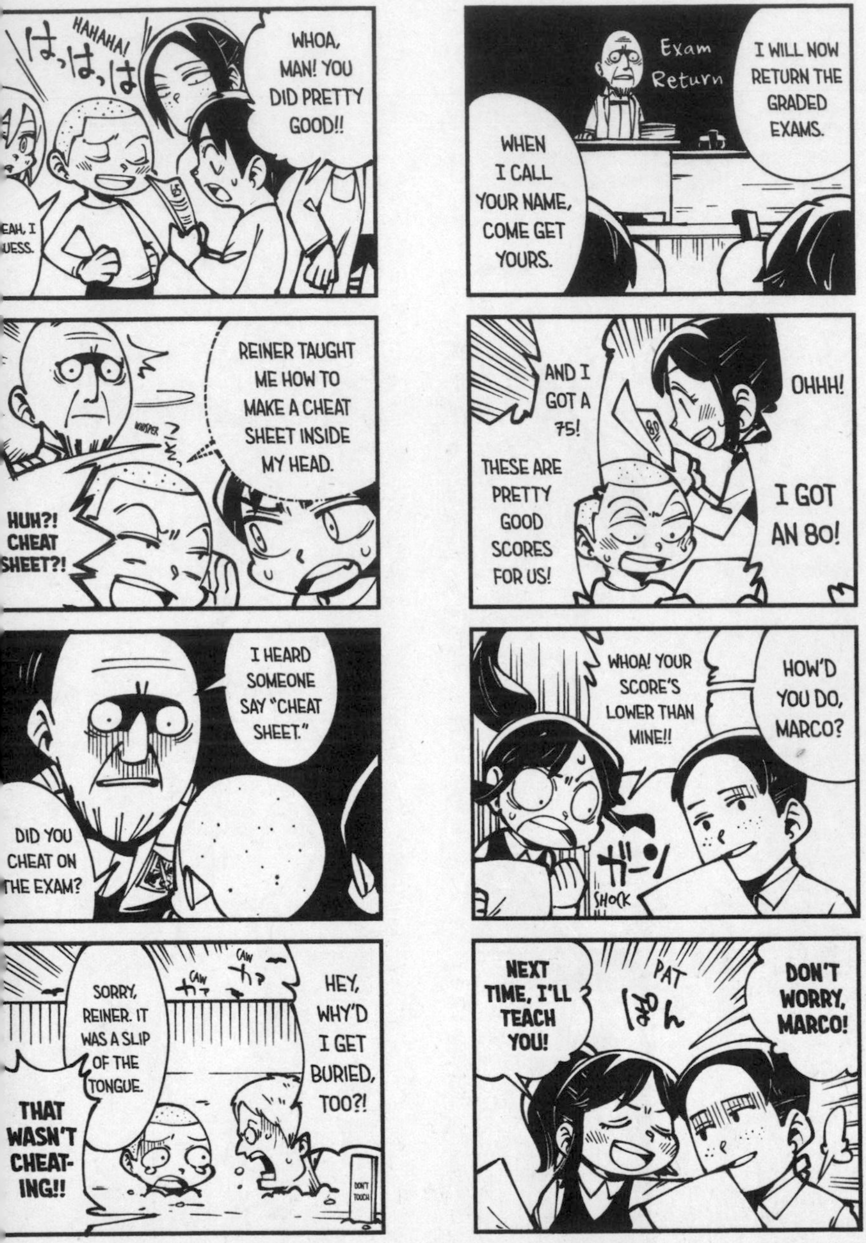

I WILL NOW RETURN THE GRADED EXAMS.
Exam Return
WHEN I CALL YOUR NAME, COME GET YOURS.
OHHH!
I GOT AN 80!
AND I GOT A 75!
THESE ARE PRETTY GOOD SCORES FOR US!
HOW'D YOU DO, MARCO?
WHOA! YOUR SCORE'S LOWER THAN MINE!!
ガーン SHOCK
DON'T WORRY, MARCO!
PAT ぽん
NEXT TIME, I'LL TEACH YOU!
WHOA, MAN! YOU DID PRETTY GOOD!!
HAHAHA! はっはっは
EAH, I UESS.
REINER TAUGHT ME HOW TO MAKE A CHEAT SHEET INSIDE MY HEAD.
WHISPER
HUH?! CHEAT SHEET?!
I HEARD SOMEONE SAY "CHEAT SHEET."
DID YOU CHEAT ON THE EXAM?
HEY, WHY'D I GET BURIED, TOO?!
CAW カァ
CAW カァ
SORRY, REINER. IT WAS A SLIP OF THE TONGUE.
THAT WASN'T CHEATING!!
DON'T TOUCH

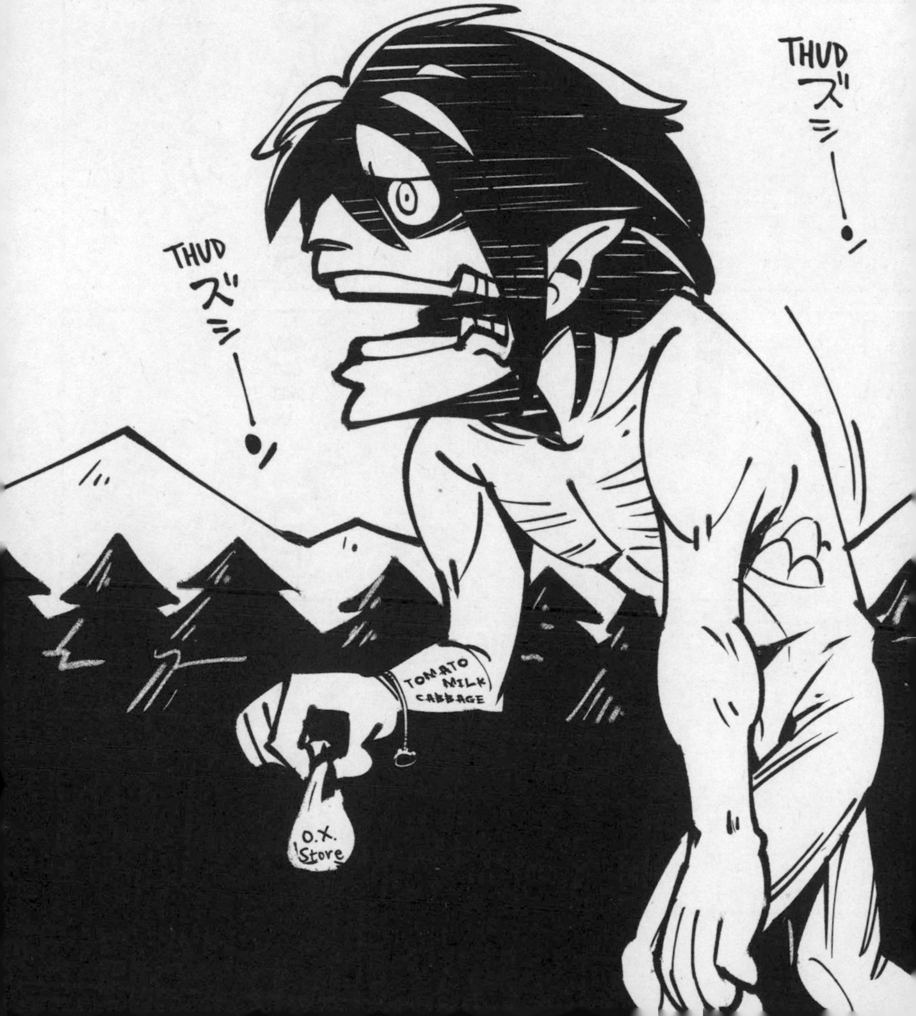
THUD
ズシーン
THUD
ズシーン
TOMATO
MILK
CABBAGE
O.X.
Store

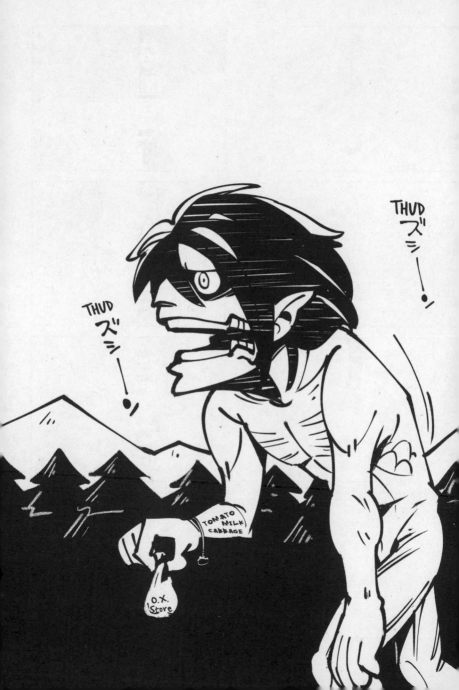

SPOOF on TITAN

SPOOF on TITAN

#11 Working Overtime with Erwin

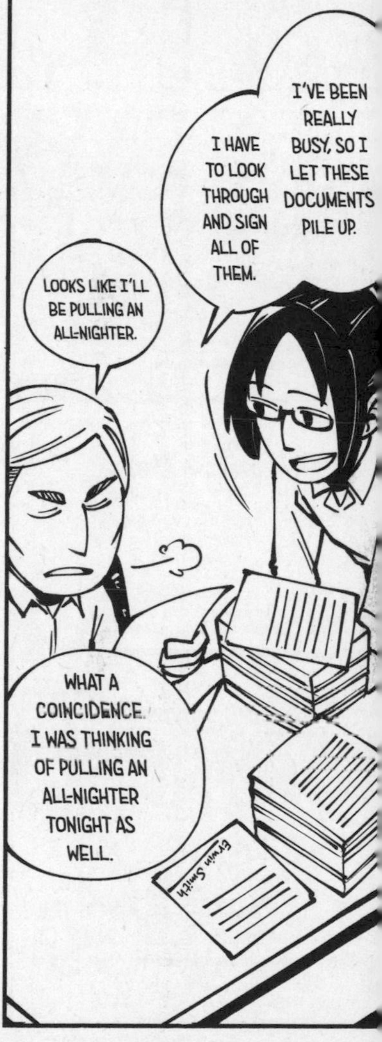
I'VE BEEN REALLY BUSY, SO I LET THESE DOCUMENTS PILE UP.
I HAVE TO LOOK THROUGH AND SIGN ALL OF THEM.
LOOKS LIKE I'LL BE PULLING AN ALL-NIGHTER.
WHAT A COINCIDENCE. I WAS THINKING OF PULLING AN ALL-NIGHTER TONIGHT AS WELL.
Erwin Smith

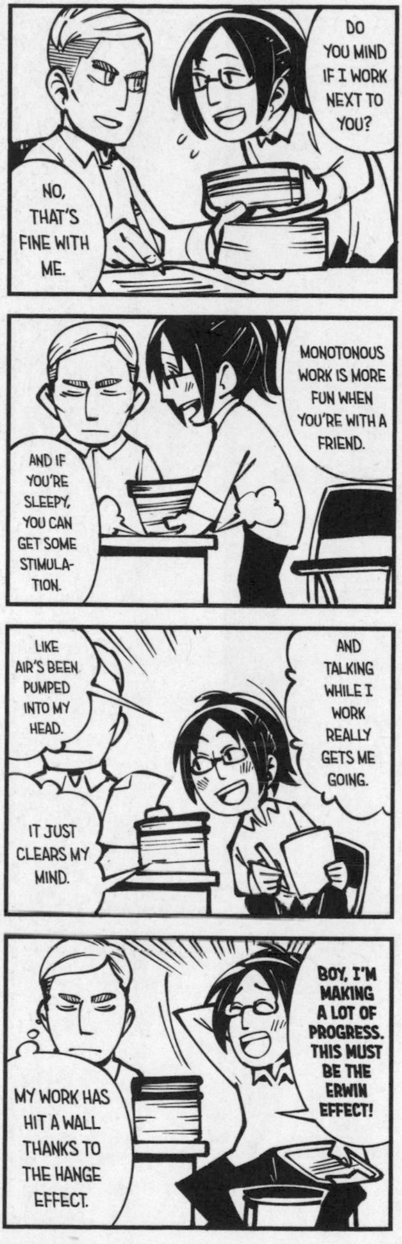
DO YOU MIND IF I WORK NEXT TO YOU?
NO, THAT'S FINE WITH ME.
MONOTONOUS WORK IS MORE FUN WHEN YOU'RE WITH A FRIEND.
AND IF YOU'RE SLEEPY, YOU CAN GET SOME STIMULA-TION.
AND TALKING WHILE I WORK REALLY GETS ME GOING.
LIKE AIR'S BEEN PUMPED INTO MY HEAD.
IT JUST CLEARS MY MIND.
BOY, I'M MAKING A LOT OF PROGRESS. THIS MUST BE THE ERWIN EFFECT!
MY WORK HAS HIT A WALL THANKS TO THE HANGE EFFECT.

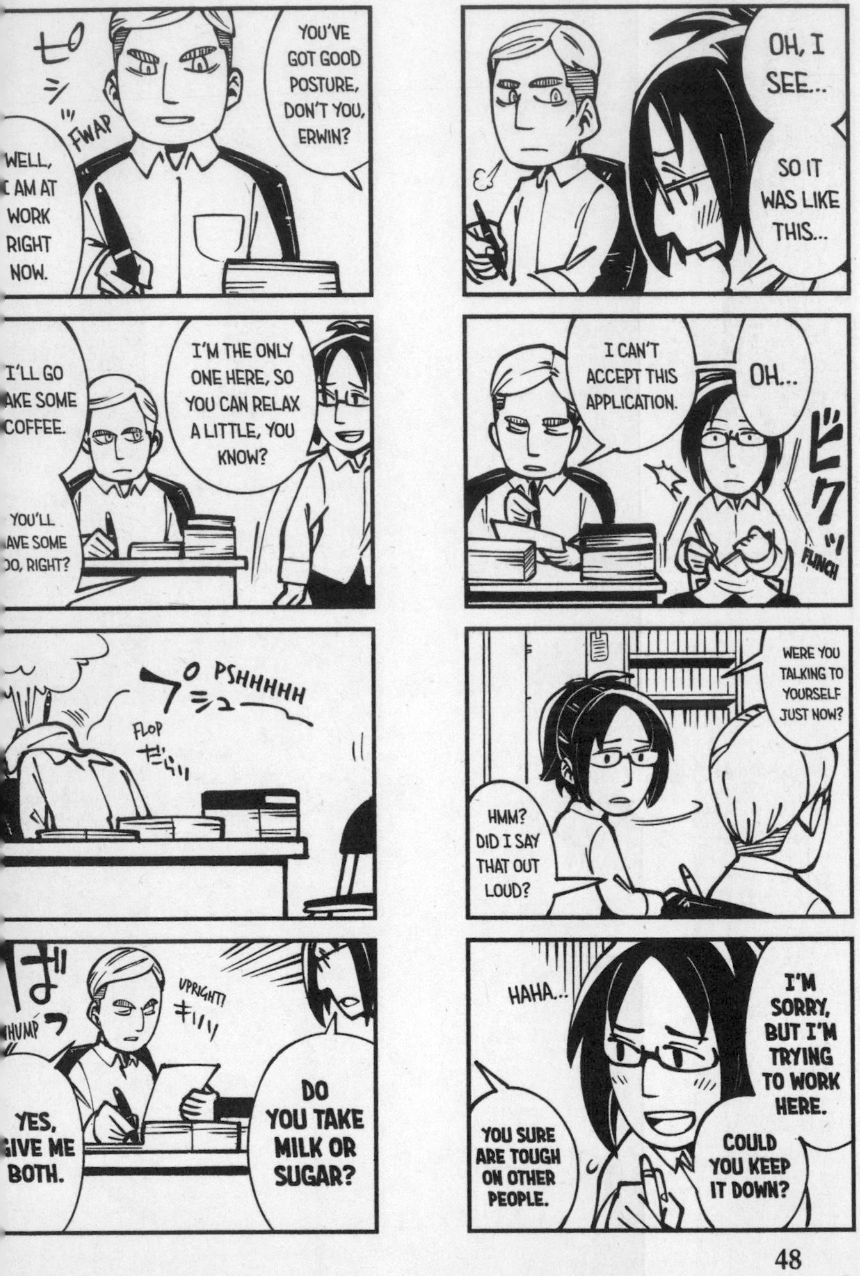
OH, I SEE...
SO IT WAS LIKE THIS...
I CAN'T ACCEPT THIS APPLICATION.
OH...
ビクッ
FLINCH
WERE YOU TALKING TO YOURSELF JUST NOW?
HMM? DID I SAY THAT OUT LOUD?
I'M SORRY, BUT I'M TRYING TO WORK HERE.
COULD YOU KEEP IT DOWN?
HAHA...
YOU SURE ARE TOUGH ON OTHER PEOPLE.
YOU'VE GOT GOOD POSTURE, DON'T YOU, ERWIN?
FWAP
WELL, I AM AT WORK RIGHT NOW.
I'M THE ONLY ONE HERE, SO YOU CAN RELAX A LITTLE, YOU KNOW?
I'LL GO AKE SOME COFFEE.
YOU'LL AVE SOME OO, RIGHT?
PSHHHHH
プシュー
FLOP
UPRIGHT!
キリッ
ばっ
THUMP
DO YOU TAKE MILK OR SUGAR?
YES, GIVE ME BOTH.

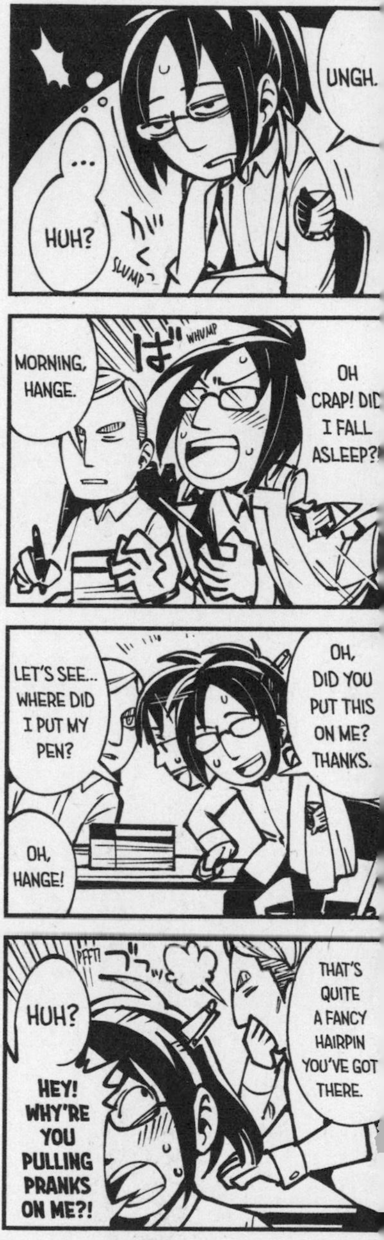
UNGH.
...
HUH?
SLUMP
OH CRAP! DID I FALL ASLEEP?!
WHUMP
MORNING, HANGE.
OH, DID YOU PUT THIS ON ME? THANKS.
LET'S SEE... WHERE DID I PUT MY PEN?
OH, HANGE!
THAT'S QUITE A FANCY HAIRPIN YOU'VE GOT THERE.
PFFT!
HUH?
HEY! WHY'RE YOU PULLING PRANKS ON ME?!

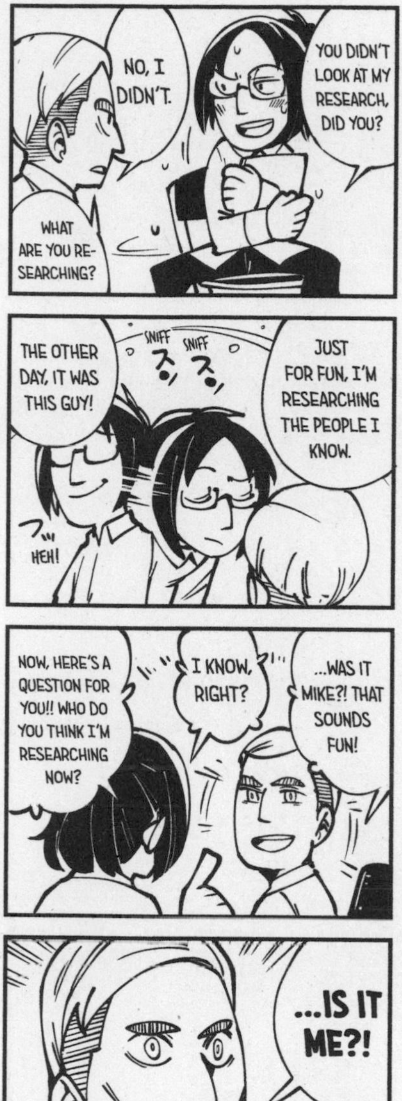
YOU DIDN'T LOOK AT MY RESEARCH, DID YOU?
NO, I DIDN'T.
WHAT ARE YOU RE-SEARCHING?
JUST FOR FUN, I'M RESEARCHING THE PEOPLE I KNOW.
SNIFF SNIFF
THE OTHER DAY, IT WAS THIS GUY!
HEH!
...WAS IT MIKE?! THAT SOUNDS FUN!
I KNOW, RIGHT?
NOW, HERE'S A QUESTION FOR YOU!! WHO DO YOU THINK I'M RESEARCHING NOW?
...IS IT ME?!
!!

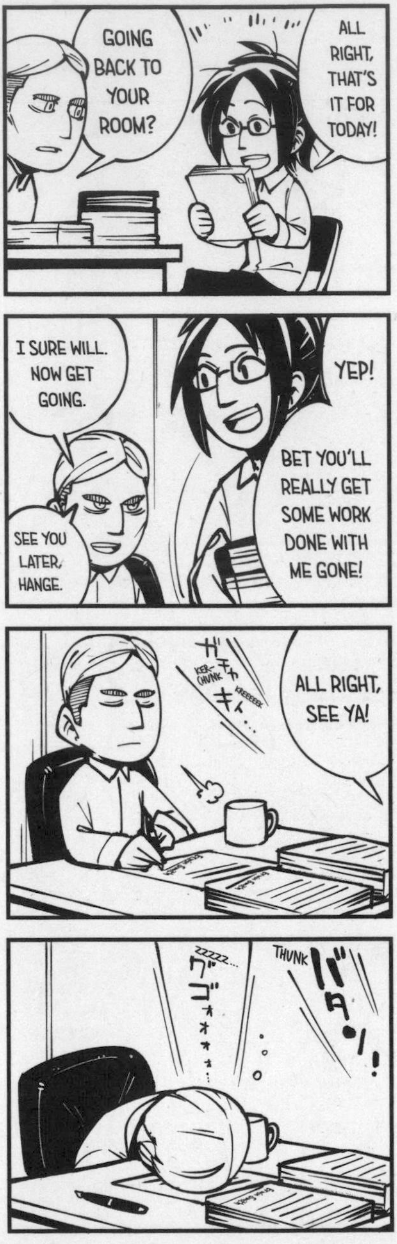
ALL RIGHT, THAT'S IT FOR TODAY!
GOING BACK TO YOUR ROOM?
YEP!
BET YOU'LL REALLY GET SOME WORK DONE WITH ME GONE!
I SURE WILL. NOW GET GOING.
SEE YOU LATER, HANGE.
ALL RIGHT, SEE YA!
KER-CHUNK
KREEEEEK
THUNK
ZZZZZ...

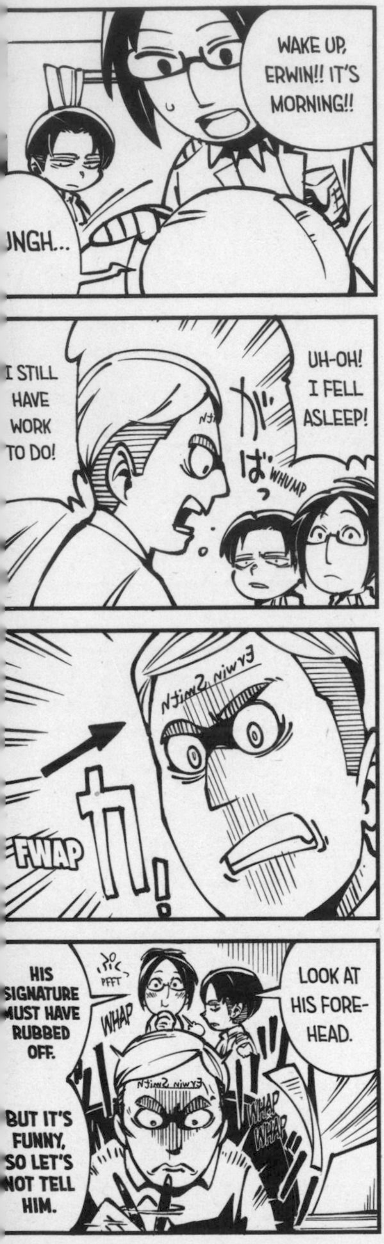
WAKE UP, ERWIN!! IT'S MORNING!!
UNGH...
UH-OH! I FELL ASLEEP!
I STILL HAVE WORK TO DO!
WHUMP
FWAP
LOOK AT HIS FOREHEAD.
PFFT
HIS SIGNATURE MUST HAVE RUBBED OFF.
WHAP
BUT IT'S FUNNY, SO LET'S NOT TELL HIM.

SPOOF on TITAN

#12 The Romantic Tale of Hannah and Franz

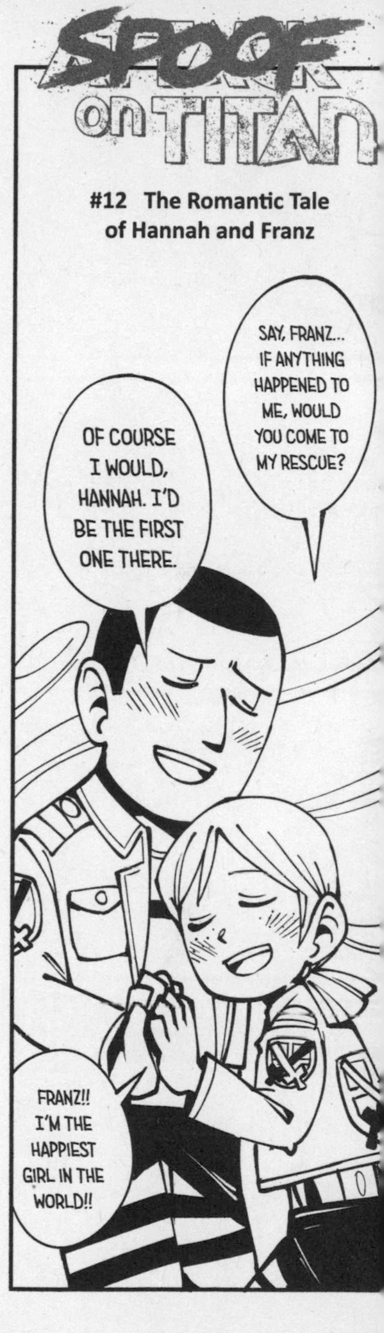
SAY, FRANZ... IF ANYTHING HAPPENED TO ME, WOULD YOU COME TO MY RESCUE?
OF COURSE I WOULD, HANNAH. I'D BE THE FIRST ONE THERE.
FRANZ!! I'M THE HAPPIEST GIRL IN THE WORLD!!

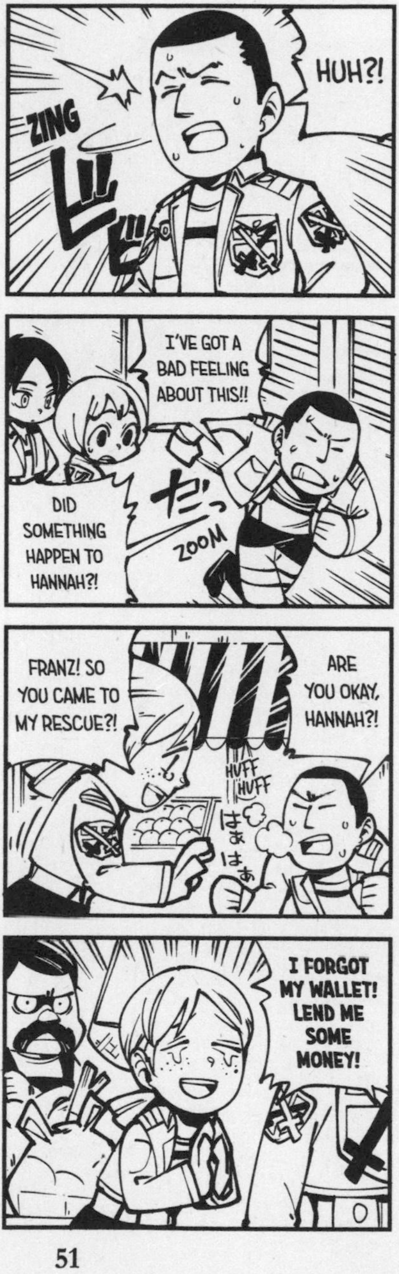
HUH?!
ZING
ビビ
I'VE GOT A BAD FEELING ABOUT THIS!!
DID SOMETHING HAPPEN TO HANNAH?!
だっ
ZOOM
ARE YOU OKAY, HANNAH?!
FRANZ! SO YOU CAME TO MY RESCUE?!
HUFF HUFF
はぁはぁ
I FORGOT MY WALLET! LEND ME SOME MONEY!

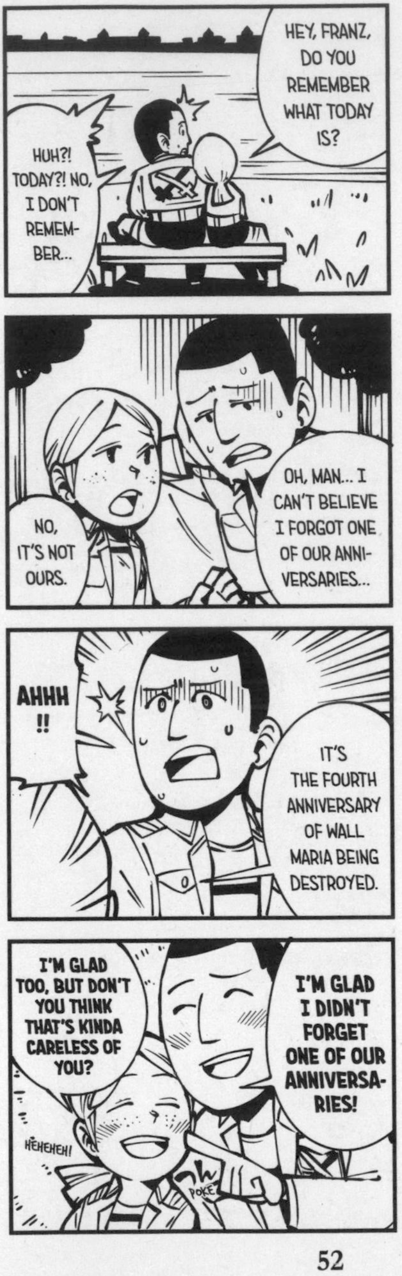
HEY, FRANZ, DO YOU REMEMBER WHAT TODAY IS?
HUH?! TODAY?! NO, I DON'T REMEMBER...
OH, MAN... I CAN'T BELIEVE I FORGOT ONE OF OUR ANNIVERSARIES...
NO, IT'S NOT OURS.
IT'S THE FOURTH ANNIVERSARY OF WALL MARIA BEING DESTROYED.
AHHH !!
I'M GLAD I DIDN'T FORGET ONE OF OUR ANNIVERSARIES!
I'M GLAD TOO, BUT DON'T YOU THINK THAT'S KINDA CARELESS OF YOU?
HEHEHEH!
POKE

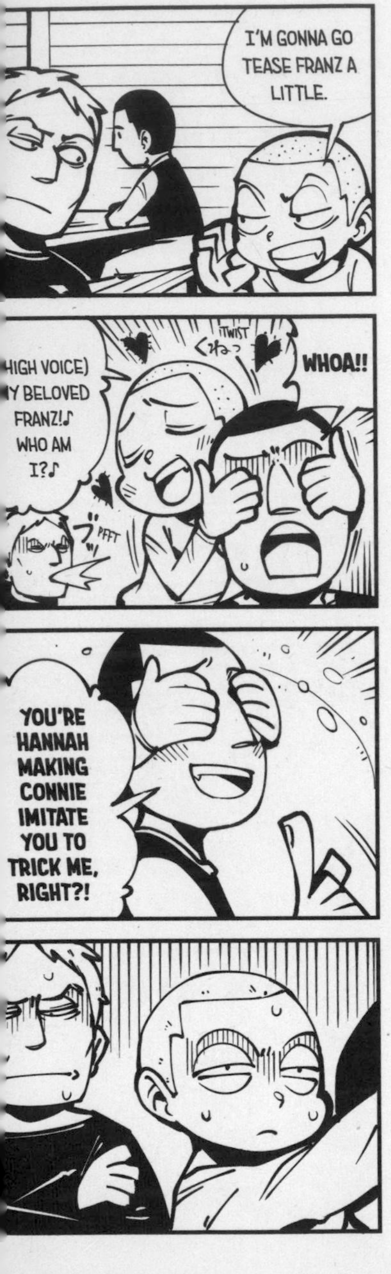
I'M GONNA GO TEASE FRANZ A LITTLE.
WHOA!!
TWIST
くねっ
HIGH VOICE) Y BELOVED FRANZ!♪ WHO AM I?♪
PFFT
YOU'RE HANNAH MAKING CONNIE IMITATE YOU TO TRICK ME, RIGHT?!

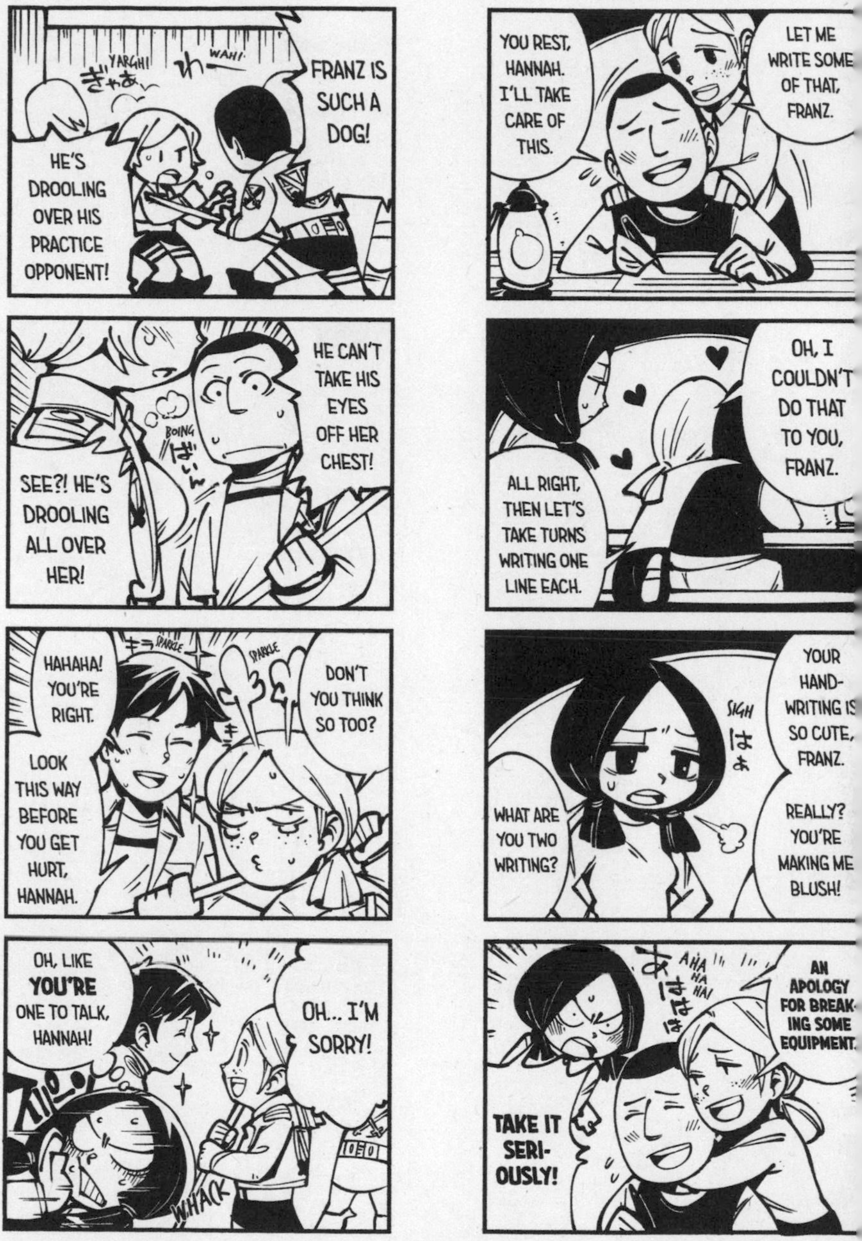
LET ME WRITE SOME OF THAT, FRANZ.
YOU REST, HANNAH. I'LL TAKE CARE OF THIS.
OH, I COULDN'T DO THAT TO YOU, FRANZ.
ALL RIGHT, THEN LET'S TAKE TURNS WRITING ONE LINE EACH.
YOUR HAND-WRITING IS SO CUTE, FRANZ.
REALLY? YOU'RE MAKING ME BLUSH!
SIGH はぁ
WHAT ARE YOU TWO WRITING?
AN APOLOGY FOR BREAKING SOME EQUIPMENT.
AHAHAHA あははは
TAKE IT SERI-OUSLY!
FRANZ IS SUCH A DOG!
WAH! わー
YARGH! ぎゃあ
HE'S DROOLING OVER HIS PRACTICE OPPONENT!
HE CAN'T TAKE HIS EYES OFF HER CHEST!
BOING ばいん
SEE?! HE'S DROOLING ALL OVER HER!
DON'T YOU THINK SO TOO?
SPARKLE
SPARKLE キラ
HAHAHA! YOU'RE RIGHT.
LOOK THIS WAY BEFORE YOU GET HURT, HANNAH.
OH... I'M SORRY!
OH, LIKE **YOU'RE** ONE TO TALK, HANNAH!
WHACK

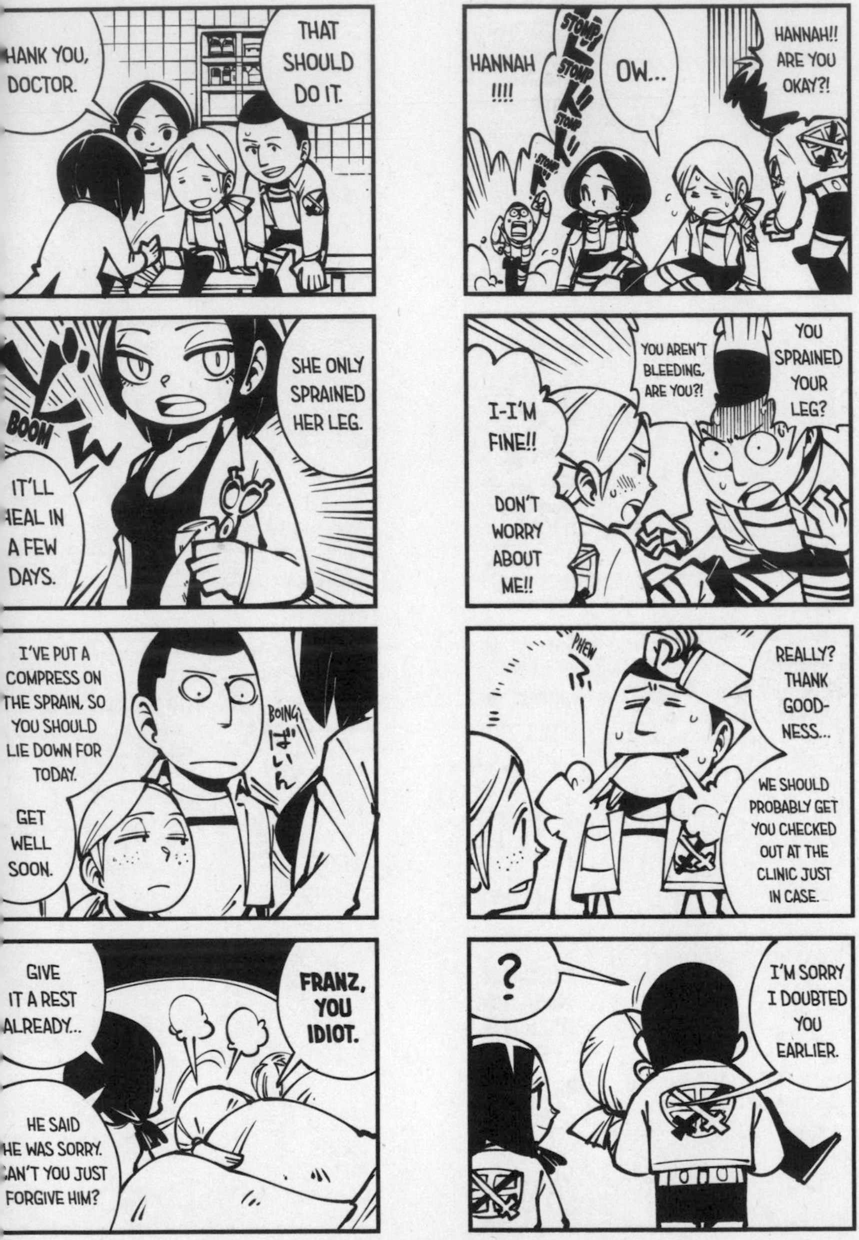
HANNAH!! ARE YOU OKAY?!
OW...
STOMP STOMP STOMP STOMP
HANNAH !!!!
YOU SPRAINED YOUR LEG?
YOU AREN'T BLEEDING, ARE YOU?!
I-I'M FINE!!
DON'T WORRY ABOUT ME!!
REALLY? THANK GOOD-NESS...
PHEW
WE SHOULD PROBABLY GET YOU CHECKED OUT AT THE CLINIC JUST IN CASE.
I'M SORRY I DOUBTED YOU EARLIER.
?
THAT SHOULD DO IT.
HANK YOU, DOCTOR.
SHE ONLY SPRAINED HER LEG.
BOOM
IT'LL HEAL IN A FEW DAYS.
BOING
I'VE PUT A COMPRESS ON THE SPRAIN, SO YOU SHOULD LIE DOWN FOR TODAY.
GET WELL SOON.
FRANZ, YOU IDIOT.
GIVE IT A REST ALREADY...
HE SAID HE WAS SORRY. CAN'T YOU JUST FORGIVE HIM?

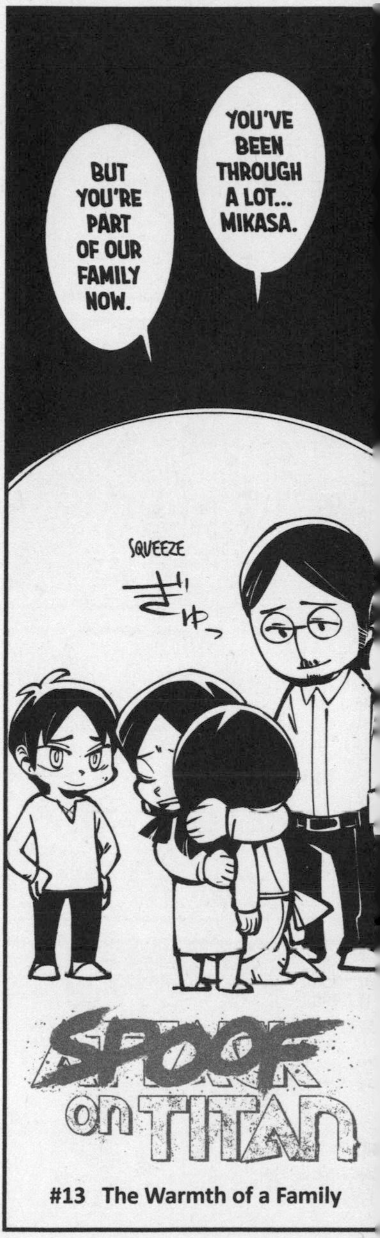
YOU'VE BEEN THROUGH A LOT... MIKASA.
BUT YOU'RE PART OF OUR FAMILY NOW.
SQUEEZE
ぎゅっ
SPOOF on TITAN
#13 The Warmth of a Family

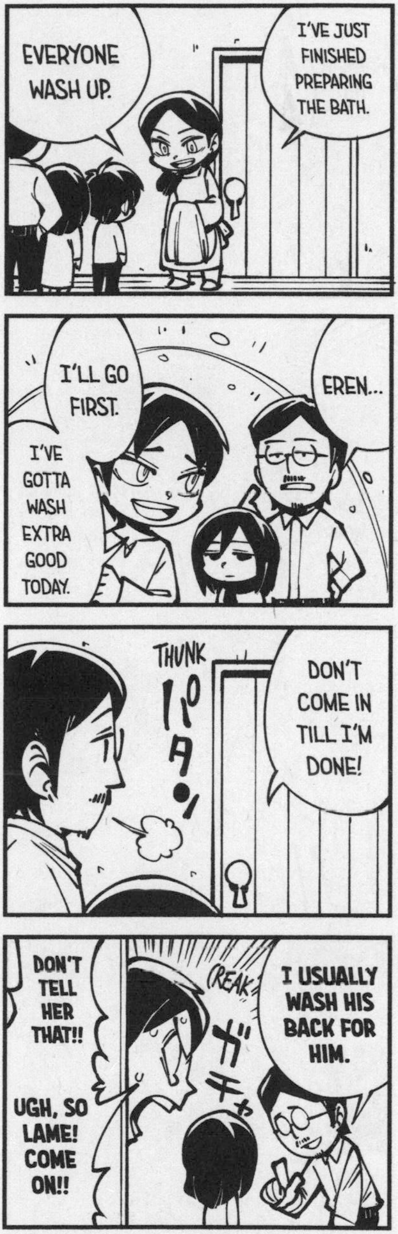
I'VE JUST FINISHED PREPARING THE BATH.
EVERYONE WASH UP.
EREN...
I'LL GO FIRST.
I'VE GOTTA WASH EXTRA GOOD TODAY.
DON'T COME IN TILL I'M DONE!
THUNK
パタン
I USUALLY WASH HIS BACK FOR HIM.
CREAK
ガチャ
DON'T TELL HER THAT!!
UGH, SO LAME! COME ON!!

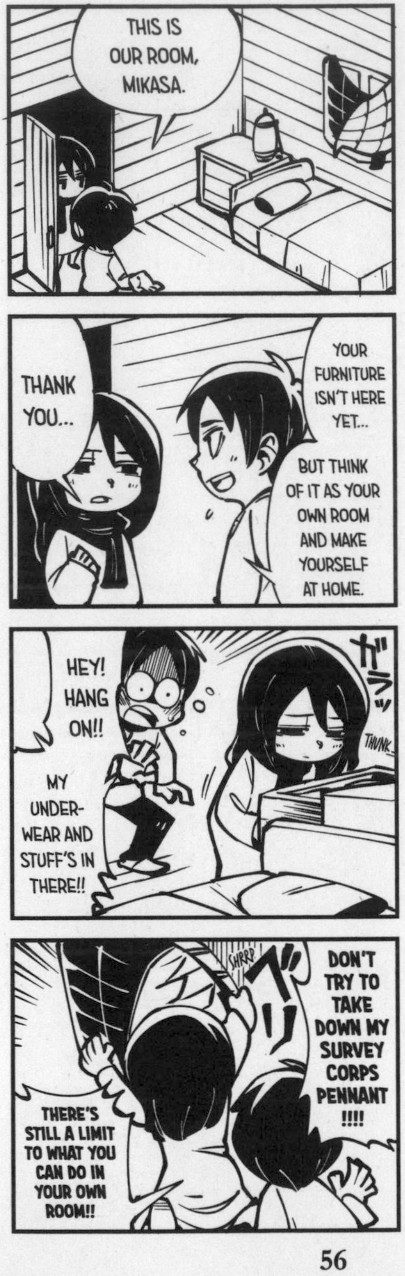
THIS IS OUR ROOM, MIKASA.
YOUR FURNITURE ISN'T HERE YET...
BUT THINK OF IT AS YOUR OWN ROOM AND MAKE YOURSELF AT HOME.
THANK YOU...
ガラッ
THUNK
HEY! HANG ON!!
MY UNDER-WEAR AND STUFF'S IN THERE!!
SHRRP
DON'T TRY TO TAKE DOWN MY SURVEY CORPS PENNANT!!!!
THERE'S STILL A LIMIT TO WHAT YOU CAN DO IN YOUR OWN ROOM!!

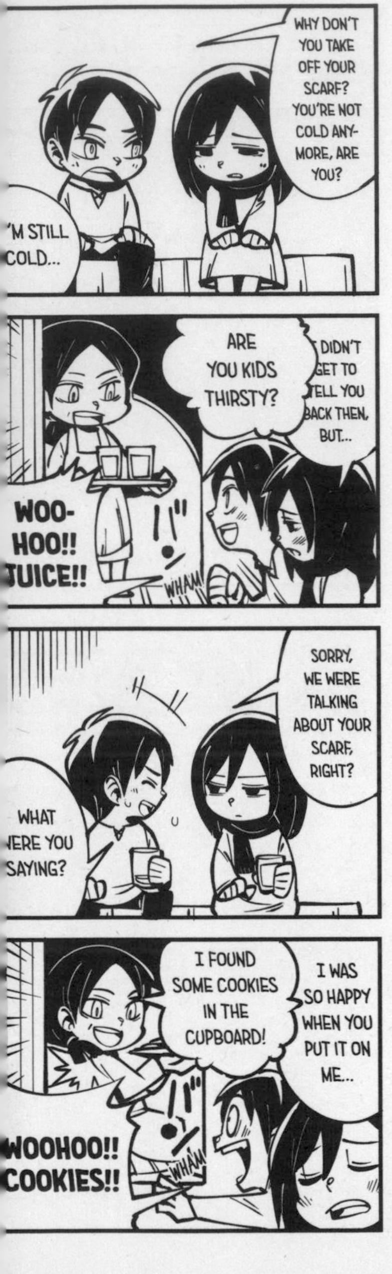
WHY DON'T YOU TAKE OFF YOUR SCARF? YOU'RE NOT COLD ANY-MORE, ARE YOU?
'M STILL COLD...
DIDN'T GET TO TELL YOU BACK THEN, BUT...
ARE YOU KIDS THIRSTY?
WOO-HOO!! JUICE!!
WHAM
SORRY, WE WERE TALKING ABOUT YOUR SCARF, RIGHT?
WHAT WERE YOU SAYING?
I WAS SO HAPPY WHEN YOU PUT IT ON ME...
I FOUND SOME COOKIES IN THE CUPBOARD!
WOOHOO!! COOKIES!!
WHAM

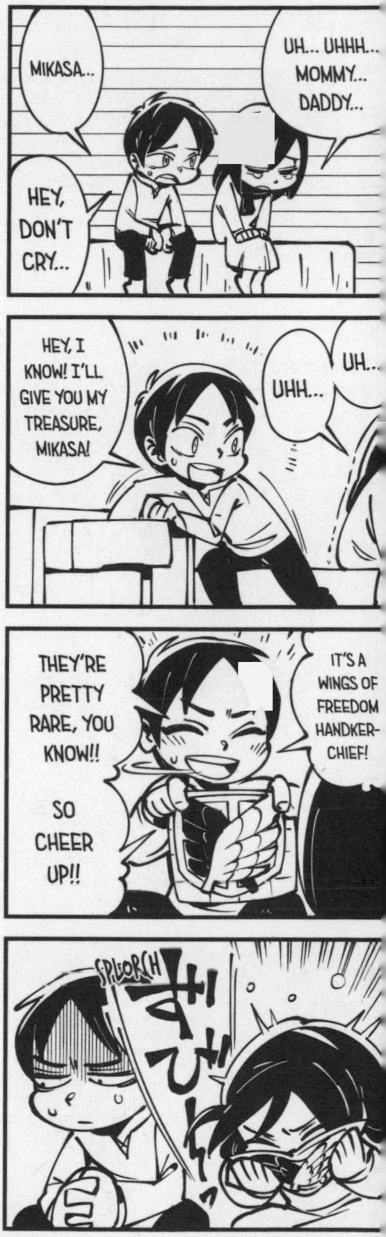
UH... UHHH... MOMMY... DADDY...
MIKASA...
HEY, DON'T CRY...
UH...
UHH...
HEY, I KNOW! I'LL GIVE YOU MY TREASURE, MIKASA!
IT'S A WINGS OF FREEDOM HANDKER-CHIEF!
THEY'RE PRETTY RARE, YOU KNOW!!
SO CHEER UP!!
SPLORCH

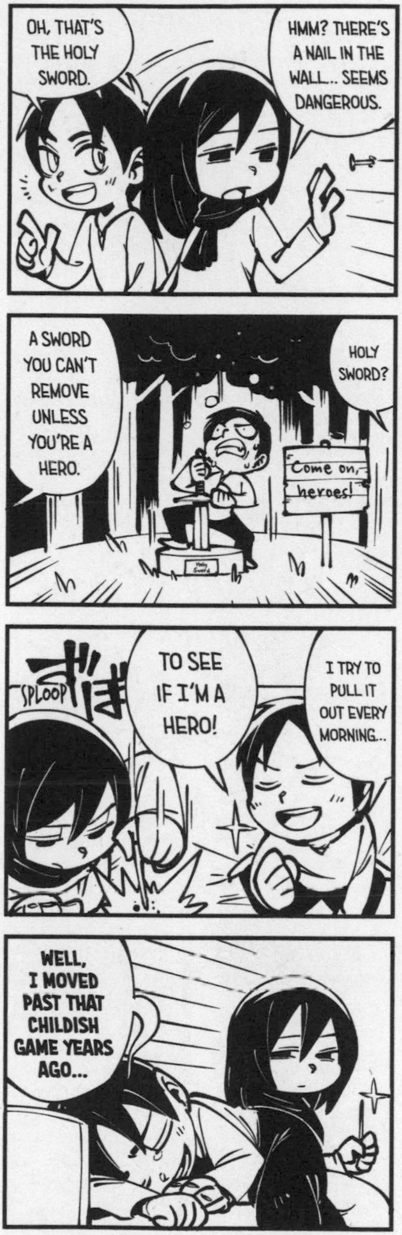
HMM? THERE'S A NAIL IN THE WALL... SEEMS DANGEROUS.
OH, THAT'S THE HOLY SWORD.
HOLY SWORD?
A SWORD YOU CAN'T REMOVE UNLESS YOU'RE A HERO.
Come on, heroes!
I TRY TO PULL IT OUT EVERY MORNING...
TO SEE IF I'M A HERO!
SPLOOP
WELL, I MOVED PAST THAT CHILDISH GAME YEARS AGO...

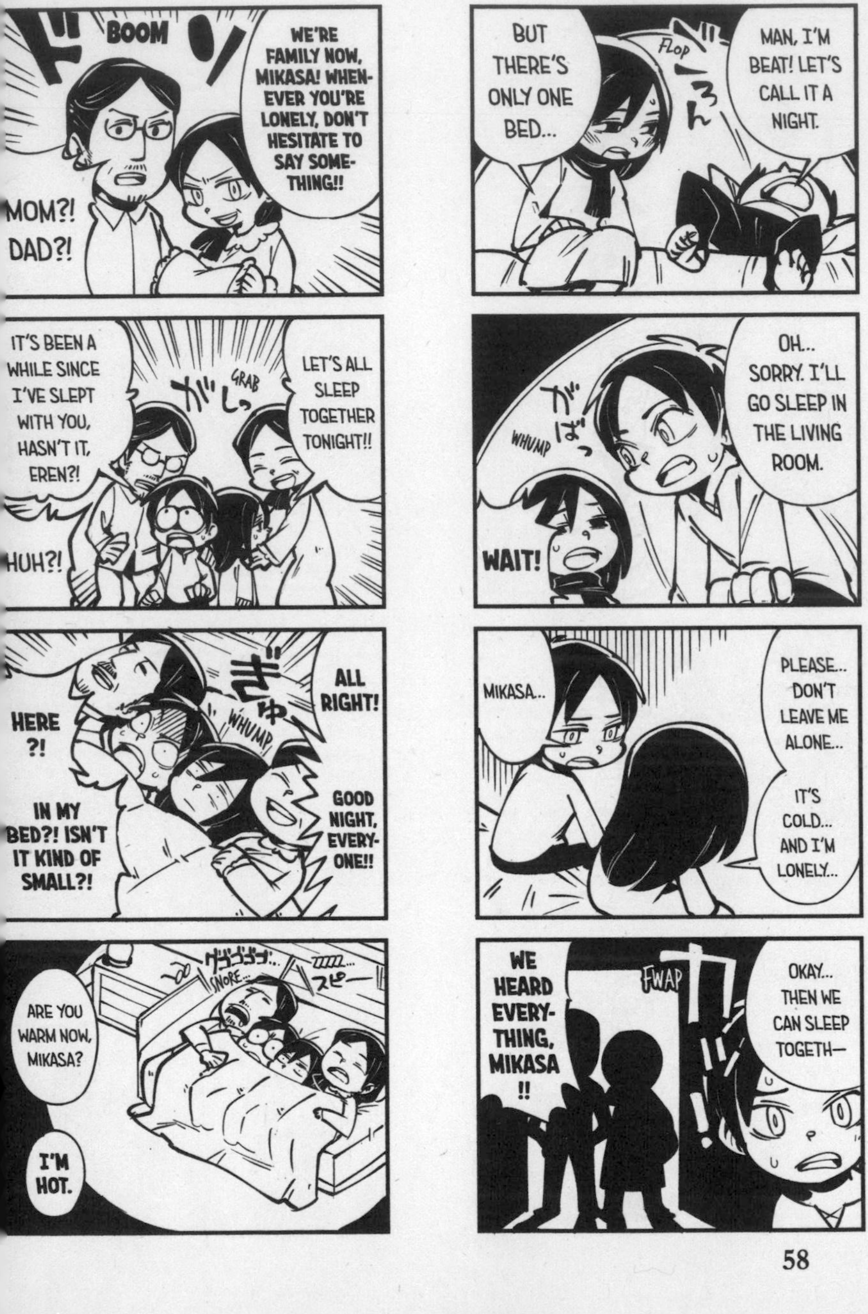
MAN, I'M BEAT! LET'S CALL IT A NIGHT.
FLOP
BUT THERE'S ONLY ONE BED...
OH... SORRY. I'LL GO SLEEP IN THE LIVING ROOM.
WHUMP
WAIT!
PLEASE... DON'T LEAVE ME ALONE...
IT'S COLD... AND I'M LONELY...
MIKASA...
OKAY... THEN WE CAN SLEEP TOGETH—
FWAP
WE HEARD EVERYTHING, MIKASA!!
WE'RE FAMILY NOW, MIKASA! WHENEVER YOU'RE LONELY, DON'T HESITATE TO SAY SOMETHING!!
BOOM
MOM?! DAD?!
LET'S ALL SLEEP TOGETHER TONIGHT!!
GRAB
IT'S BEEN A WHILE SINCE I'VE SLEPT WITH YOU, HASN'T IT, EREN?!
HUH?!
ALL RIGHT!
WHUMP
GOOD NIGHT, EVERYONE!!
HERE?!
IN MY BED?! ISN'T IT KIND OF SMALL?!
SNORE...
ARE YOU WARM NOW, MIKASA?
I'M HOT.

#14 Asking Too Much! The Survey Corps Welcoming Party

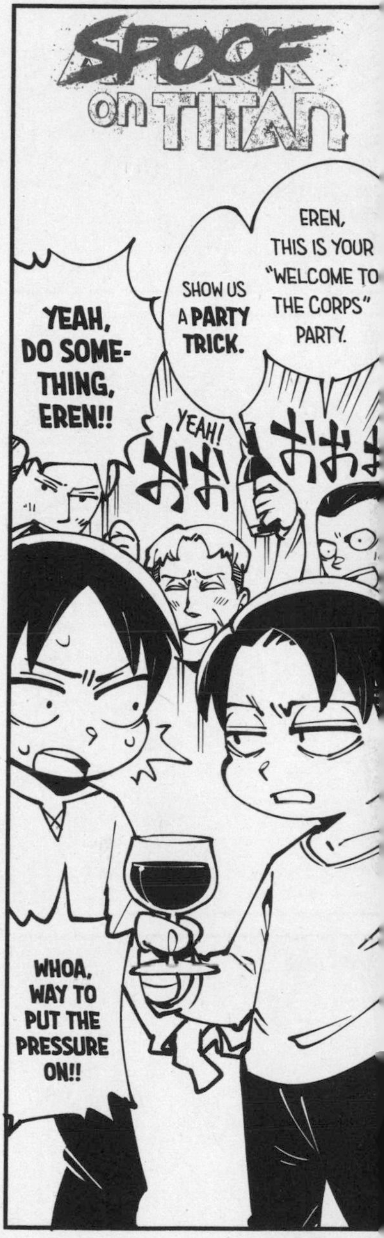
SPOOF on TITAN
EREN, THIS IS YOUR "WELCOME TO THE CORPS" PARTY.
SHOW US A PARTY TRICK.
YEAH, DO SOME-THING, EREN!!
YEAH!
おお
WHOA, WAY TO PUT THE PRESSURE ON!!

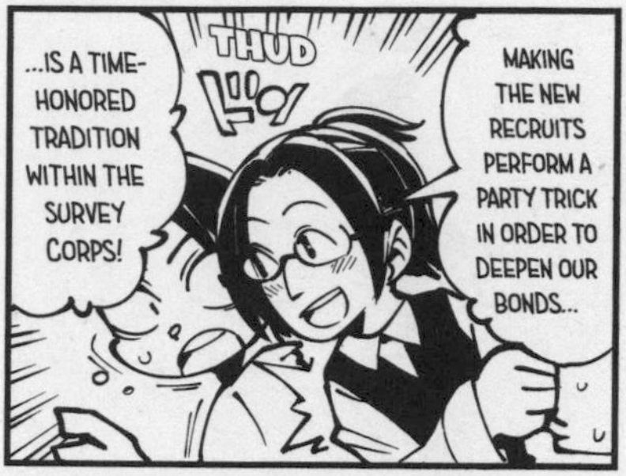
MAKING THE NEW RECRUITS PERFORM A PARTY TRICK IN ORDER TO DEEPEN OUR BONDS...
THUD
...IS A TIME-HONORED TRADITION WITHIN THE SURVEY CORPS!

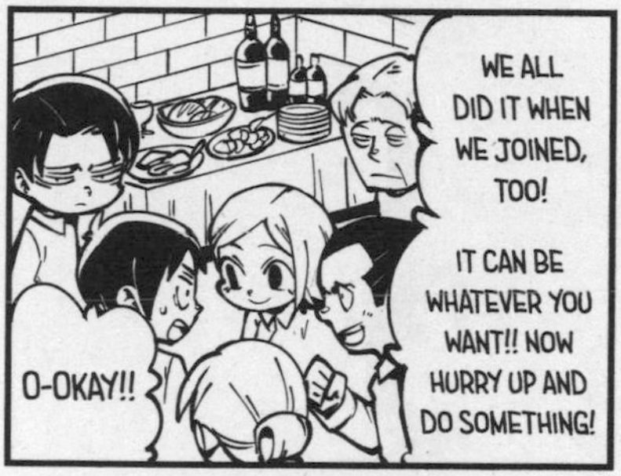
WE ALL DID IT WHEN WE JOINED, TOO!
IT CAN BE WHATEVER YOU WANT!! NOW HURRY UP AND DO SOMETHING!
O-OKAY!!

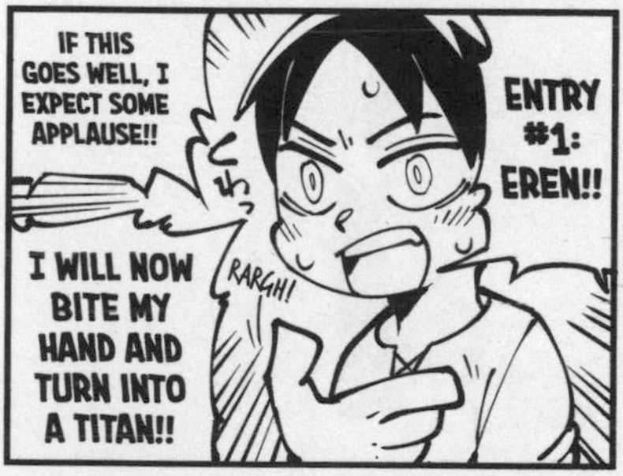
ENTRY #1: EREN!!
IF THIS GOES WELL, I EXPECT SOME APPLAUSE!!
RARGH!
I WILL NOW BITE MY HAND AND TURN INTO A TITAN!!

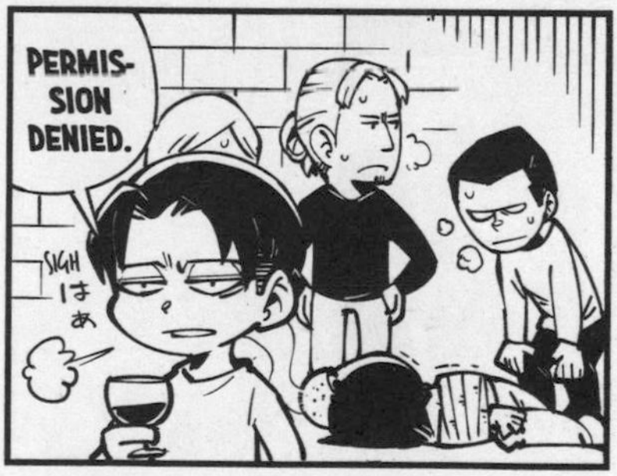
PERMIS-SION DENIED.
SIGH
はあ

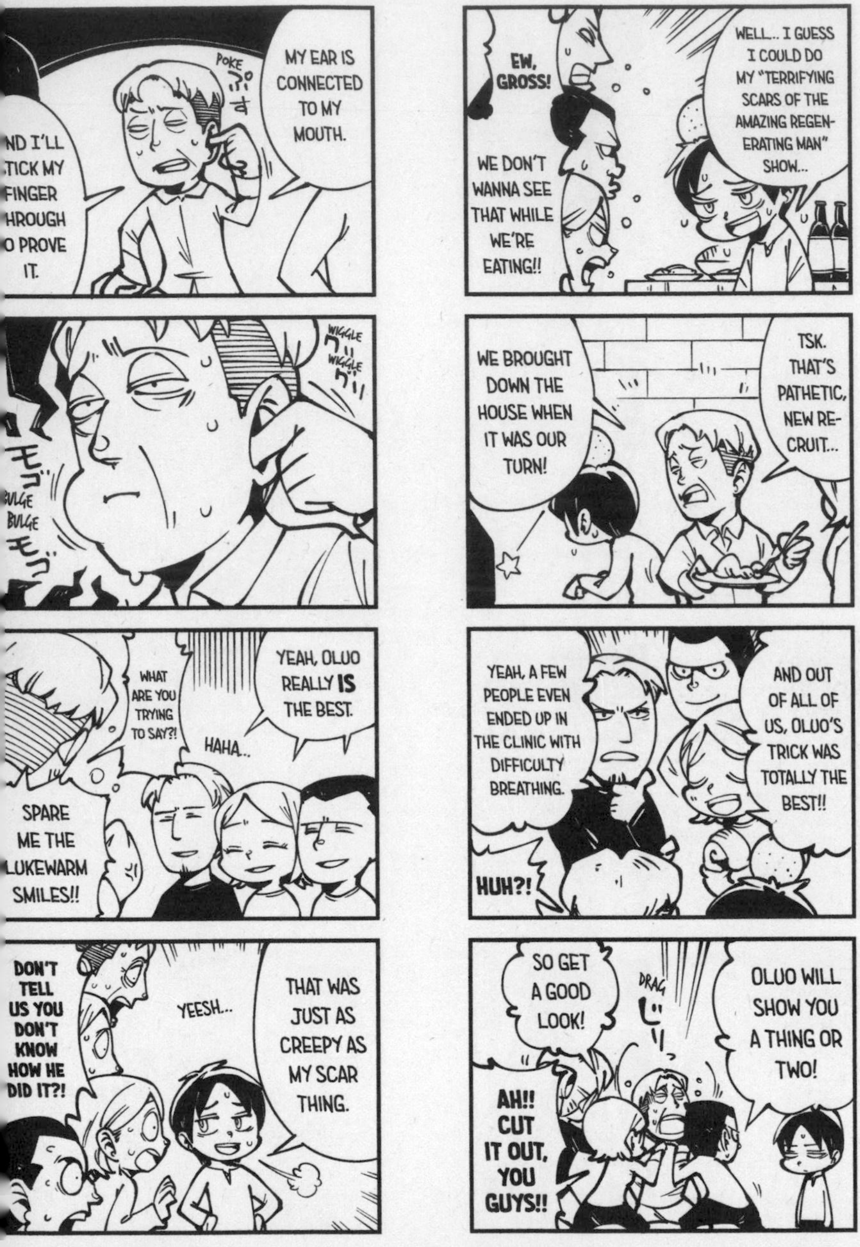
WELL... I GUESS I COULD DO MY "TERRIFYING SCARS OF THE AMAZING REGEN-ERATING MAN" SHOW...
EW, GROSS!
WE DON'T WANNA SEE THAT WHILE WE'RE EATING!!
TSK. THAT'S PATHETIC, NEW RE-CRUIT...
WE BROUGHT DOWN THE HOUSE WHEN IT WAS OUR TURN!
AND OUT OF ALL OF US, OLUO'S TRICK WAS TOTALLY THE BEST!!
YEAH, A FEW PEOPLE EVEN ENDED UP IN THE CLINIC WITH DIFFICULTY BREATHING.
HUH?!
OLUO WILL SHOW YOU A THING OR TWO!
DRAG じ
SO GET A GOOD LOOK!
AH!! CUT IT OUT, YOU GUYS!!
MY EAR IS CONNECTED TO MY MOUTH.
POKE ぷす
ND I'LL TICK MY FINGER HROUGH O PROVE IT.
WIGGLE グリ
WIGGLE グリ
BULGE モゴ
BULGE モゴ
YEAH, OLUO REALLY IS THE BEST.
WHAT ARE YOU TRYING TO SAY?!
HAHA..
SPARE ME THE LUKEWARM SMILES!!
THAT WAS JUST AS CREEPY AS MY SCAR THING.
YEESH...
DON'T TELL US YOU DON'T KNOW HOW HE DID IT?!

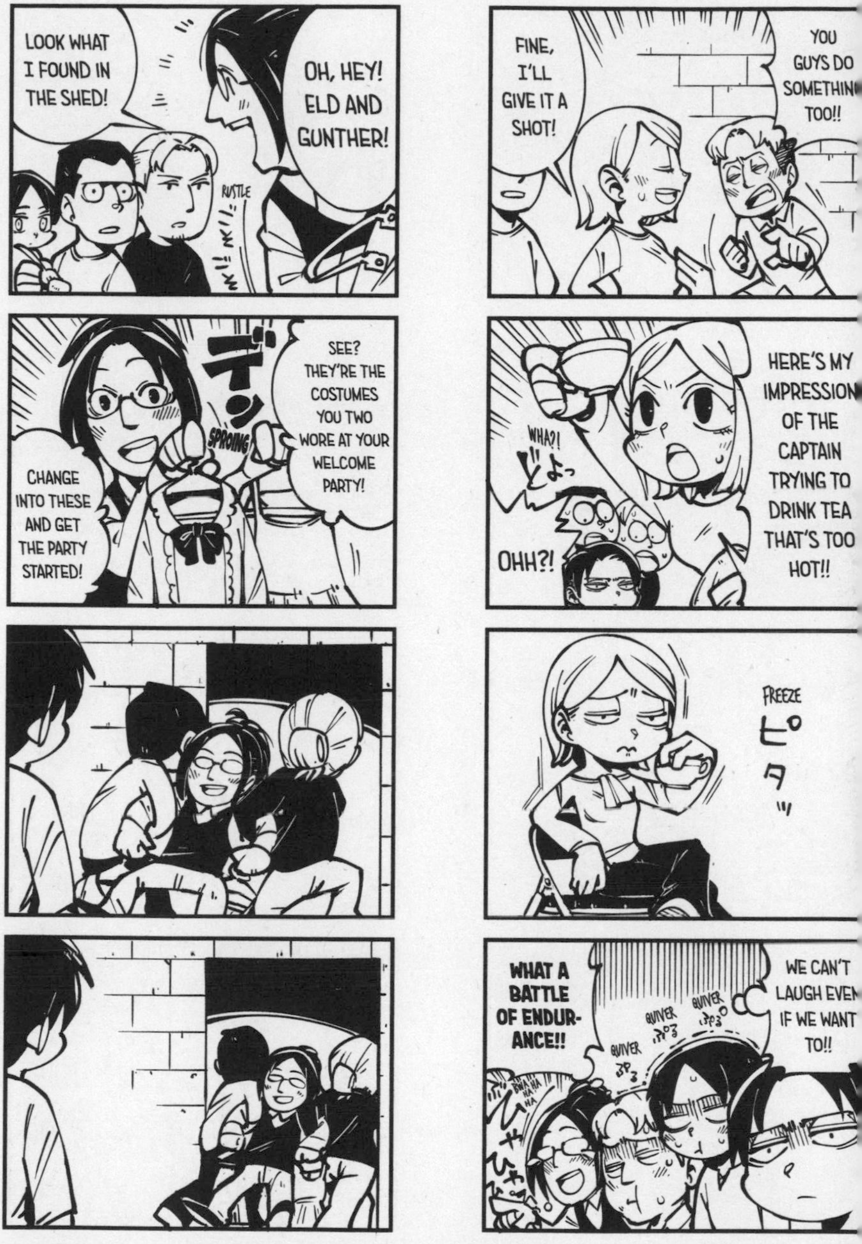
YOU GUYS DO SOMETHIN TOO!!
FINE, I'LL GIVE IT A SHOT!
HERE'S MY IMPRESSION OF THE CAPTAIN TRYING TO DRINK TEA THAT'S TOO HOT!!
WHA?! どよっ
OHH?!
FREEZE ピタッ
WE CAN'T LAUGH EVE IF WE WANT TO!!
QUIVER ぷる
QUIVER ぷる
QUIVER ぷる
WHAT A BATTLE OF ENDUR-ANCE!!
BWA HA HA HA
OH, HEY! ELD AND GUNTHER!
LOOK WHAT I FOUND IN THE SHED!
RUSTLE
SEE? THEY'RE THE COSTUMES YOU TWO WORE AT YOUR WELCOME PARTY!
デン
SPROING
CHANGE INTO THESE AND GET THE PARTY STARTED!

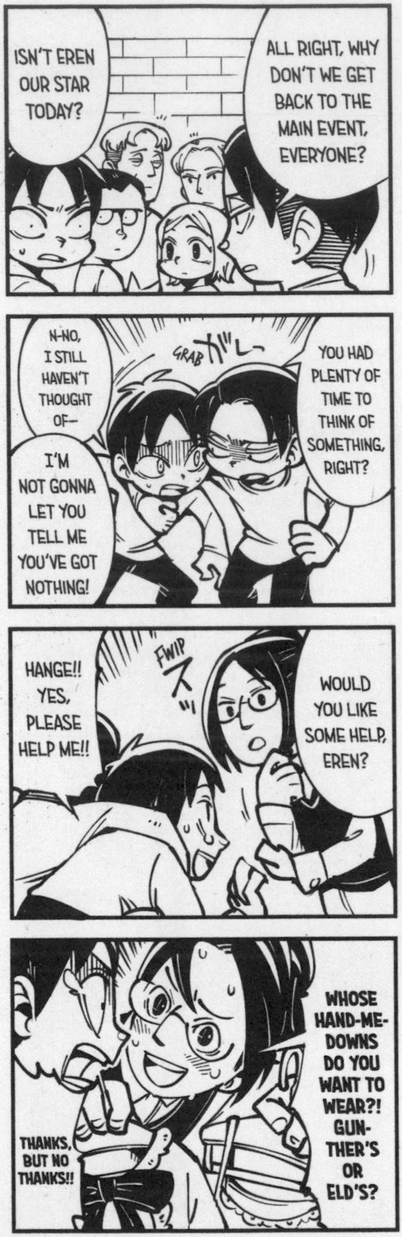
ALL RIGHT, WHY DON'T WE GET BACK TO THE MAIN EVENT, EVERYONE?
ISN'T EREN OUR STAR TODAY?
YOU HAD PLENTY OF TIME TO THINK OF SOMETHING, RIGHT?
GRAB
N-NO, I STILL HAVEN'T THOUGHT OF—
I'M NOT GONNA LET YOU TELL ME YOU'VE GOT NOTHING!
WOULD YOU LIKE SOME HELP, EREN?
FWIP
HANGE!! YES, PLEASE HELP ME!!
WHOSE HAND-ME-DOWNS DO YOU WANT TO WEAR?! GUNTHER'S OR ELD'S?
THANKS, BUT NO THANKS!!

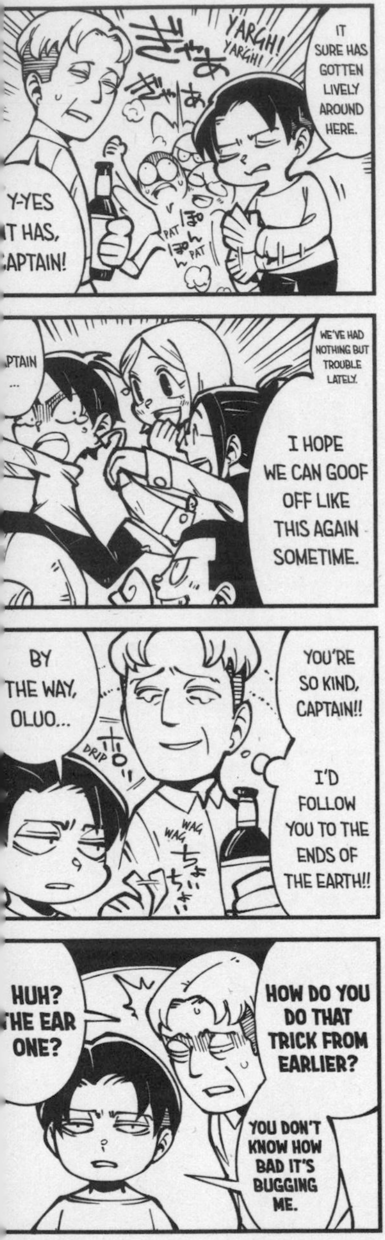
IT SURE HAS GOTTEN LIVELY AROUND HERE.
YARGH! YARGH!
PAT PAT
Y-YES T HAS, APTAIN!
WE'VE HAD NOTHING BUT TROUBLE LATELY.
I HOPE WE CAN GOOF OFF LIKE THIS AGAIN SOMETIME.
PTAIN ...
YOU'RE SO KIND, CAPTAIN!!
I'D FOLLOW YOU TO THE ENDS OF THE EARTH!!
DRIP
WAG WAG
BY THE WAY, OLUO...
HOW DO YOU DO THAT TRICK FROM EARLIER?
HUH? THE EAR ONE?
YOU DON'T KNOW HOW BAD IT'S BUGGING ME.

SPOOF on TITAN

SPOOF on TITAN

#15 Krista's Cookies

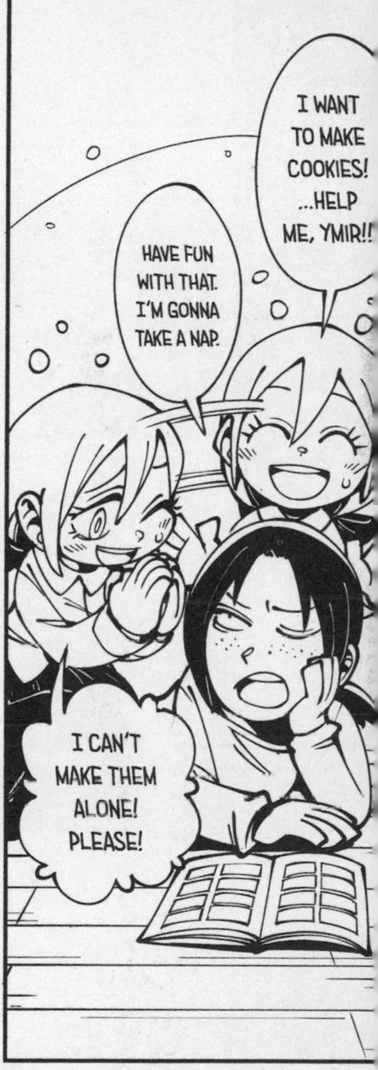
I WANT TO MAKE COOKIES! ...HELP ME, YMIR!!
HAVE FUN WITH THAT. I'M GONNA TAKE A NAP.
I CAN'T MAKE THEM ALONE! PLEASE!

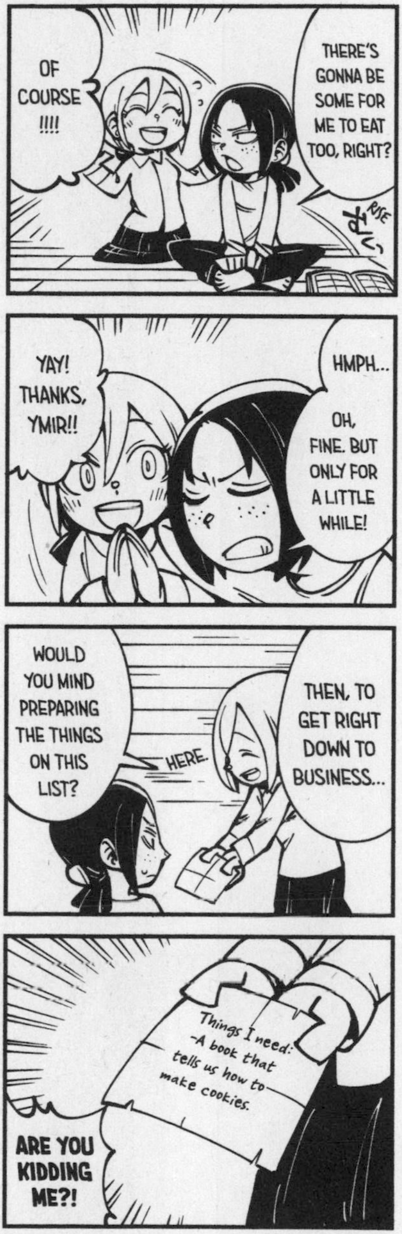
THERE'S GONNA BE SOME FOR ME TO EAT TOO, RIGHT?
RISE
OF COURSE !!!!
HMPH...
OH, FINE. BUT ONLY FOR A LITTLE WHILE!
YAY! THANKS, YMIR!!
THEN, TO GET RIGHT DOWN TO BUSINESS...
HERE.
WOULD YOU MIND PREPARING THE THINGS ON THIS LIST?
Things I need: -A book that tells us how to make cookies.
ARE YOU KIDDING ME?!

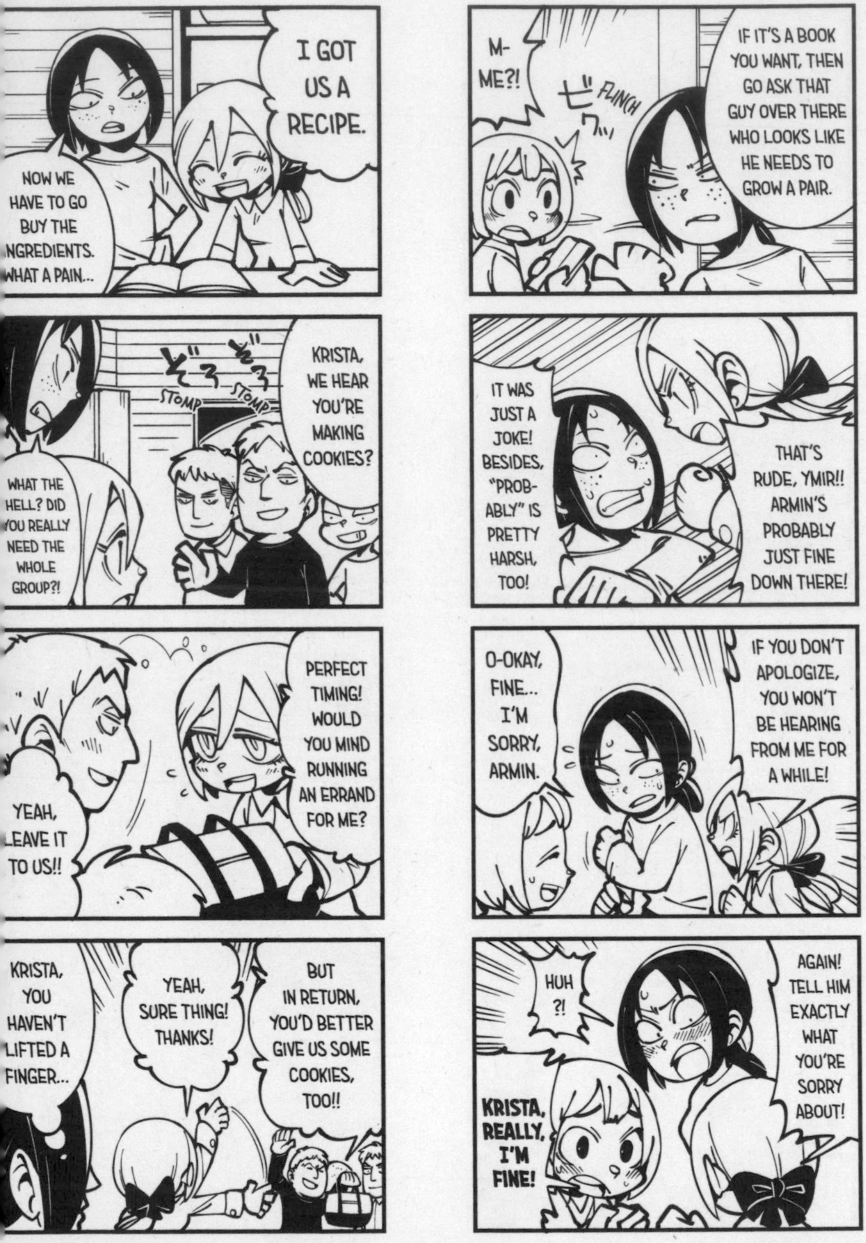
IF IT'S A BOOK YOU WANT, THEN GO ASK THAT GUY OVER THERE WHO LOOKS LIKE HE NEEDS TO GROW A PAIR.
FLINCH
M-ME?!
THAT'S RUDE, YMIR!! ARMIN'S PROBABLY JUST FINE DOWN THERE!
IT WAS JUST A JOKE! BESIDES, "PROB-ABLY" IS PRETTY HARSH, TOO!
IF YOU DON'T APOLOGIZE, YOU WON'T BE HEARING FROM ME FOR A WHILE!
O-OKAY, FINE... I'M SORRY, ARMIN.
AGAIN! TELL HIM EXACTLY WHAT YOU'RE SORRY ABOUT!
HUH?!
KRISTA, REALLY, I'M FINE!
I GOT US A RECIPE.
NOW WE HAVE TO GO BUY THE NGREDIENTS. WHAT A PAIN...
KRISTA, WE HEAR YOU'RE MAKING COOKIES?
STOMP
STOMP
WHAT THE HELL? DID OU REALLY NEED THE WHOLE GROUP?!
PERFECT TIMING! WOULD YOU MIND RUNNING AN ERRAND FOR ME?
YEAH, EAVE IT TO US!!
BUT IN RETURN, YOU'D BETTER GIVE US SOME COOKIES, TOO!!
YEAH, SURE THING! THANKS!
KRISTA, YOU HAVEN'T LIFTED A FINGER...

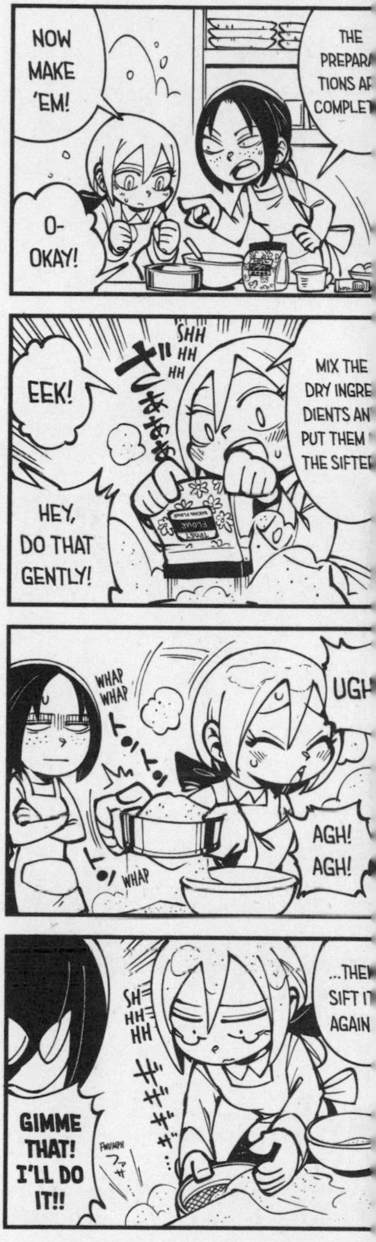
THE PREPARA TIONS AR COMPLET
NOW MAKE 'EM!
O- OKAY!
MIX THE DRY INGRE DIENTS AN PUT THEM THE SIFTE
SHH HH HH
さあああ
EEK!
HEY, DO THAT GENTLY!
UGH
WHAP WHAP
トン トン
AGH! AGH!
WHAP
...THE SIFT IT AGAIN
SH HH HH
ザザザ...
GIMME THAT! I'LL DO IT!!
FWUMPH
ファサ...

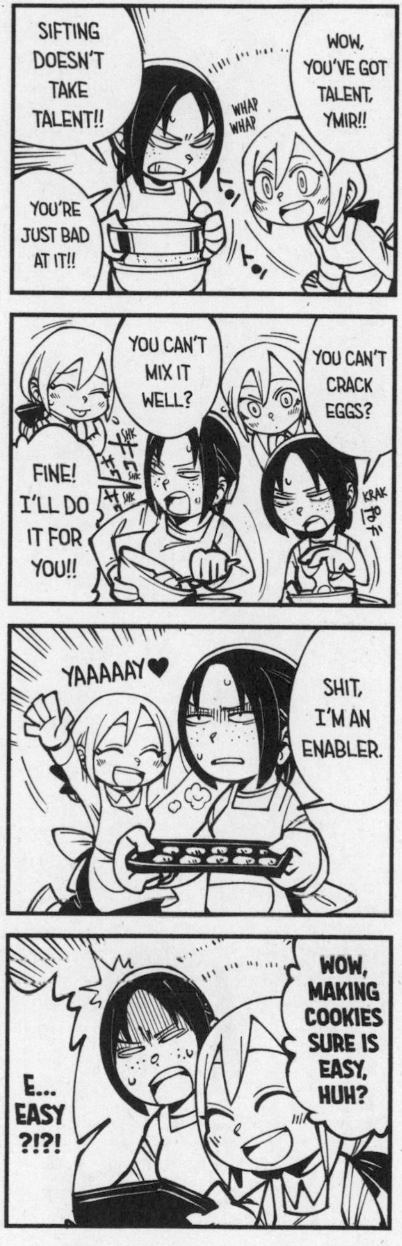
WOW, YOU'VE GOT TALENT, YMIR!!
WHAP WHAP
トン トン
SIFTING DOESN'T TAKE TALENT!!
YOU'RE JUST BAD AT IT!!
YOU CAN'T CRACK EGGS?
KRAK
ぱか
YOU CAN'T MIX IT WELL?
SHK SHK SHK
シャカ シャカ
FINE! I'LL DO IT FOR YOU!!
SHIT, I'M AN ENABLER.
YAAAAAY♥
WOW, MAKING COOKIES SURE IS EASY, HUH?
E... EASY ?!?!

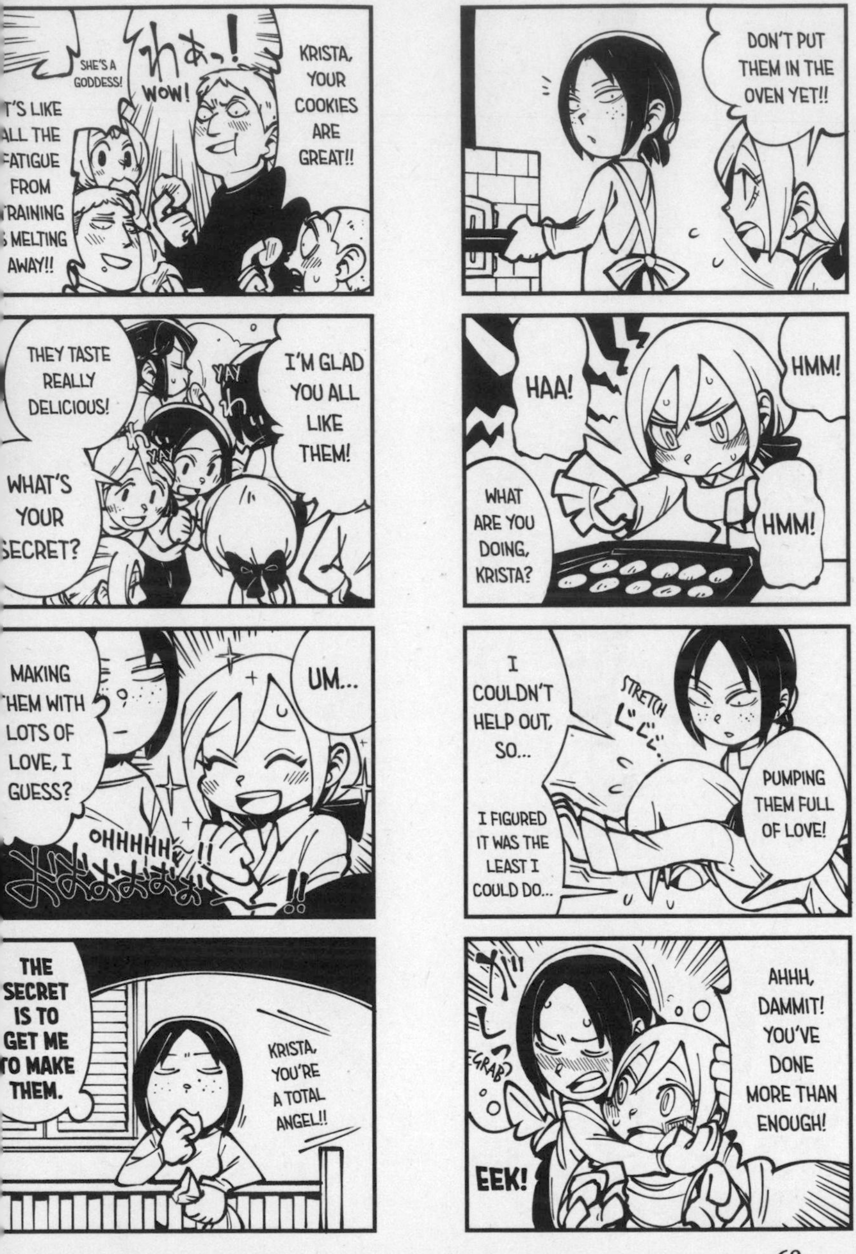
DON'T PUT THEM IN THE OVEN YET!!
HMM!
HAA!
HMM!
WHAT ARE YOU DOING, KRISTA?
STRETCH じじじ...
I COULDN'T HELP OUT, SO...
PUMPING THEM FULL OF LOVE!
I FIGURED IT WAS THE LEAST I COULD DO...
AHHH, DAMMIT! YOU'VE DONE MORE THAN ENOUGH!
ガバッ GRAB
EEK!
KRISTA, YOUR COOKIES ARE GREAT!!
わあっ! WOW!
SHE'S A GODDESS!
T'S LIKE ALL THE FATIGUE FROM RAINING S MELTING AWAY!!
I'M GLAD YOU ALL LIKE THEM!
YAY わ
THEY TASTE REALLY DELICIOUS!
YAY
WHAT'S YOUR ECRET?
UM...
MAKING HEM WITH LOTS OF LOVE, I GUESS?
OHHHHH~!! おおおおおお!!
KRISTA, YOU'RE A TOTAL ANGEL!!
THE SECRET IS TO GET ME O MAKE THEM.

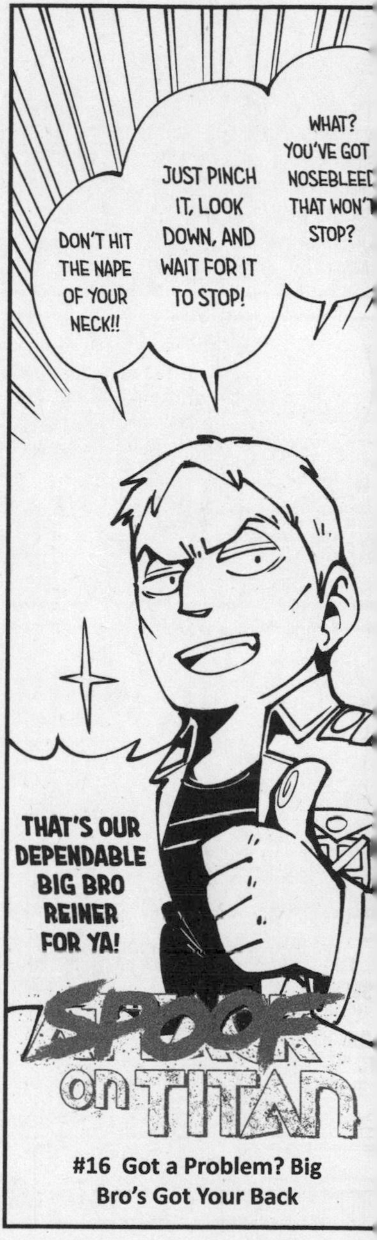
WHAT? YOU'VE GOT NOSEBLEED THAT WON'T STOP?
JUST PINCH IT, LOOK DOWN, AND WAIT FOR IT TO STOP!
DON'T HIT THE NAPE OF YOUR NECK!!
THAT'S OUR DEPENDABLE BIG BRO REINER FOR YA!
SPOOF on TITAN
#16 Got a Problem? Big Bro's Got Your Back

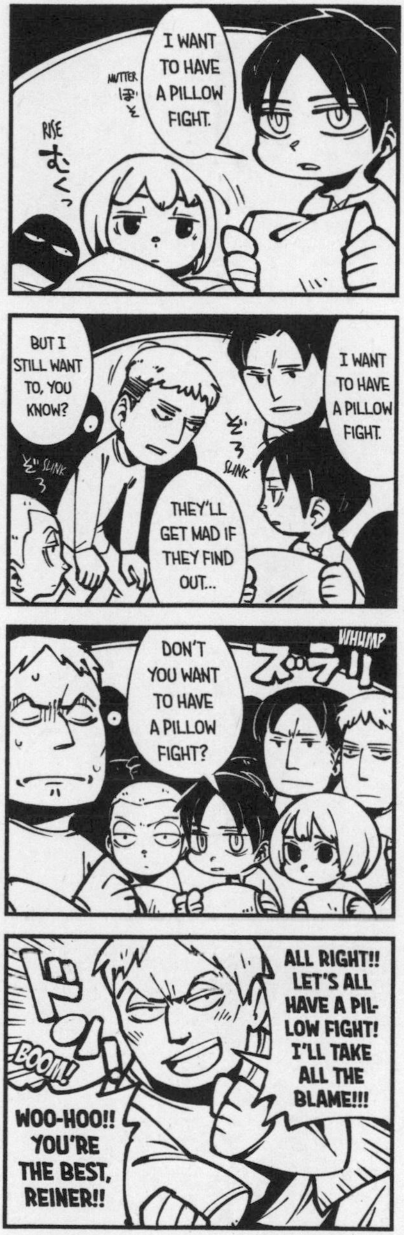
I WANT TO HAVE A PILLOW FIGHT.
MUTTER
ぼそ
RISE
むくっ
I WANT TO HAVE A PILLOW FIGHT.
ぞろ
SLINK
THEY'LL GET MAD IF THEY FIND OUT...
BUT I STILL WANT TO, YOU KNOW?
ぞろ SLINK
WHUMP
ズラリ
DON'T YOU WANT TO HAVE A PILLOW FIGHT?
ALL RIGHT!! LET'S ALL HAVE A PIL-LOW FIGHT! I'LL TAKE ALL THE BLAME!!!
ドン
BOOM!
WOO-HOO!! YOU'RE THE BEST, REINER!!

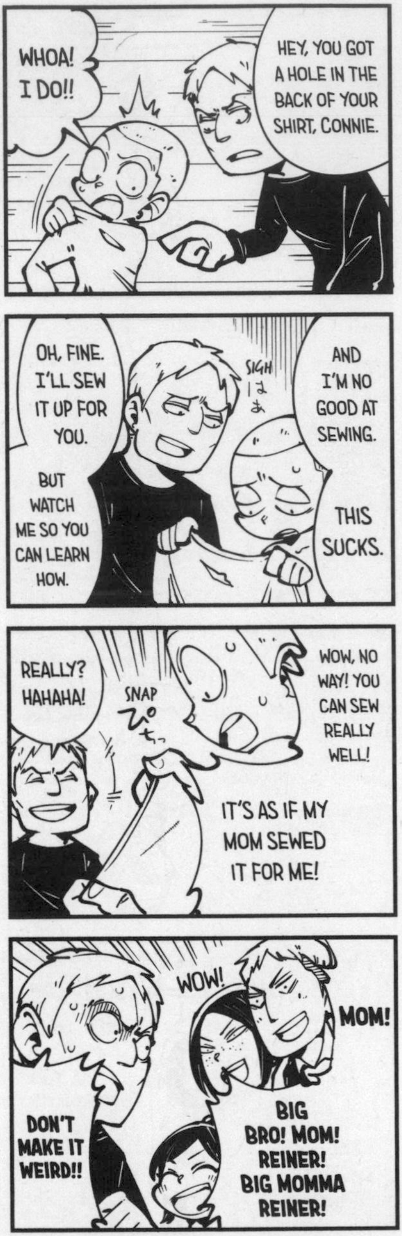
HEY, YOU GOT A HOLE IN THE BACK OF YOUR SHIRT, CONNIE.
WHOA! I DO!!
AND I'M NO GOOD AT SEWING.
SIGH はぁ
THIS SUCKS.
OH, FINE. I'LL SEW IT UP FOR YOU.
BUT WATCH ME SO YOU CAN LEARN HOW.
WOW, NO WAY! YOU CAN SEW REALLY WELL!
IT'S AS IF MY MOM SEWED IT FOR ME!
SNAP ぴちっ
REALLY? HAHAHA!
MOM!
WOW!
BIG BRO! MOM! REINER! BIG MOMMA REINER!
DON'T MAKE IT WEIRD!!

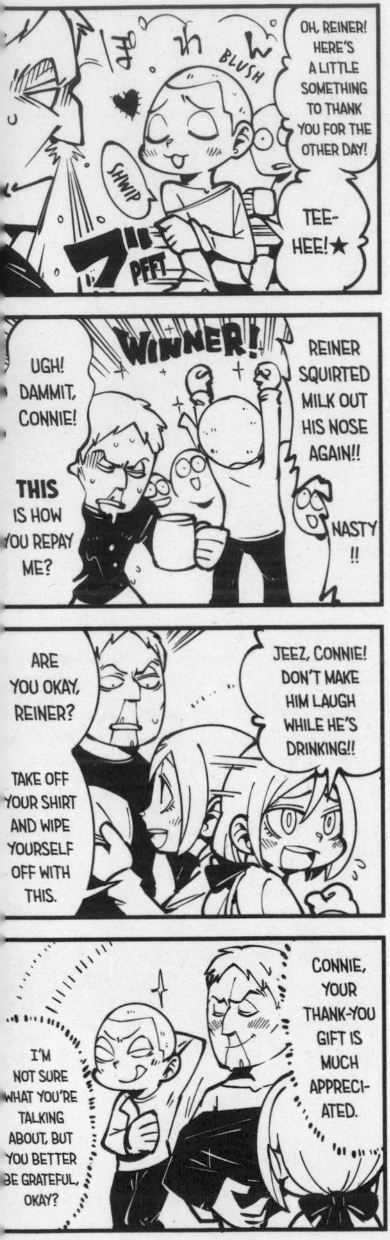
OH, REINER! HERE'S A LITTLE SOMETHING TO THANK YOU FOR THE OTHER DAY!
TEE-HEE!★
BLUSH
ぽわん
SHWIP
PFFT
REINER SQUIRTED MILK OUT HIS NOSE AGAIN!!
WINNER!
NASTY!!
UGH! DAMMIT, CONNIE!
THIS IS HOW YOU REPAY ME?
JEEZ, CONNIE! DON'T MAKE HIM LAUGH WHILE HE'S DRINKING!!
ARE YOU OKAY, REINER?
TAKE OFF YOUR SHIRT AND WIPE YOURSELF OFF WITH THIS.
CONNIE, YOUR THANK-YOU GIFT IS MUCH APPRECIATED.
I'M NOT SURE WHAT YOU'RE TALKING ABOUT, BUT YOU BETTER BE GRATEFUL, OKAY?

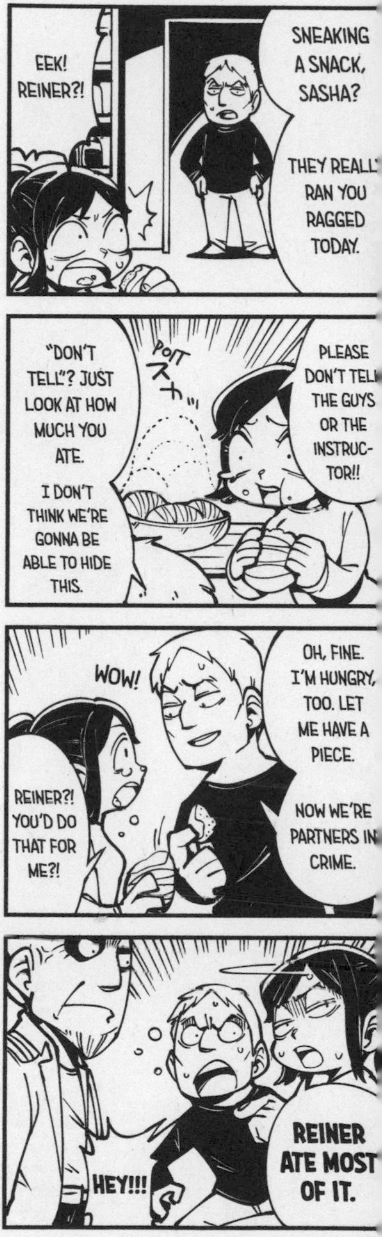
SNEAKING A SNACK, SASHA?
EEK! REINER?!
THEY REALL RAN YOU RAGGED TODAY.
PLEASE DON'T TELI THE GUYS OR THE INSTRUC-TOR!!
POIT
"DON'T TELL"? JUST LOOK AT HOW MUCH YOU ATE.
I DON'T THINK WE'RE GONNA BE ABLE TO HIDE THIS.
OH, FINE. I'M HUNGRY, TOO. LET ME HAVE A PIECE.
WOW!
NOW WE'RE PARTNERS IN CRIME.
REINER?! YOU'D DO THAT FOR ME?!
REINER ATE MOST OF IT.
HEY!!!

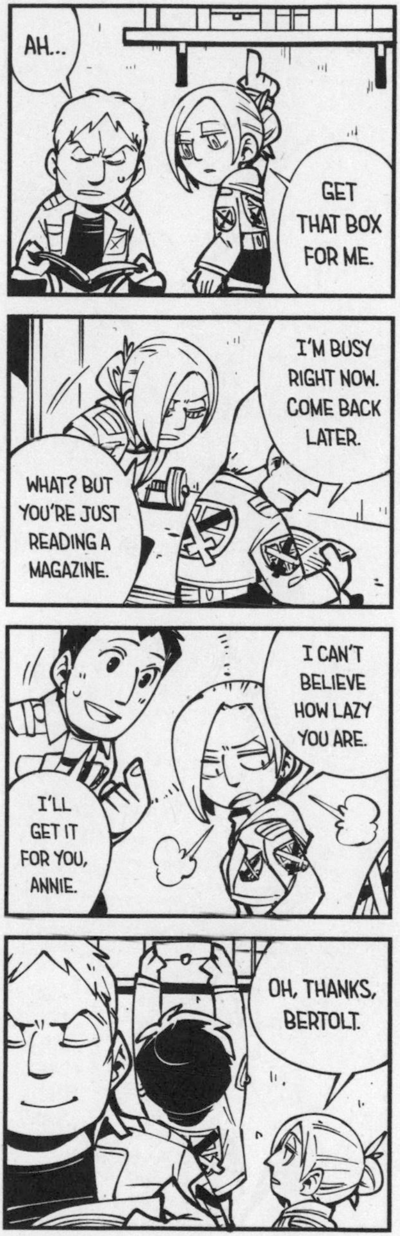
AH...
GET THAT BOX FOR ME.
I'M BUSY RIGHT NOW. COME BACK LATER.
WHAT? BUT YOU'RE JUST READING A MAGAZINE.
I CAN'T BELIEVE HOW LAZY YOU ARE.
I'LL GET IT FOR YOU, ANNIE.
OH, THANKS, BERTOLT.

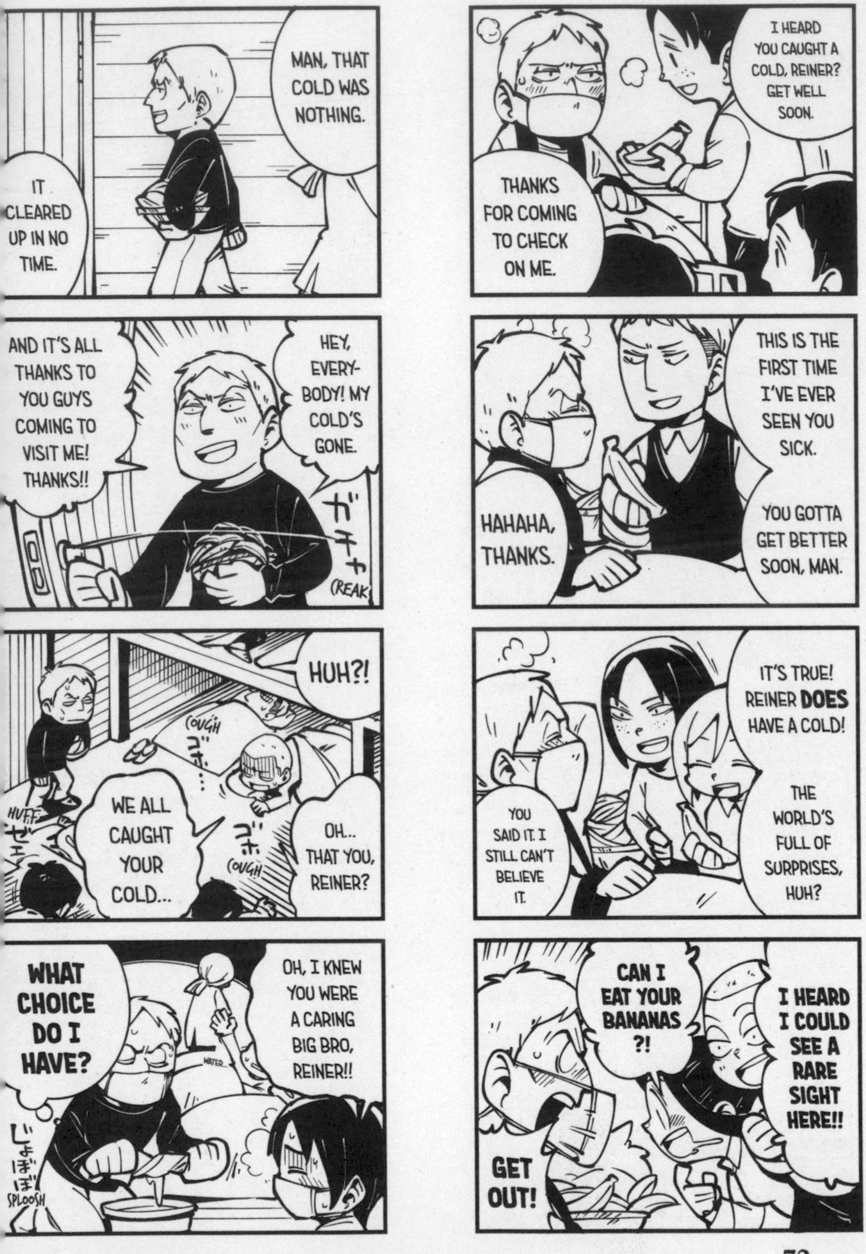
I HEARD YOU CAUGHT A COLD, REINER? GET WELL SOON.
THANKS FOR COMING TO CHECK ON ME.
THIS IS THE FIRST TIME I'VE EVER SEEN YOU SICK.
YOU GOTTA GET BETTER SOON, MAN.
HAHAHA, THANKS.
IT'S TRUE! REINER **DOES** HAVE A COLD!
THE WORLD'S FULL OF SURPRISES, HUH?
YOU SAID IT. I STILL CAN'T BELIEVE IT.
I HEARD I COULD SEE A RARE SIGHT HERE!!
CAN I EAT YOUR BANANAS?!
GET OUT!
MAN, THAT COLD WAS NOTHING.
IT CLEARED UP IN NO TIME.
HEY, EVERYBODY! MY COLD'S GONE.
AND IT'S ALL THANKS TO YOU GUYS COMING TO VISIT ME! THANKS!!
ガチャ
CREAK
HUH?!
OH... THAT YOU, REINER?
ゴホ…
COUGH
ゴホ
COUGH
WE ALL CAUGHT YOUR COLD...
ゼェ
HUFF
OH, I KNEW YOU WERE A CARING BIG BRO, REINER!!
WATER...
WHAT CHOICE DO I HAVE?
じょぼぼぼ
SPLOOSH

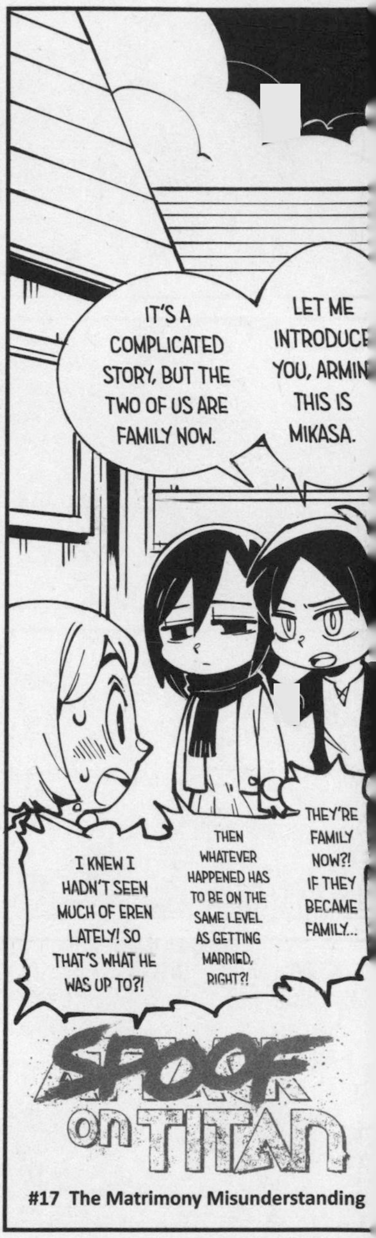
LET ME INTRODUC YOU, ARMIN THIS IS MIKASA.
IT'S A COMPLICATED STORY, BUT THE TWO OF US ARE FAMILY NOW.
THEY'RE FAMILY NOW?! IF THEY BECAME FAMILY...
THEN WHATEVER HAPPENED HAS TO BE ON THE SAME LEVEL AS GETTING MARRIED, RIGHT?!
I KNEW I HADN'T SEEN MUCH OF EREN LATELY! SO THAT'S WHAT HE WAS UP TO?!
SPOOF on TITAN
#17 The Matrimony Misunderstanding

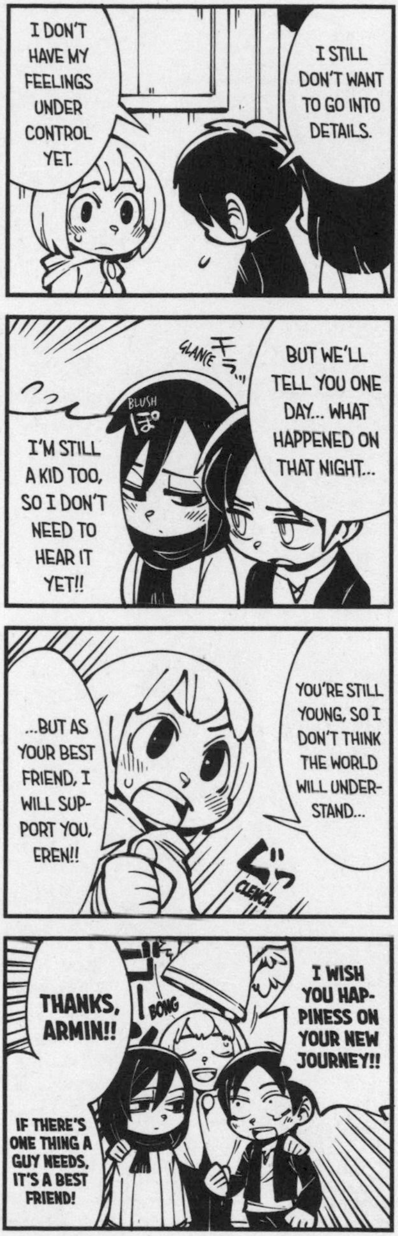
I STILL DON'T WANT TO GO INTO DETAILS.
I DON'T HAVE MY FEELINGS UNDER CONTROL YET.
BUT WE'LL TELL YOU ONE DAY... WHAT HAPPENED ON THAT NIGHT...
GLANCE
BLUSH
I'M STILL A KID TOO, SO I DON'T NEED TO HEAR IT YET!!
YOU'RE STILL YOUNG, SO I DON'T THINK THE WORLD WILL UNDER-STAND...
CLENCH
...BUT AS YOUR BEST FRIEND, I WILL SUP-PORT YOU, EREN!!
I WISH YOU HAP-PINESS ON YOUR NEW JOURNEY!!
BONG
THANKS, ARMIN!!
IF THERE'S ONE THING A GUY NEEDS, IT'S A BEST FRIEND!

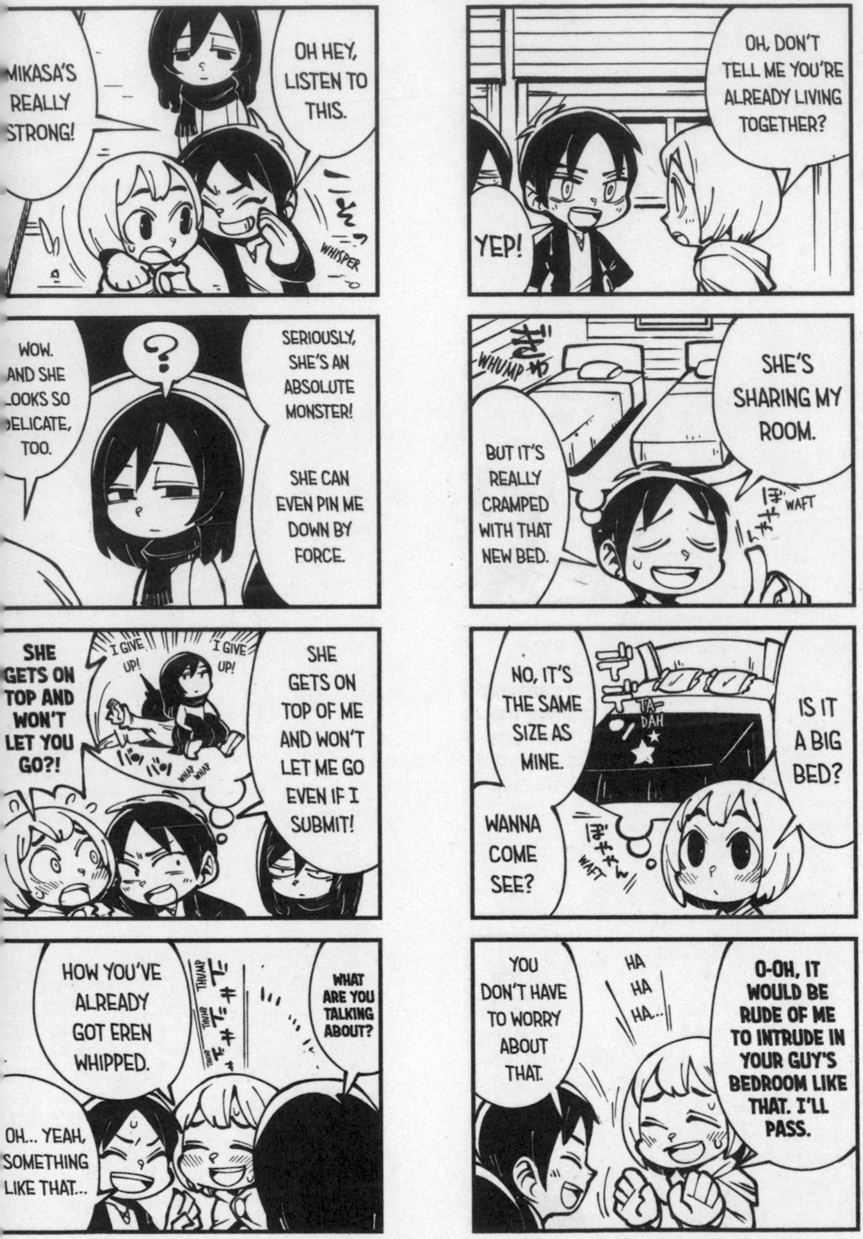
OH, DON'T TELL ME YOU'RE ALREADY LIVING TOGETHER?
YEP!
SHE'S SHARING MY ROOM.
WHUMP
BUT IT'S REALLY CRAMPED WITH THAT NEW BED.
WAFT
IS IT A BIG BED?
NO, IT'S THE SAME SIZE AS MINE.
TA-DAH
WANNA COME SEE?
WAFT
O-OH, IT WOULD BE RUDE OF ME TO INTRUDE IN YOUR GUY'S BEDROOM LIKE THAT. I'LL PASS.
HA HA HA...
YOU DON'T HAVE TO WORRY ABOUT THAT.
OH HEY, LISTEN TO THIS.
WHISPER
MIKASA'S REALLY STRONG!
SERIOUSLY, SHE'S AN ABSOLUTE MONSTER!
SHE CAN EVEN PIN ME DOWN BY FORCE.
WOW. AND SHE LOOKS SO DELICATE, TOO.
SHE GETS ON TOP OF ME AND WON'T LET ME GO EVEN IF I SUBMIT!
I GIVE UP!
I GIVE UP!
WHAP WHAP
SHE GETS ON TOP AND WON'T LET YOU GO?!
WHAT ARE YOU TALKING ABOUT?
THUMP THUMP THUMP
HOW YOU'VE ALREADY GOT EREN WHIPPED.
OH... YEAH, SOMETHING LIKE THAT...

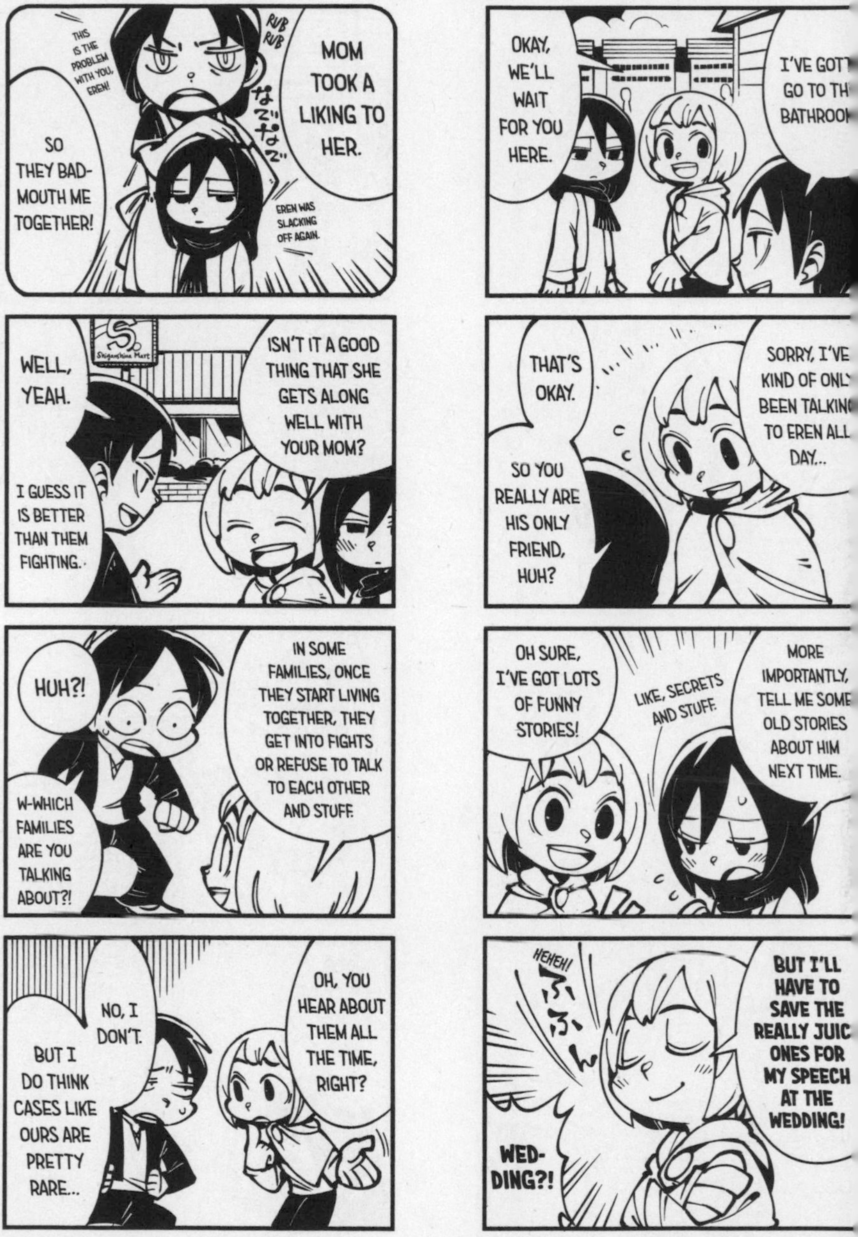
I'VE GOT GO TO TH BATHROO
OKAY, WE'LL WAIT FOR YOU HERE.
SORRY, I'VE KIND OF ONL BEEN TALKIN TO EREN ALL DAY...
THAT'S OKAY.
SO YOU REALLY ARE HIS ONLY FRIEND, HUH?
MORE IMPORTANTLY, TELL ME SOME OLD STORIES ABOUT HIM NEXT TIME.
LIKE, SECRETS AND STUFF.
OH SURE, I'VE GOT LOTS OF FUNNY STORIES!
BUT I'LL HAVE TO SAVE THE REALLY JUIC ONES FOR MY SPEECH AT THE WEDDING!
HEHEH!
ふふん
WED-DING?!
MOM TOOK A LIKING TO HER.
RUB RUB
なでなで
THIS IS THE PROBLEM WITH YOU, EREN!
SO THEY BAD-MOUTH ME TOGETHER!
EREN WAS SLACKING OFF AGAIN.
ISN'T IT A GOOD THING THAT SHE GETS ALONG WELL WITH YOUR MOM?
Shiganshina Mart
WELL, YEAH.
I GUESS IT IS BETTER THAN THEM FIGHTING.
IN SOME FAMILIES, ONCE THEY START LIVING TOGETHER, THEY GET INTO FIGHTS OR REFUSE TO TALK TO EACH OTHER AND STUFF.
HUH?!
W-WHICH FAMILIES ARE YOU TALKING ABOUT?!
OH, YOU HEAR ABOUT THEM ALL THE TIME, RIGHT?
NO, I DON'T.
BUT I DO THINK CASES LIKE OURS ARE PRETTY RARE...

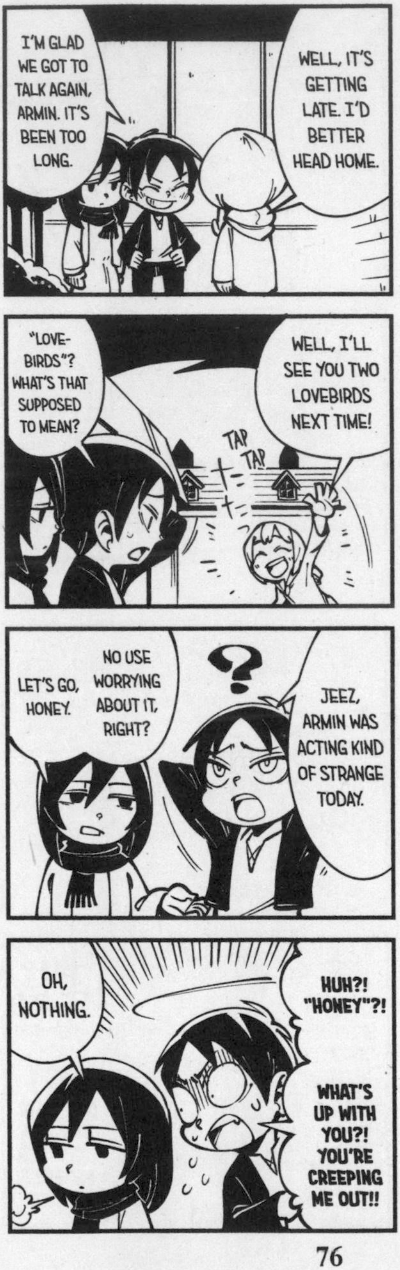
WELL, IT'S GETTING LATE. I'D BETTER HEAD HOME.
I'M GLAD WE GOT TO TALK AGAIN, ARMIN. IT'S BEEN TOO LONG.
WELL, I'LL SEE YOU TWO LOVEBIRDS NEXT TIME!
TAP TAP
"LOVE-BIRDS"? WHAT'S THAT SUPPOSED TO MEAN?
JEEZ, ARMIN WAS ACTING KIND OF STRANGE TODAY.
?
NO USE WORRYING ABOUT IT, RIGHT?
LET'S GO, HONEY.
HUH?! "HONEY"?!
OH, NOTHING.
WHAT'S UP WITH YOU?! YOU'RE CREEPING ME OUT!!
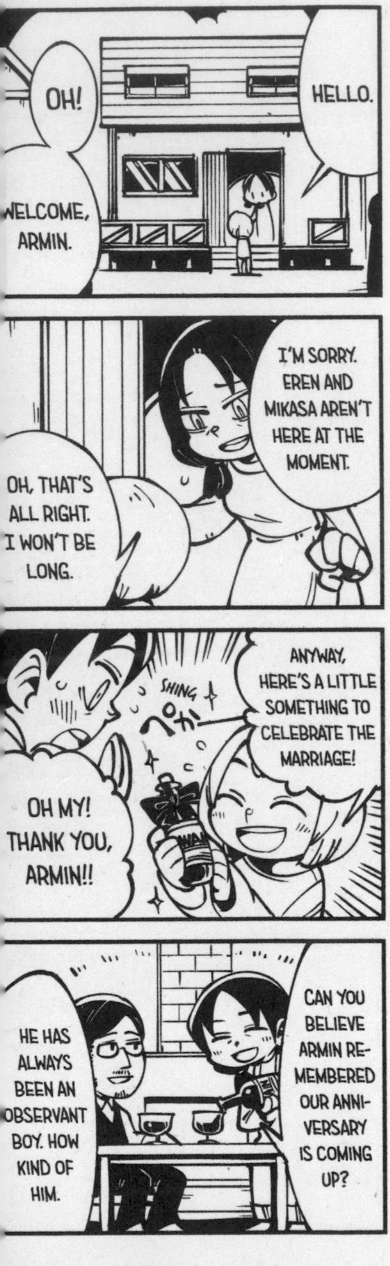
HELLO.
OH!
WELCOME, ARMIN.
I'M SORRY. EREN AND MIKASA AREN'T HERE AT THE MOMENT.
OH, THAT'S ALL RIGHT. I WON'T BE LONG.
ANYWAY, HERE'S A LITTLE SOMETHING TO CELEBRATE THE MARRIAGE!
SHING
OH MY! THANK YOU, ARMIN!!
CAN YOU BELIEVE ARMIN RE-MEMBERED OUR ANNI-VERSARY IS COMING UP?
HE HAS ALWAYS BEEN AN OBSERVANT BOY. HOW KIND OF HIM.

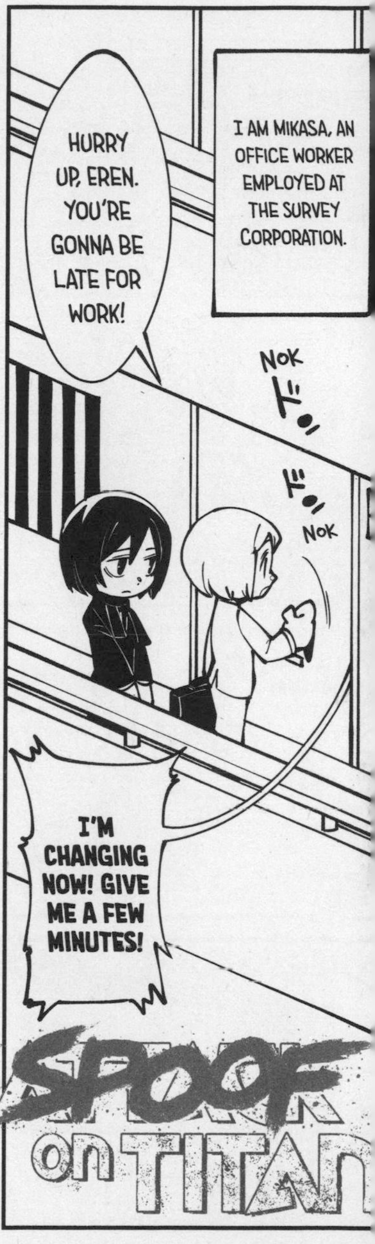
I AM MIKASA, AN OFFICE WORKER EMPLOYED AT THE SURVEY CORPORATION.
HURRY UP, EREN. YOU'RE GONNA BE LATE FOR WORK!
NOK
NOK
I'M CHANGING NOW! GIVE ME A FEW MINUTES!
SPOOF on TITAN

#18 A Day in Mikasa's Life at the Office

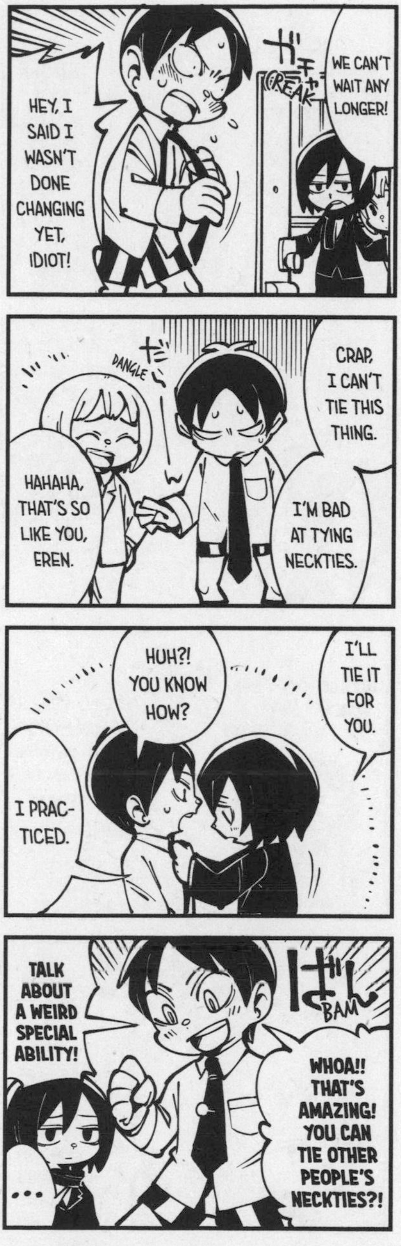
WE CAN'T WAIT ANY LONGER!
CREAK
HEY, I SAID I WASN'T DONE CHANGING YET, IDIOT!
CRAP, I CAN'T TIE THIS THING.
I'M BAD AT TYING NECKTIES.
DANGLE
HAHAHA, THAT'S SO LIKE YOU, EREN.
I'LL TIE IT FOR YOU.
HUH?! YOU KNOW HOW?
I PRACTICED.
BAM
WHOA!! THAT'S AMAZING! YOU CAN TIE OTHER PEOPLE'S NECKTIES?!
TALK ABOUT A WEIRD SPECIAL ABILITY!
...

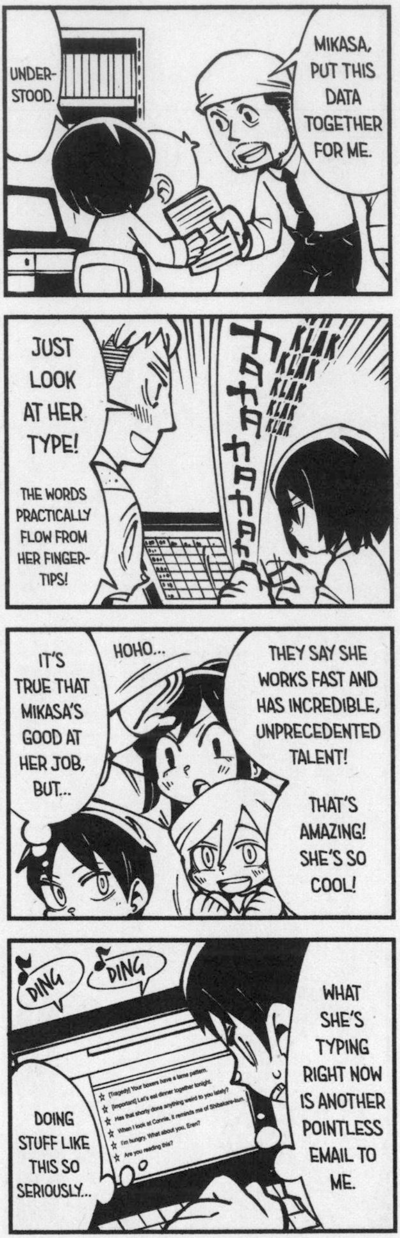
MIKASA, PUT THIS DATA TOGETHER FOR ME.
UNDER-STOOD.
KLAK KLAK KLAK KLAK KLAK
JUST LOOK AT HER TYPE!
THE WORDS PRACTICALLY FLOW FROM HER FINGER-TIPS!
THEY SAY SHE WORKS FAST AND HAS INCREDIBLE, UNPRECEDENTED TALENT!
THAT'S AMAZING! SHE'S SO COOL!
HOHO...
IT'S TRUE THAT MIKASA'S GOOD AT HER JOB, BUT...
WHAT SHE'S TYPING RIGHT NOW IS ANOTHER POINTLESS EMAIL TO ME.
DING
DING
☆ [Tragedy] Your boxers have a lame pattern.
☆ [Important] Let's eat dinner together tonight.
☆ Has that shorty done anything weird to you lately?
☆ When I look at Connie, it reminds me of Shibakare-kun.
☆ I'm hungry. What about you, Eren?
☆ Are you reading this?
DOING STUFF LIKE THIS SO SERIOUSLY...

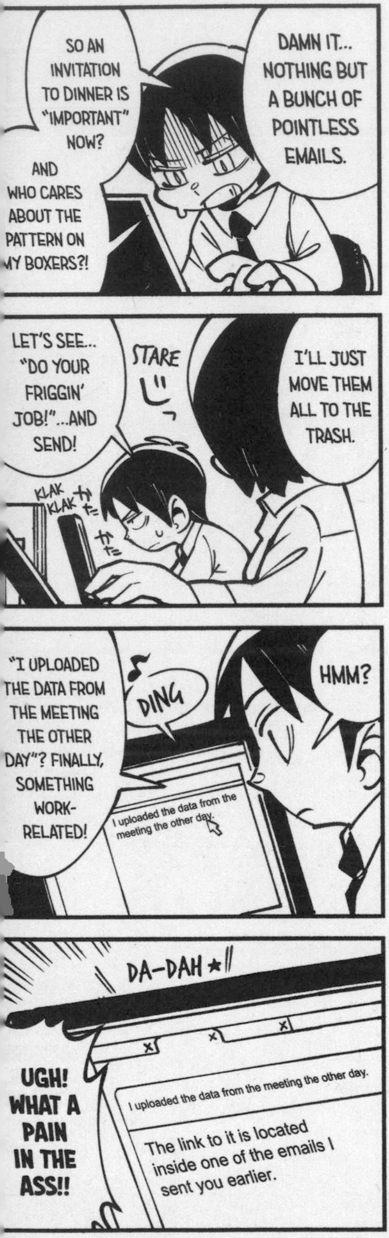
DAMN IT... NOTHING BUT A BUNCH OF POINTLESS EMAILS.
SO AN INVITATION TO DINNER IS "IMPORTANT" NOW?
AND WHO CARES ABOUT THE PATTERN ON MY BOXERS?!
I'LL JUST MOVE THEM ALL TO THE TRASH.
STARE
LET'S SEE... "DO YOUR FRIGGIN' JOB!"...AND SEND!
KLAK KLAK
HMM?
DING
"I UPLOADED THE DATA FROM THE MEETING THE OTHER DAY"? FINALLY, SOMETHING WORK-RELATED!
I uploaded the data from the meeting the other day.
DA-DAH ★//
I uploaded the data from the meeting the other day.
The link to it is located inside one of the emails I sent you earlier.
UGH! WHAT A PAIN IN THE ASS!!

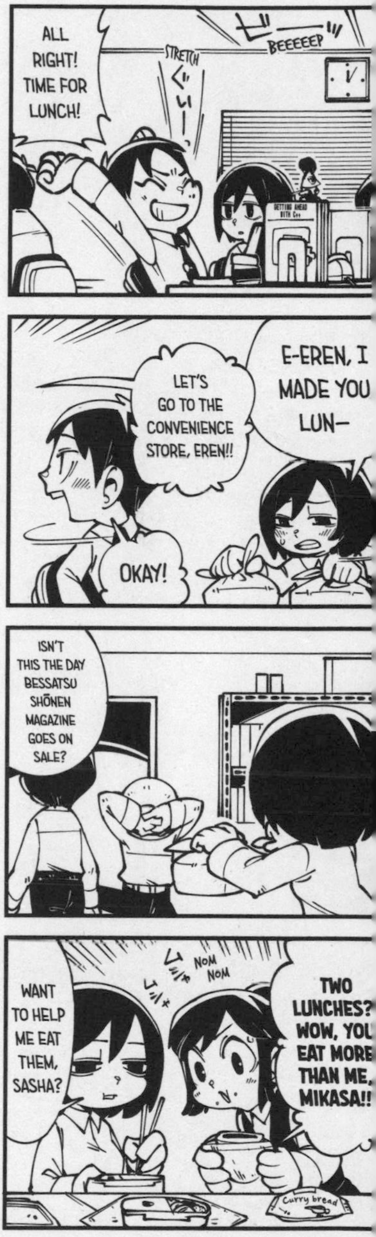
BEEEEEP
STRETCH
ALL RIGHT! TIME FOR LUNCH!
E-EREN, I MADE YOU LUN—
LET'S GO TO THE CONVENIENCE STORE, EREN!!
OKAY!
ISN'T THIS THE DAY BESSATSU SHŌNEN MAGAZINE GOES ON SALE?
TWO LUNCHES? WOW, YOU EAT MORE THAN ME, MIKASA!!
NOM NOM
WANT TO HELP ME EAT THEM, SASHA?
Curry bread
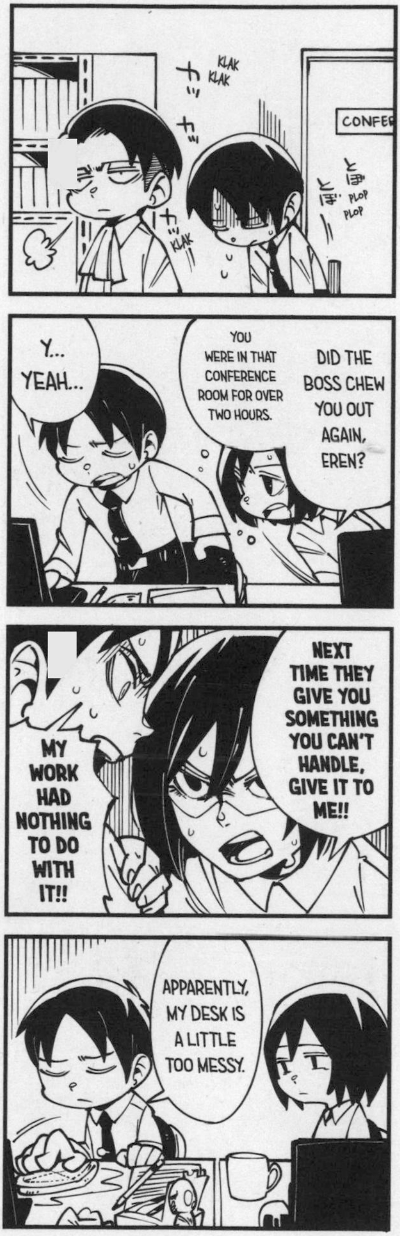
CONFER
KLAK KLAK
PLOP PLOP
KLAK
DID THE BOSS CHEW YOU OUT AGAIN, EREN?
YOU WERE IN THAT CONFERENCE ROOM FOR OVER TWO HOURS.
Y... YEAH...
NEXT TIME THEY GIVE YOU SOMETHING YOU CAN'T HANDLE, GIVE IT TO ME!!
MY WORK HAD NOTHING TO DO WITH IT!!
APPARENTLY, MY DESK IS A LITTLE TOO MESSY.

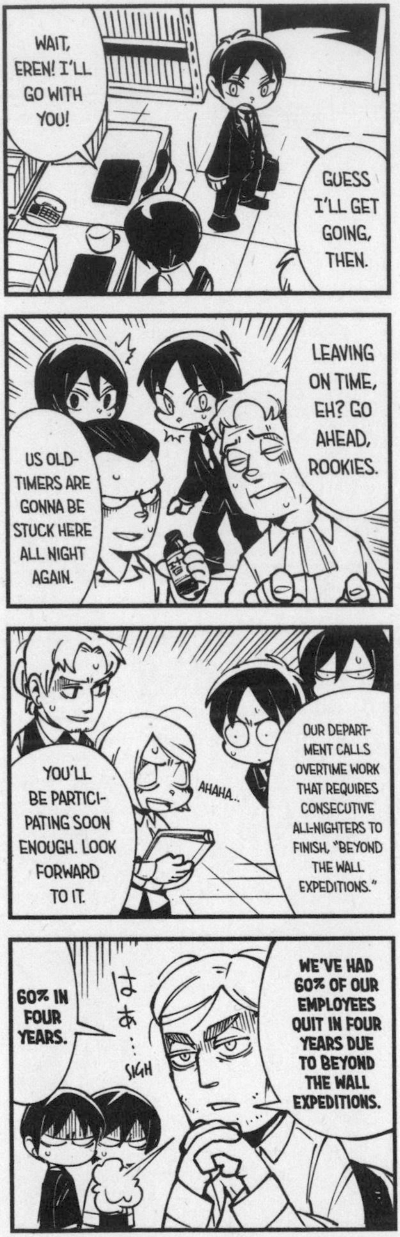
GUESS I'LL GET GOING, THEN.
WAIT, EREN! I'LL GO WITH YOU!
LEAVING ON TIME, EH? GO AHEAD, ROOKIES.
US OLD-TIMERS ARE GONNA BE STUCK HERE ALL NIGHT AGAIN.
OUR DEPARTMENT CALLS OVERTIME WORK THAT REQUIRES CONSECUTIVE ALL-NIGHTERS TO FINISH, "BEYOND THE WALL EXPEDITIONS."
AHAHA..
YOU'LL BE PARTICIPATING SOON ENOUGH. LOOK FORWARD TO IT.
WE'VE HAD 60% OF OUR EMPLOYEES QUIT IN FOUR YEARS DUE TO BEYOND THE WALL EXPEDITIONS.
はぁ… SIGH
60% IN FOUR YEARS.

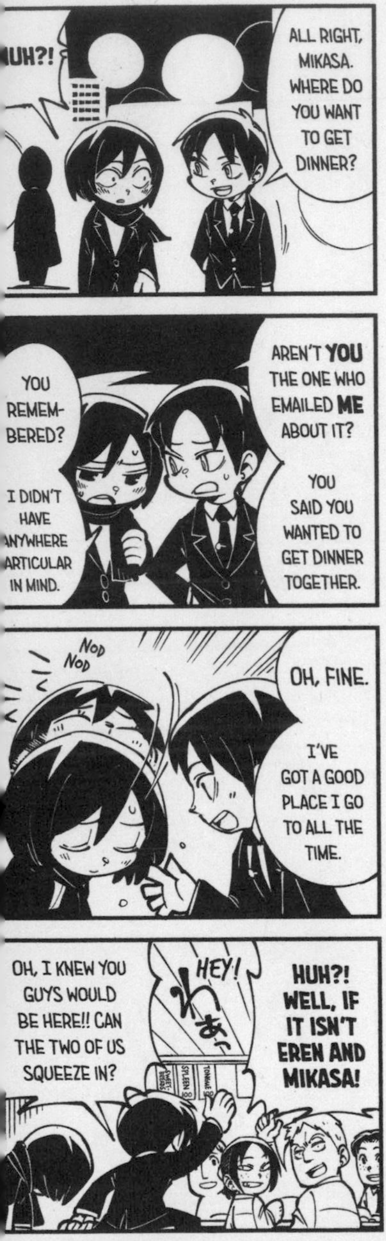
ALL RIGHT, MIKASA. WHERE DO YOU WANT TO GET DINNER?
HUH?!
AREN'T **YOU** THE ONE WHO EMAILED **ME** ABOUT IT?
YOU SAID YOU WANTED TO GET DINNER TOGETHER.
YOU REMEMBERED?
I DIDN'T HAVE ANYWHERE ARTICULAR IN MIND.
OH, FINE.
I'VE GOT A GOOD PLACE I GO TO ALL THE TIME.
NOD NOD
HUH?! WELL, IF IT ISN'T EREN AND MIKASA!
HEY!
わあっ
TONGUE
SPLEEN
OH, I KNEW YOU GUYS WOULD BE HERE!! CAN THE TWO OF US SQUEEZE IN?

SPOOF on TITAN

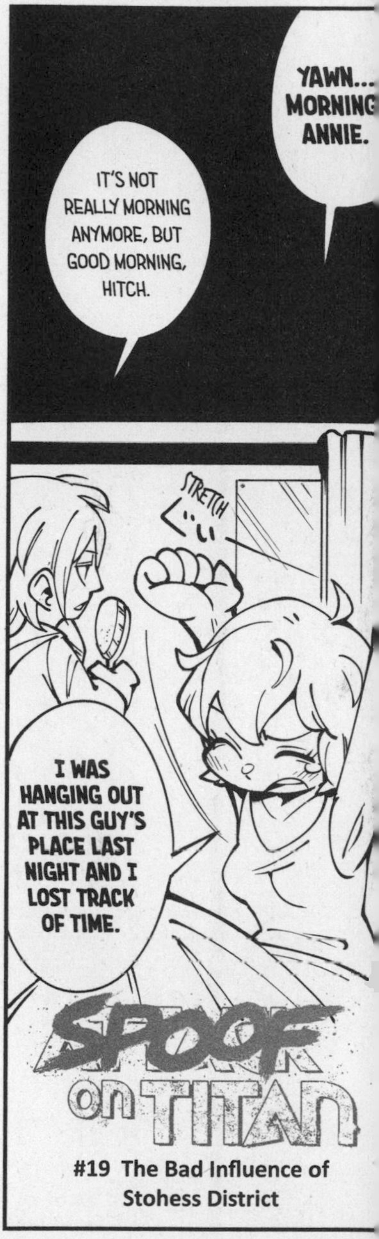
YAWN... MORNING ANNIE.
IT'S NOT REALLY MORNING ANYMORE, BUT GOOD MORNING, HITCH.
STRETCH
I WAS HANGING OUT AT THIS GUY'S PLACE LAST NIGHT AND I LOST TRACK OF TIME.
SPOOF on TITAN
#19 The Bad Influence of Stohess District

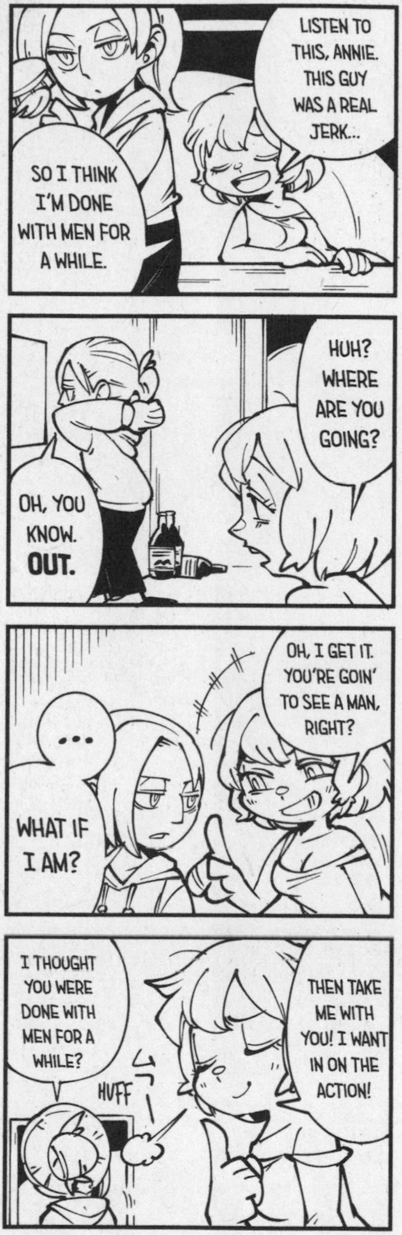
LISTEN TO THIS, ANNIE. THIS GUY WAS A REAL JERK...
SO I THINK I'M DONE WITH MEN FOR A WHILE.
HUH? WHERE ARE YOU GOING?
OH, YOU KNOW. **OUT.**
OH, I GET IT. YOU'RE GOIN' TO SEE A MAN, RIGHT?
...
WHAT IF I AM?
THEN TAKE ME WITH YOU! I WANT IN ON THE ACTION!
HUFF
I THOUGHT YOU WERE DONE WITH MEN FOR A WHILE?

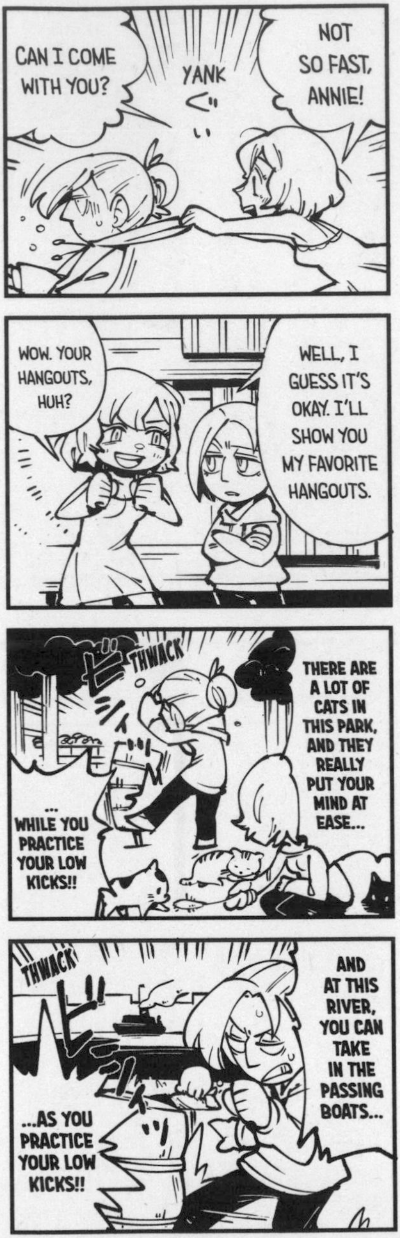
NOT SO FAST, ANNIE!
YANK
CAN I COME WITH YOU?
WELL, I GUESS IT'S OKAY. I'LL SHOW YOU MY FAVORITE HANGOUTS.
WOW. YOUR HANGOUTS, HUH?
THERE ARE A LOT OF CATS IN THIS PARK, AND THEY REALLY PUT YOUR MIND AT EASE...
THWACK
...WHILE YOU PRACTICE YOUR LOW KICKS!!
AND AT THIS RIVER, YOU CAN TAKE IN THE PASSING BOATS...
THWACK
...AS YOU PRACTICE YOUR LOW KICKS!!

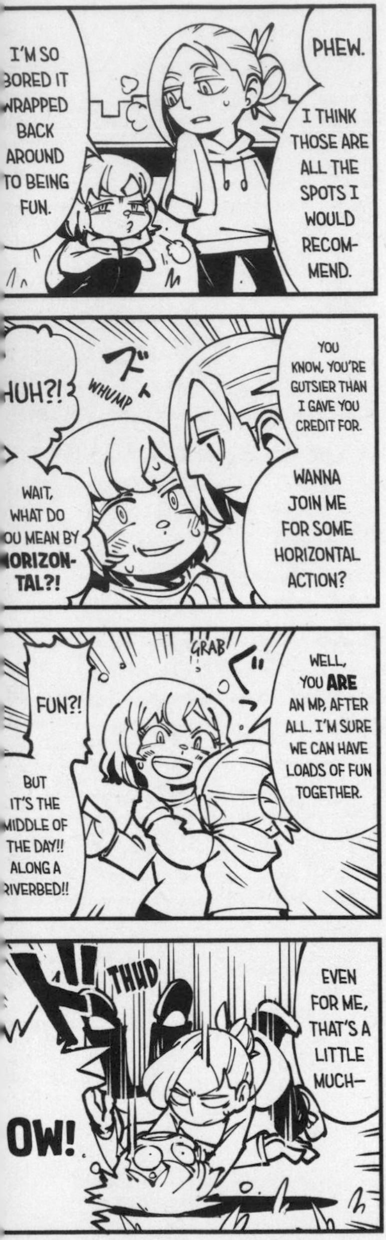
PHEW.
I THINK THOSE ARE ALL THE SPOTS I WOULD RECOMMEND.
I'M SO BORED IT WRAPPED BACK AROUND TO BEING FUN.
YOU KNOW, YOU'RE GUTSIER THAN I GAVE YOU CREDIT FOR.
WANNA JOIN ME FOR SOME HORIZONTAL ACTION?
WHUMP
HUH?!
WAIT, WHAT DO YOU MEAN BY HORIZONTAL?!
WELL, YOU **ARE** AN MP, AFTER ALL. I'M SURE WE CAN HAVE LOADS OF FUN TOGETHER.
GRAB
FUN?!
BUT IT'S THE MIDDLE OF THE DAY!! ALONG A RIVERBED!!
EVEN FOR ME, THAT'S A LITTLE MUCH—
THUD
OW!

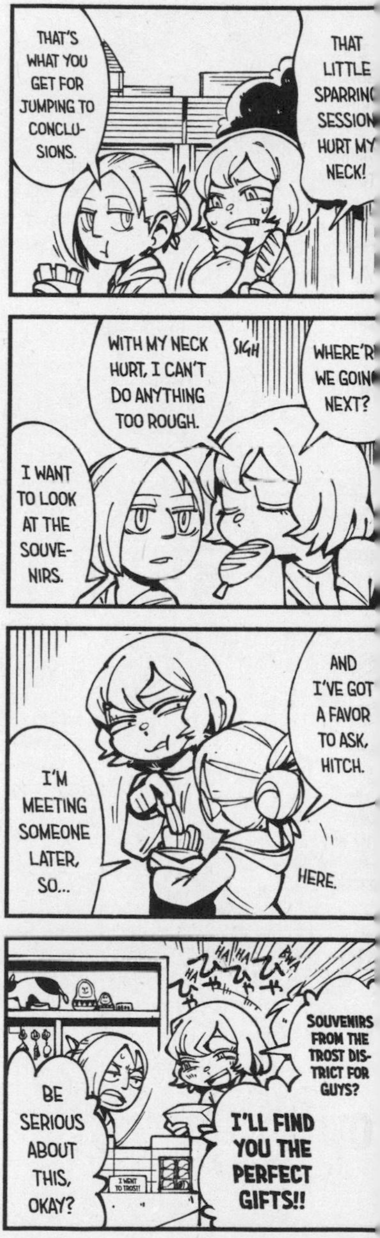
THAT LITTLE SPARRING SESSION HURT MY NECK!
THAT'S WHAT YOU GET FOR JUMPING TO CONCLUSIONS.
WHERE'RE WE GOING NEXT?
SIGH
WITH MY NECK HURT, I CAN'T DO ANYTHING TOO ROUGH.
I WANT TO LOOK AT THE SOUVENIRS.
AND I'VE GOT A FAVOR TO ASK, HITCH.
HERE.
I'M MEETING SOMEONE LATER, SO...
BWA HA HA HA HA
SOUVENIRS FROM THE TROST DISTRICT FOR GUYS?
I'LL FIND YOU THE PERFECT GIFTS!!
BE SERIOUS ABOUT THIS, OKAY?
I WANT TO TROST!
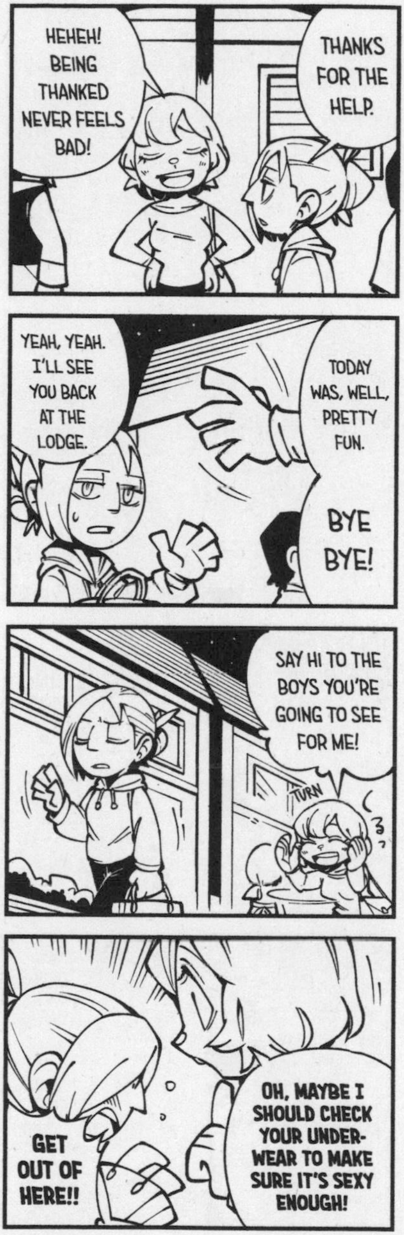
THANKS FOR THE HELP.
HEHEH! BEING THANKED NEVER FEELS BAD!
TODAY WAS, WELL, PRETTY FUN.
BYE BYE!
YEAH, YEAH. I'LL SEE YOU BACK AT THE LODGE.
SAY HI TO THE BOYS YOU'RE GOING TO SEE FOR ME!
TURN
OH, MAYBE I SHOULD CHECK YOUR UNDER-WEAR TO MAKE SURE IT'S SEXY ENOUGH!
GET OUT OF HERE!!

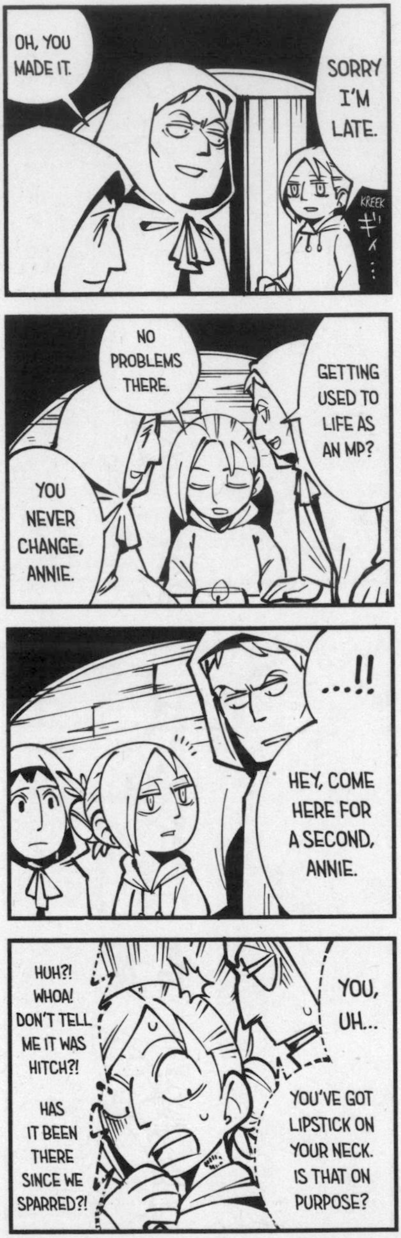
SORRY I'M LATE.
KREEK
OH, YOU MADE IT.
GETTING USED TO LIFE AS AN MP?
NO PROBLEMS THERE.
YOU NEVER CHANGE, ANNIE.
...!!
HEY, COME HERE FOR A SECOND, ANNIE.
YOU, UH...
YOU'VE GOT LIPSTICK ON YOUR NECK. IS THAT ON PURPOSE?
HUH?! WHOA! DON'T TELL ME IT WAS HITCH?!
HAS IT BEEN THERE SINCE WE SPARRED?!

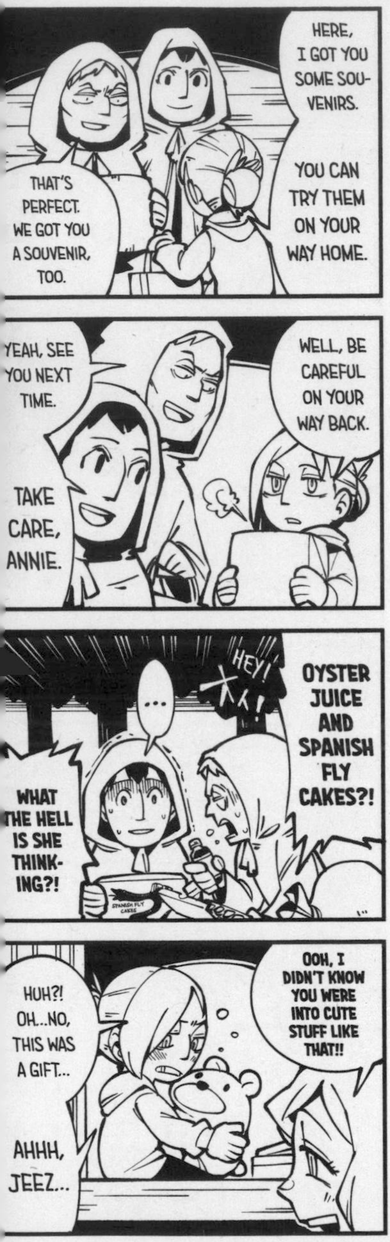
HERE, I GOT YOU SOME SOU-VENIRS.
YOU CAN TRY THEM ON YOUR WAY HOME.
THAT'S PERFECT. WE GOT YOU A SOUVENIR, TOO.
WELL, BE CAREFUL ON YOUR WAY BACK.
YEAH, SEE YOU NEXT TIME.
TAKE CARE, ANNIE.
OYSTER JUICE AND SPANISH FLY CAKES?!
HEY!
...
WHAT THE HELL IS SHE THINKING?!
SPANISH FLY CAKES
OOH, I DIDN'T KNOW YOU WERE INTO CUTE STUFF LIKE THAT!!
HUH?! OH...NO, THIS WAS A GIFT...
AHHH, JEEZ...

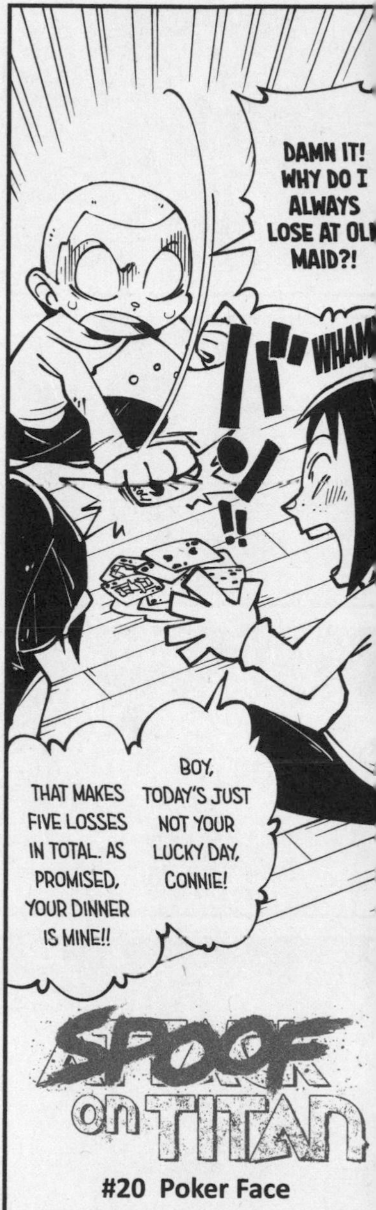
DAMN IT! WHY DO I ALWAYS LOSE AT OL MAID?!
WHAM
BOY, TODAY'S JUST NOT YOUR LUCKY DAY, CONNIE!
THAT MAKES FIVE LOSSES IN TOTAL. AS PROMISED, YOUR DINNER IS MINE!!
SPOOF on TITAN
#20 Poker Face

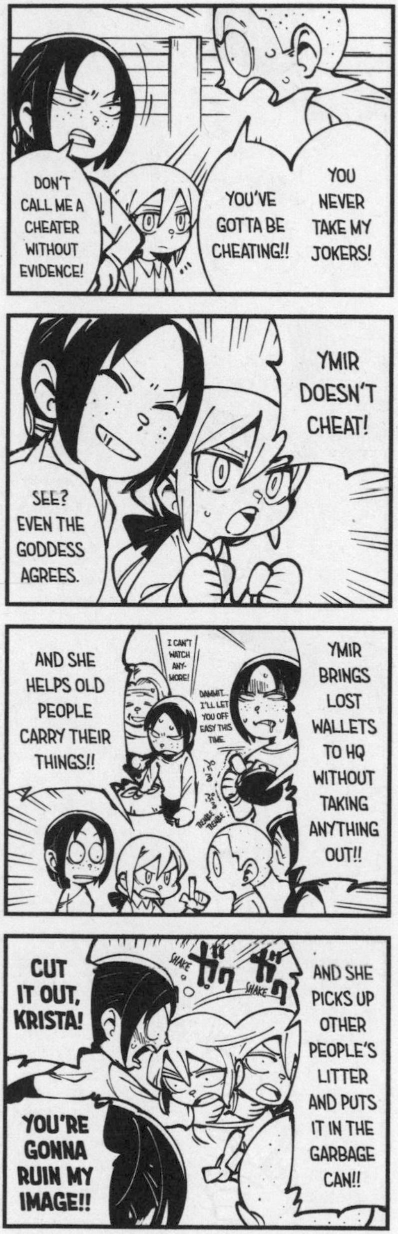
YOU NEVER TAKE MY JOKERS!
YOU'VE GOTTA BE CHEATING!!
DON'T CALL ME A CHEATER WITHOUT EVIDENCE!
YMIR DOESN'T CHEAT!
SEE? EVEN THE GODDESS AGREES.
YMIR BRINGS LOST WALLETS TO HQ WITHOUT TAKING ANYTHING OUT!!
DAMMIT... I'LL LET YOU OFF EASY THIS TIME.
I CAN'T WATCH ANYMORE!
AND SHE HELPS OLD PEOPLE CARRY THEIR THINGS!!
TREMBLE TREMBLE
AND SHE PICKS UP OTHER PEOPLE'S LITTER AND PUTS IT IN THE GARBAGE CAN!!
SHAKE
SHAKE
CUT IT OUT, KRISTA!
YOU'RE GONNA RUIN MY IMAGE!!

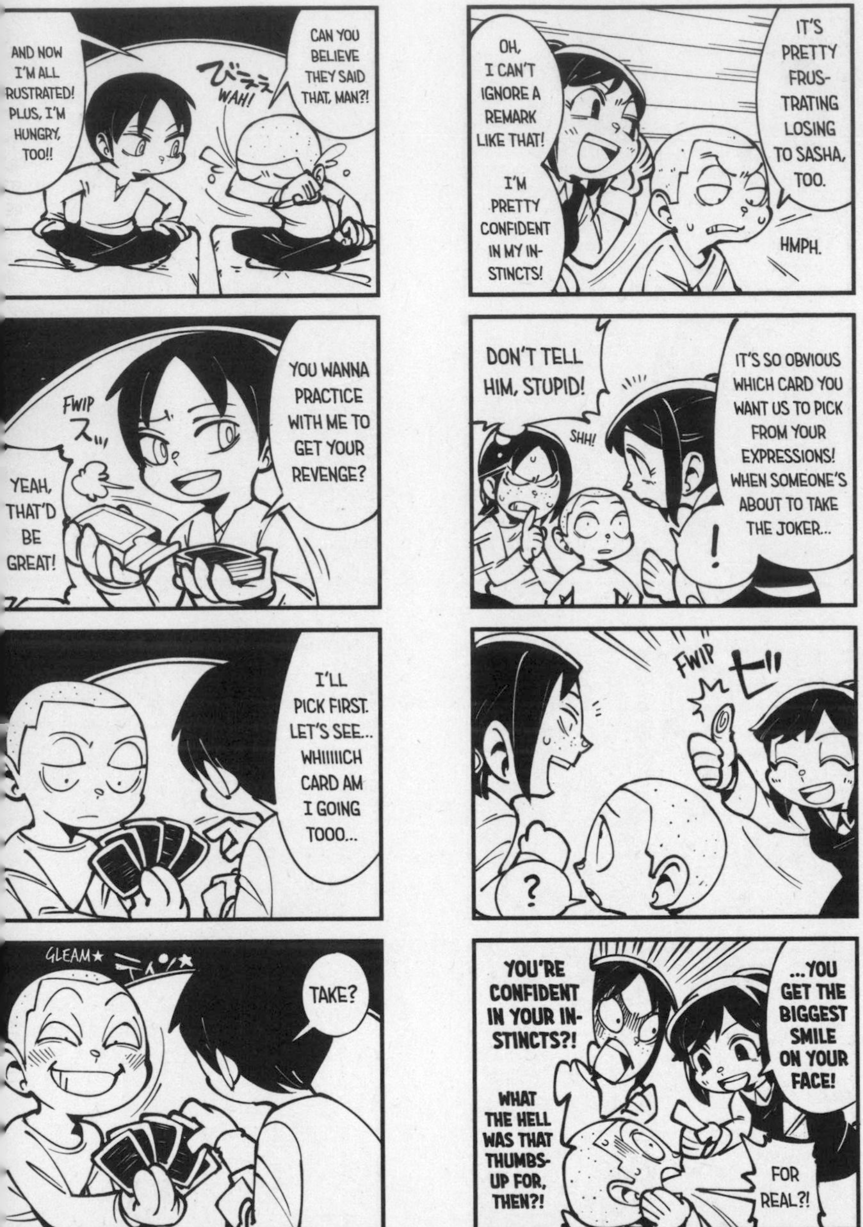
IT'S PRETTY FRUS-TRATING LOSING TO SASHA, TOO.
HMPH.
OH, I CAN'T IGNORE A REMARK LIKE THAT!
I'M PRETTY CONFIDENT IN MY IN-STINCTS!
IT'S SO OBVIOUS WHICH CARD YOU WANT US TO PICK FROM YOUR EXPRESSIONS! WHEN SOMEONE'S ABOUT TO TAKE THE JOKER...
!
DON'T TELL HIM, STUPID!
SHH!
FWIP
?
...YOU GET THE BIGGEST SMILE ON YOUR FACE!
FOR REAL?!
YOU'RE CONFIDENT IN YOUR IN-STINCTS?!
WHAT THE HELL WAS THAT THUMBS-UP FOR, THEN?!
CAN YOU BELIEVE THEY SAID THAT, MAN?!
WAH!
AND NOW I'M ALL RUSTRATED! PLUS, I'M HUNGRY, TOO!!
YOU WANNA PRACTICE WITH ME TO GET YOUR REVENGE?
FWIP
YEAH, THAT'D BE GREAT!
I'LL PICK FIRST. LET'S SEE... WHIIIIICH CARD AM I GOING TOOO...
TAKE?
GLEAM★

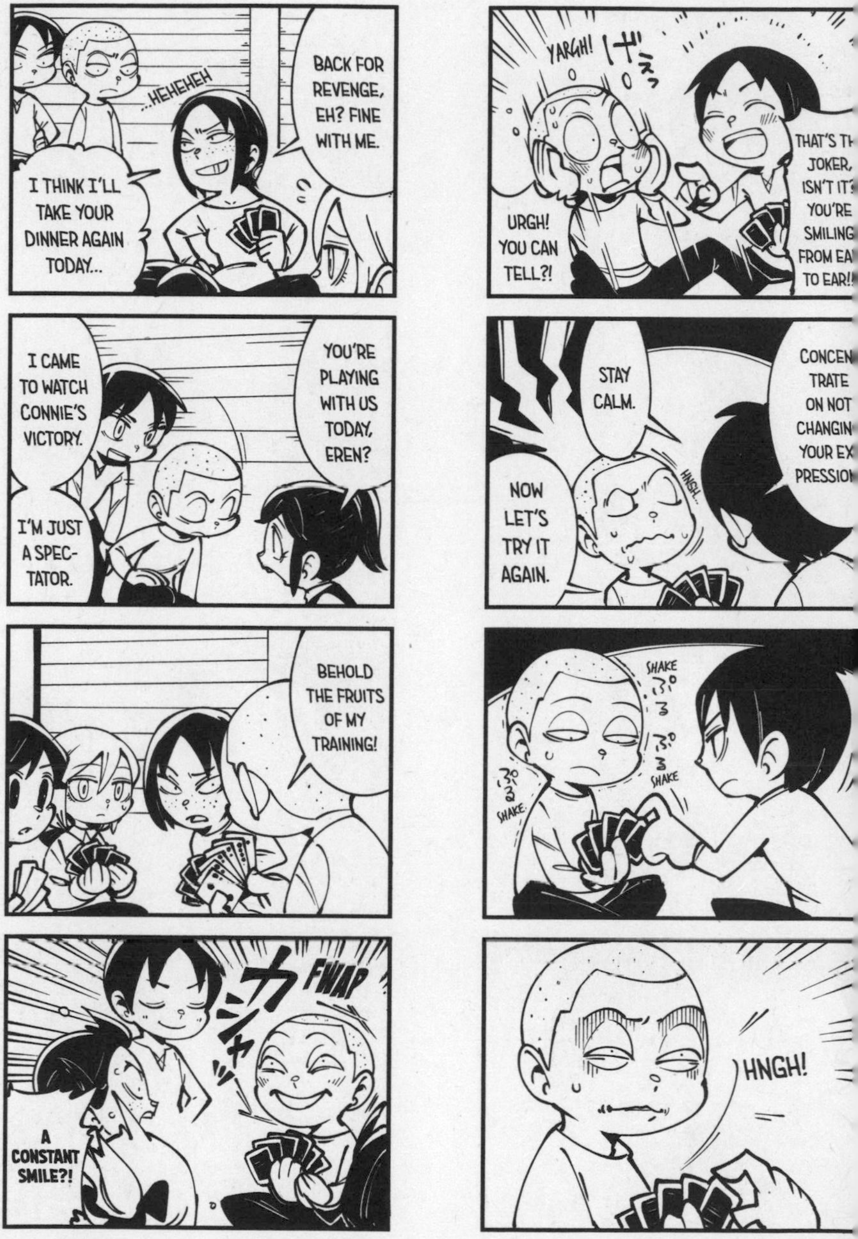
YARGH!
THAT'S TH JOKER, ISN'T IT? YOU'RE SMILING FROM EA TO EAR!
URGH! YOU CAN TELL?!
CONCEN TRATE ON NOT CHANGIN YOUR EX PRESSIO
STAY CALM.
HNGH...
NOW LET'S TRY IT AGAIN.
SHAKE ぶる
ぶる SHAKE
ぷる SHAKE
HNGH!
BACK FOR REVENGE, EH? FINE WITH ME.
...HEHEHEH
I THINK I'LL TAKE YOUR DINNER AGAIN TODAY...
YOU'RE PLAYING WITH US TODAY, EREN?
I CAME TO WATCH CONNIE'S VICTORY.
I'M JUST A SPECTATOR.
BEHOLD THE FRUITS OF MY TRAINING!
FWAP
A CONSTANT SMILE?!

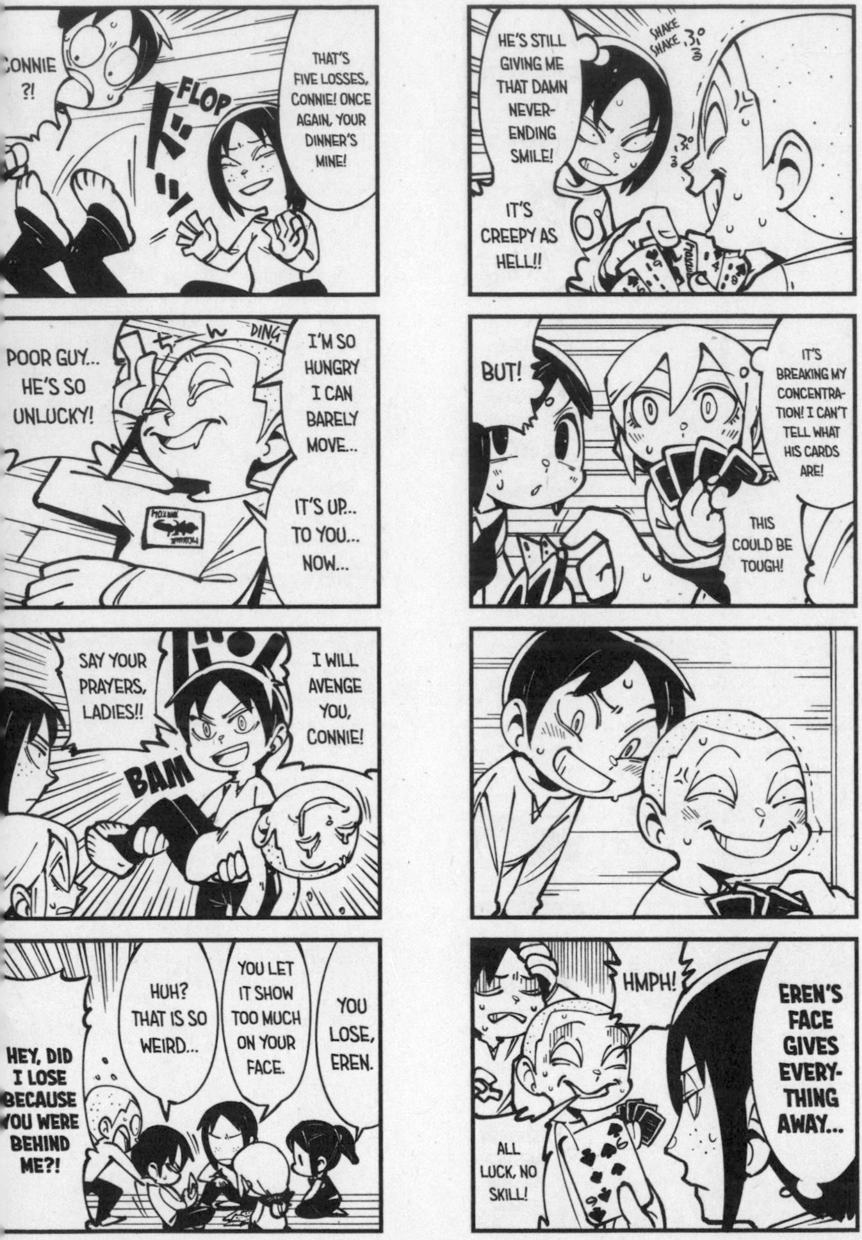
SHAKE SHAKE
HE'S STILL GIVING ME THAT DAMN NEVER-ENDING SMILE!
IT'S CREEPY AS HELL!!
IT'S BREAKING MY CONCENTRATION! I CAN'T TELL WHAT HIS CARDS ARE!
THIS COULD BE TOUGH!
BUT!
EREN'S FACE GIVES EVERYTHING AWAY...
HMPH!
ALL LUCK, NO SKILL!
THAT'S FIVE LOSSES, CONNIE! ONCE AGAIN, YOUR DINNER'S MINE!
FLOP
CONNIE ?!
DING
I'M SO HUNGRY I CAN BARELY MOVE...
IT'S UP... TO YOU... NOW...
POOR GUY... HE'S SO UNLUCKY!
I WILL AVENGE YOU, CONNIE!
SAY YOUR PRAYERS, LADIES!!
BAM
YOU LOSE, EREN.
YOU LET IT SHOW TOO MUCH ON YOUR FACE.
HUH? THAT IS SO WEIRD...
HEY, DID I LOSE BECAUSE YOU WERE BEHIND ME?!

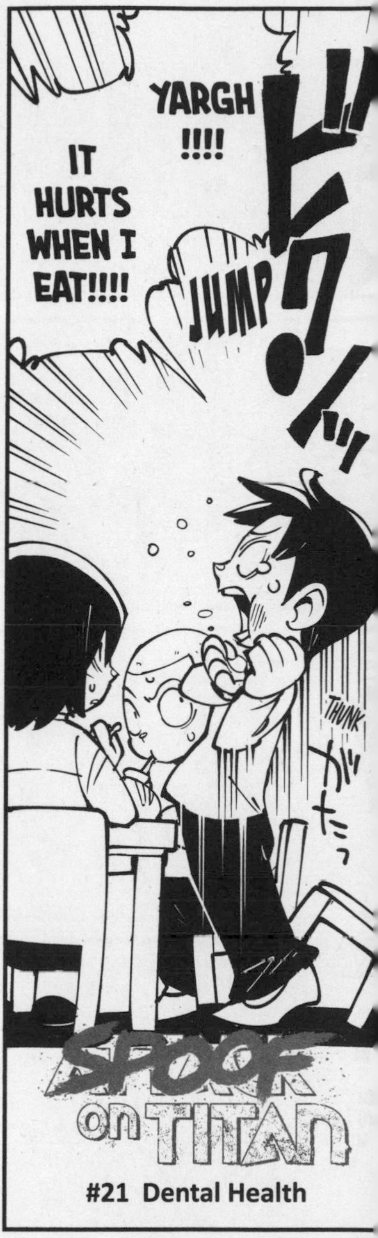
YARGH !!!!
IT HURTS WHEN I EAT!!!!
JUMP
THUNK
SPOOF on TITAN
#21 Dental Health

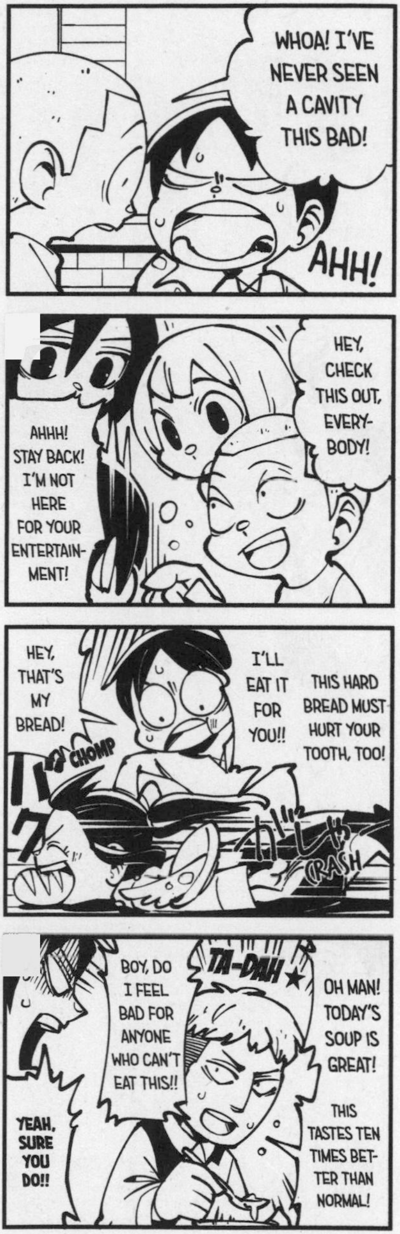
WHOA! I'VE NEVER SEEN A CAVITY THIS BAD!
AHH!
HEY, CHECK THIS OUT, EVERY-BODY!
AHHH! STAY BACK! I'M NOT HERE FOR YOUR ENTERTAIN-MENT!
THIS HARD BREAD MUST HURT YOUR TOOTH, TOO!
I'LL EAT IT FOR YOU!!
HEY, THAT'S MY BREAD!
CHOMP
CRASH
OH MAN! TODAY'S SOUP IS GREAT!
THIS TASTES TEN TIMES BET-TER THAN NORMAL!
TA-DAH★
BOY, DO I FEEL BAD FOR ANYONE WHO CAN'T EAT THIS!!
YEAH, SURE YOU DO!!

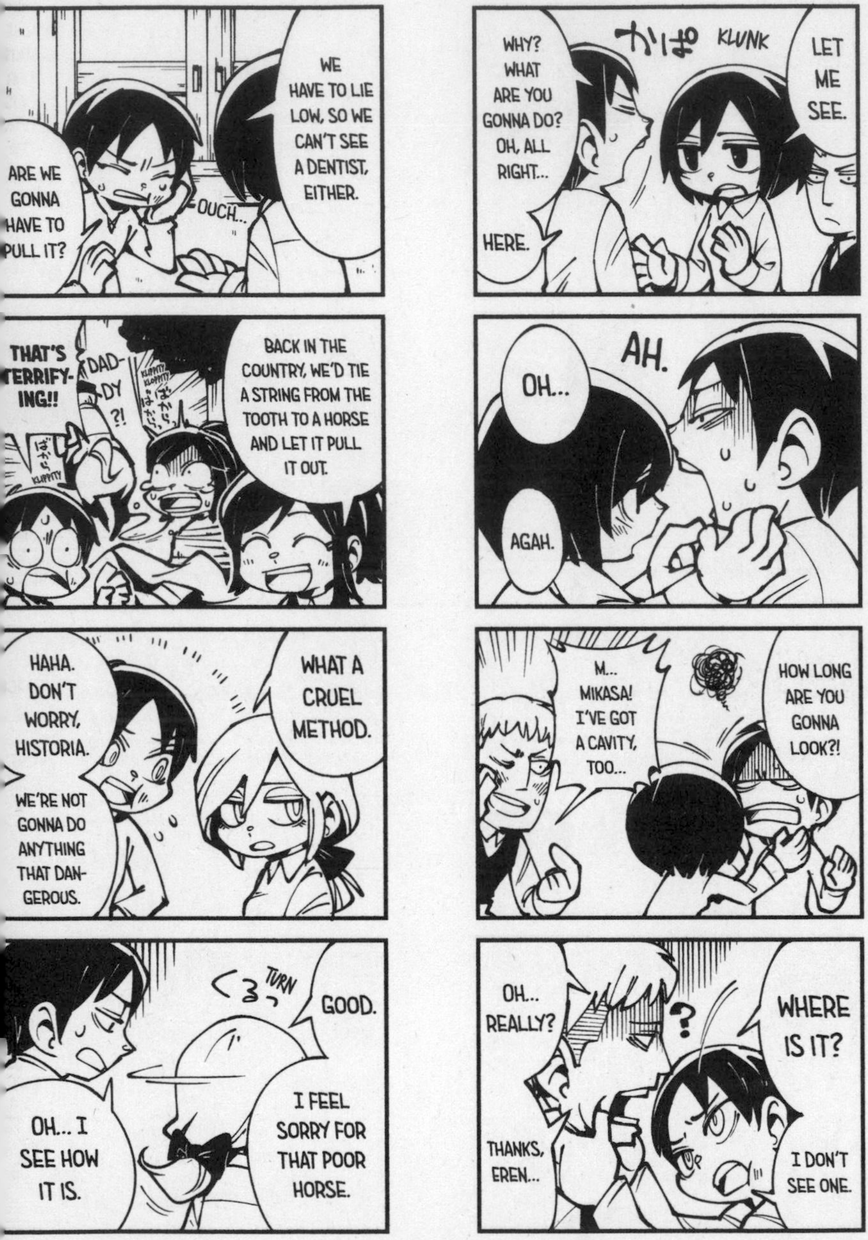
LET ME SEE.
かぽ KLUNK
WHY? WHAT ARE YOU GONNA DO? OH, ALL RIGHT...
HERE.
AH.
OH...
AGAH.
HOW LONG ARE YOU GONNA LOOK?!
M... MIKASA! I'VE GOT A CAVITY, TOO...
WHERE IS IT?
I DON'T SEE ONE.
OH... REALLY?
THANKS, EREN...
WE HAVE TO LIE LOW, SO WE CAN'T SEE A DENTIST, EITHER.
OUCH...
ARE WE GONNA HAVE TO PULL IT?
BACK IN THE COUNTRY, WE'D TIE A STRING FROM THE TOOTH TO A HORSE AND LET IT PULL IT OUT.
ぱかぱか KLIPPITY KLOPPITY
DADDY?!
THAT'S TERRIFYING!!
ぱかぱか KLIPPITY
WHAT A CRUEL METHOD.
HAHA. DON'T WORRY, HISTORIA.
WE'RE NOT GONNA DO ANYTHING THAT DANGEROUS.
GOOD.
くるっ TURN
I FEEL SORRY FOR THAT POOR HORSE.
OH... I SEE HOW IT IS.

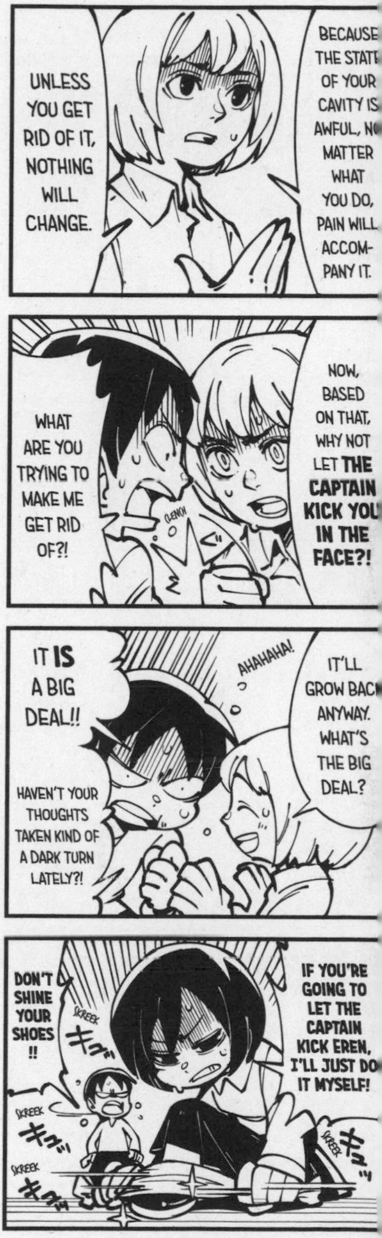
BECAUSE THE STAT OF YOUR CAVITY IS AWFUL, N MATTER WHAT YOU DO, PAIN WILL ACCOMPANY IT.
UNLESS YOU GET RID OF IT, NOTHING WILL CHANGE.
NOW, BASED ON THAT, WHY NOT LET THE CAPTAIN KICK YOU IN THE FACE?!
CLENCH
WHAT ARE YOU TRYING TO MAKE ME GET RID OF?!
IT'LL GROW BAC ANYWAY. WHAT'S THE BIG DEAL?
AHAHAHA!
IT IS A BIG DEAL!!
HAVEN'T YOUR THOUGHTS TAKEN KIND OF A DARK TURN LATELY?!
IF YOU'RE GOING TO LET THE CAPTAIN KICK EREN, I'LL JUST DO IT MYSELF!
SKREEK
DON'T SHINE YOUR SHOES!!
SKREEK
SKREEK
SKREEK

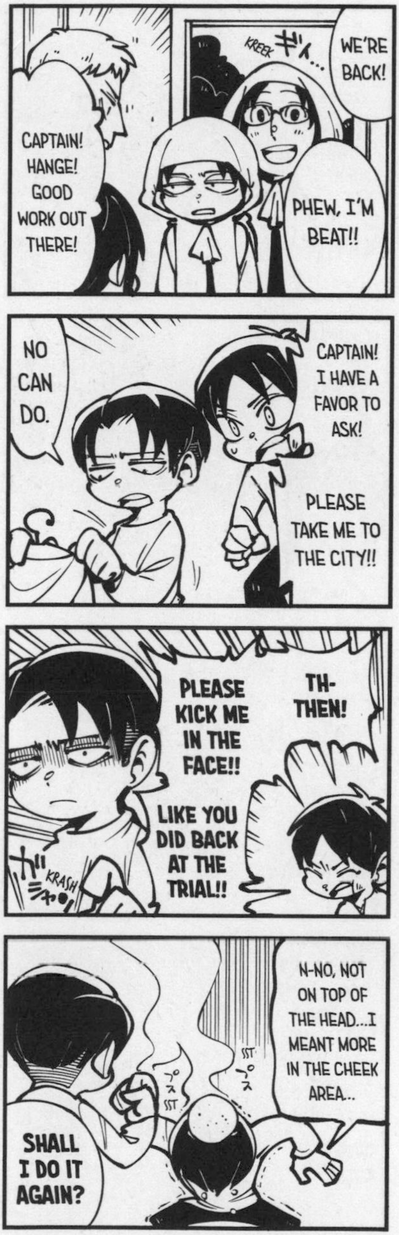
WE'RE BACK!
KREEK
CAPTAIN! HANGE! GOOD WORK OUT THERE!
PHEW, I'M BEAT!!
CAPTAIN! I HAVE A FAVOR TO ASK!
PLEASE TAKE ME TO THE CITY!!
NO CAN DO.
TH-THEN!
PLEASE KICK ME IN THE FACE!!
LIKE YOU DID BACK AT THE TRIAL!!
KRASH
N-NO, NOT ON TOP OF THE HEAD...I MEANT MORE IN THE CHEEK AREA...
SST
SST
SHALL I DO IT AGAIN?

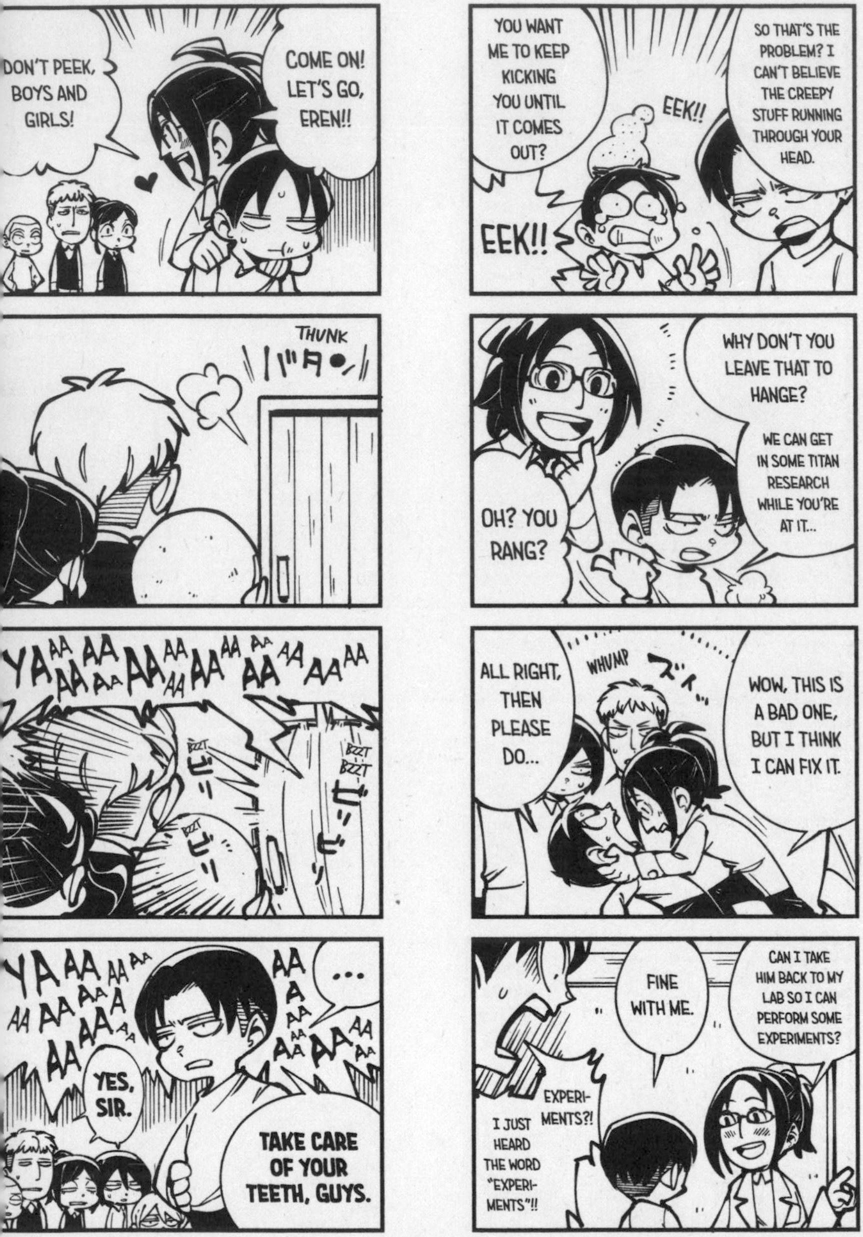
SO THAT'S THE PROBLEM? I CAN'T BELIEVE THE CREEPY STUFF RUNNING THROUGH YOUR HEAD.
EEK!!
YOU WANT ME TO KEEP KICKING YOU UNTIL IT COMES OUT?
EEK!!
WHY DON'T YOU LEAVE THAT TO HANGE?
WE CAN GET IN SOME TITAN RESEARCH WHILE YOU'RE AT IT...
OH? YOU RANG?
WOW, THIS IS A BAD ONE, BUT I THINK I CAN FIX IT.
WHUMP
ALL RIGHT, THEN PLEASE DO...
CAN I TAKE HIM BACK TO MY LAB SO I CAN PERFORM SOME EXPERIMENTS?
FINE WITH ME.
EXPERI-MENTS?!
I JUST HEARD THE WORD "EXPERI-MENTS"!!
COME ON! LET'S GO, EREN!!
DON'T PEEK, BOYS AND GIRLS!
THUNK
YAAAAAAAAAAAAAAAAAAAAAAA
BZZT
BZZT BZZT
BZZT
YAAAAAAAAAAAAAAAAAAAAAAA
...
YES, SIR.
TAKE CARE OF YOUR TEETH, GUYS.

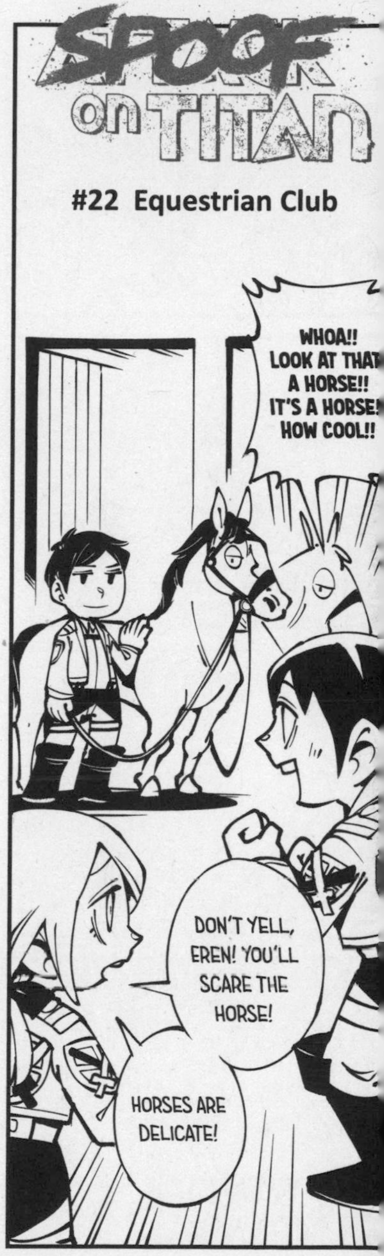
SPOOF on TITAN
#22 Equestrian Club
WHOA!! LOOK AT THAT A HORSE!! IT'S A HORSE! HOW COOL!!
DON'T YELL, EREN! YOU'LL SCARE THE HORSE!
HORSES ARE DELICATE!

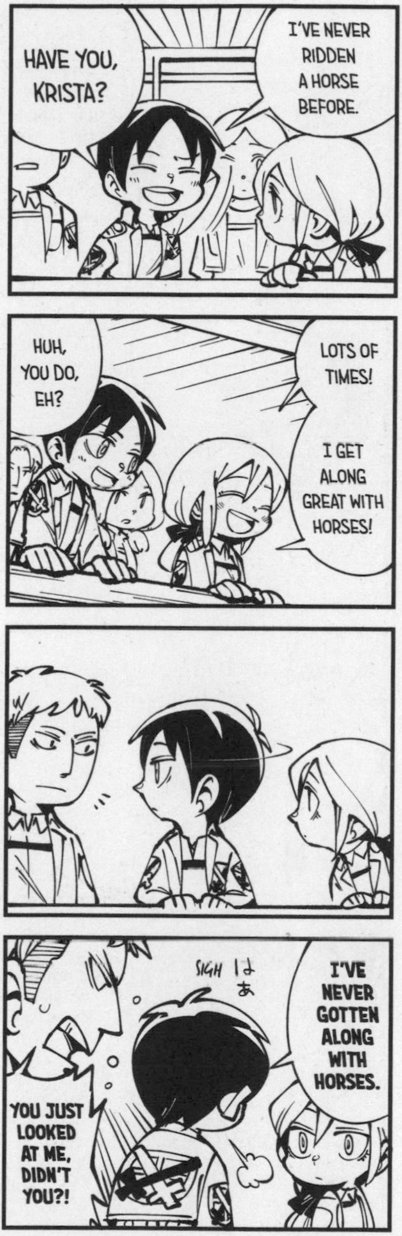
I'VE NEVER RIDDEN A HORSE BEFORE.
HAVE YOU, KRISTA?
LOTS OF TIMES!
I GET ALONG GREAT WITH HORSES!
HUH, YOU DO, EH?
I'VE NEVER GOTTEN ALONG WITH HORSES.
SIGH はあ
YOU JUST LOOKED AT ME, DIDN'T YOU?!

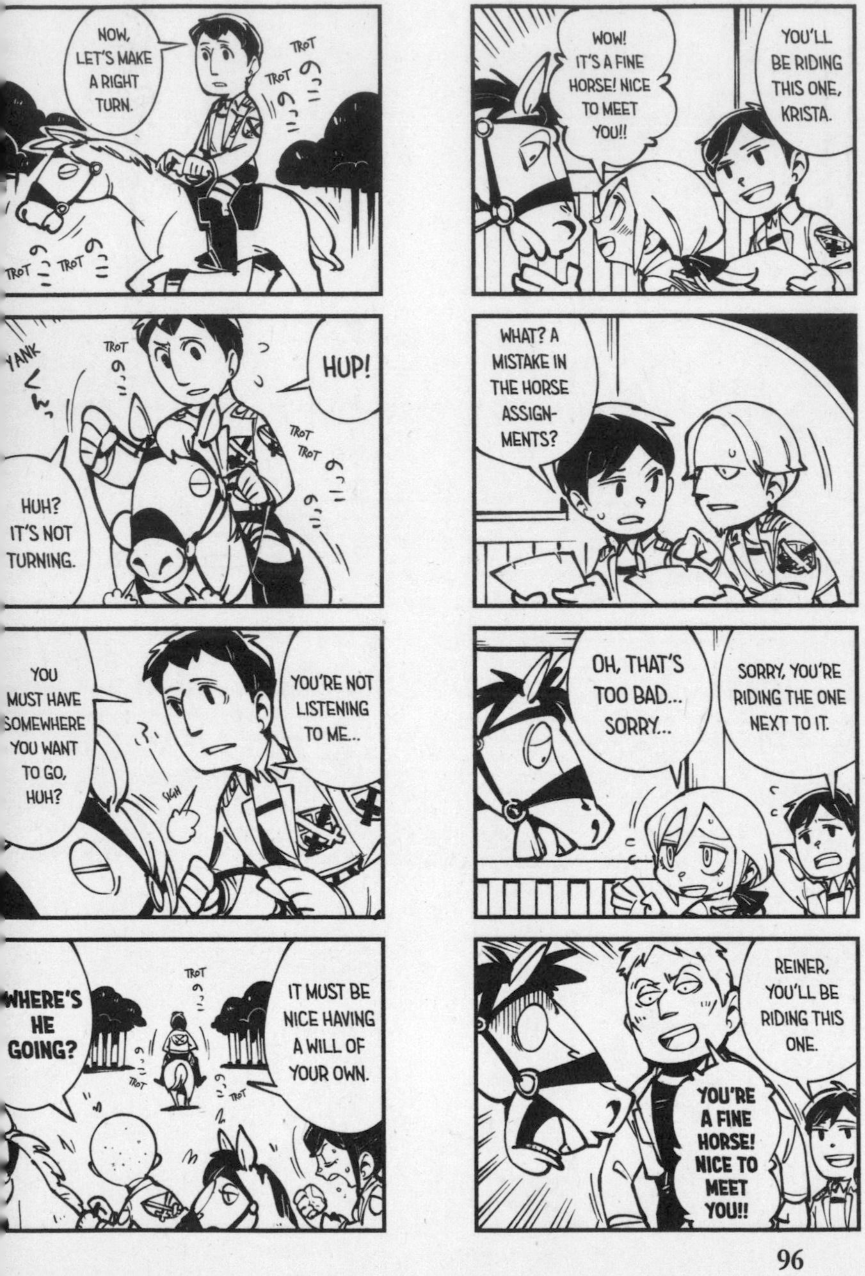
YOU'LL BE RIDING THIS ONE, KRISTA.
WOW! IT'S A FINE HORSE! NICE TO MEET YOU!!
WHAT? A MISTAKE IN THE HORSE ASSIGN-MENTS?
SORRY, YOU'RE RIDING THE ONE NEXT TO IT.
OH, THAT'S TOO BAD... SORRY...
REINER, YOU'LL BE RIDING THIS ONE.
YOU'RE A FINE HORSE! NICE TO MEET YOU!!
TROT
TROT
NOW, LET'S MAKE A RIGHT TURN.
TROT
TROT
HUP!
TROT
YANK
TROT
TROT
HUH? IT'S NOT TURNING.
YOU'RE NOT LISTENING TO ME...
SIGH
YOU MUST HAVE SOMEWHERE YOU WANT TO GO, HUH?
IT MUST BE NICE HAVING A WILL OF YOUR OWN.
TROT
TROT
TROT
WHERE'S HE GOING?

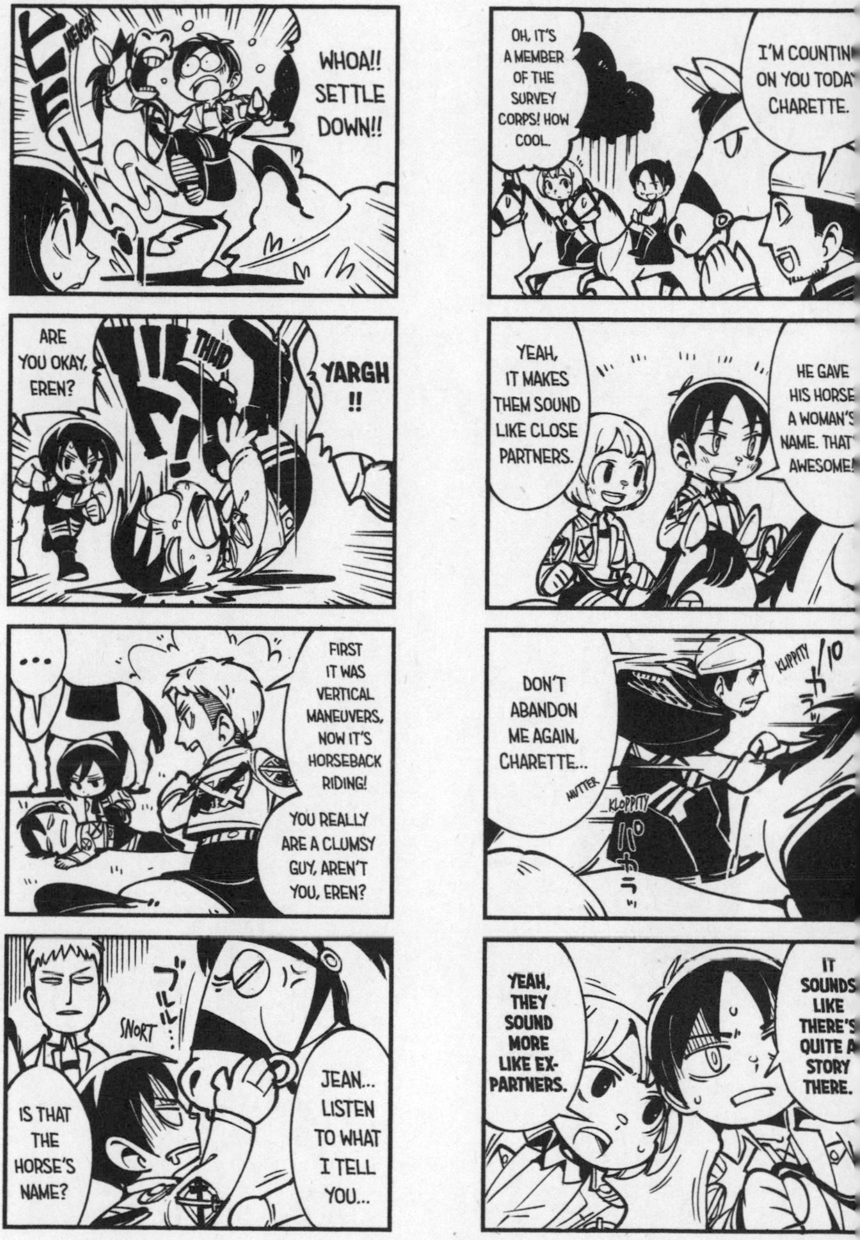
I'M COUNTIN ON YOU TODA CHARETTE.
OH, IT'S A MEMBER OF THE SURVEY CORPS! HOW COOL.
HE GAVE HIS HORSE A WOMAN'S NAME. THAT AWESOME!
YEAH, IT MAKES THEM SOUND LIKE CLOSE PARTNERS.
KLIPPITY
DON'T ABANDON ME AGAIN, CHARETTE...
MUTTER
KLOPPITY
IT SOUNDS LIKE THERE'S QUITE A STORY THERE.
YEAH, THEY SOUND MORE LIKE EX-PARTNERS.
WHOA!! SETTLE DOWN!!
NEIGH
YARGH!!
THUD
ARE YOU OKAY, EREN?
FIRST IT WAS VERTICAL MANEUVERS, NOW IT'S HORSEBACK RIDING!
YOU REALLY ARE A CLUMSY GUY, AREN'T YOU, EREN?
...
JEAN... LISTEN TO WHAT I TELL YOU...
SNORT
IS THAT THE HORSE'S NAME?

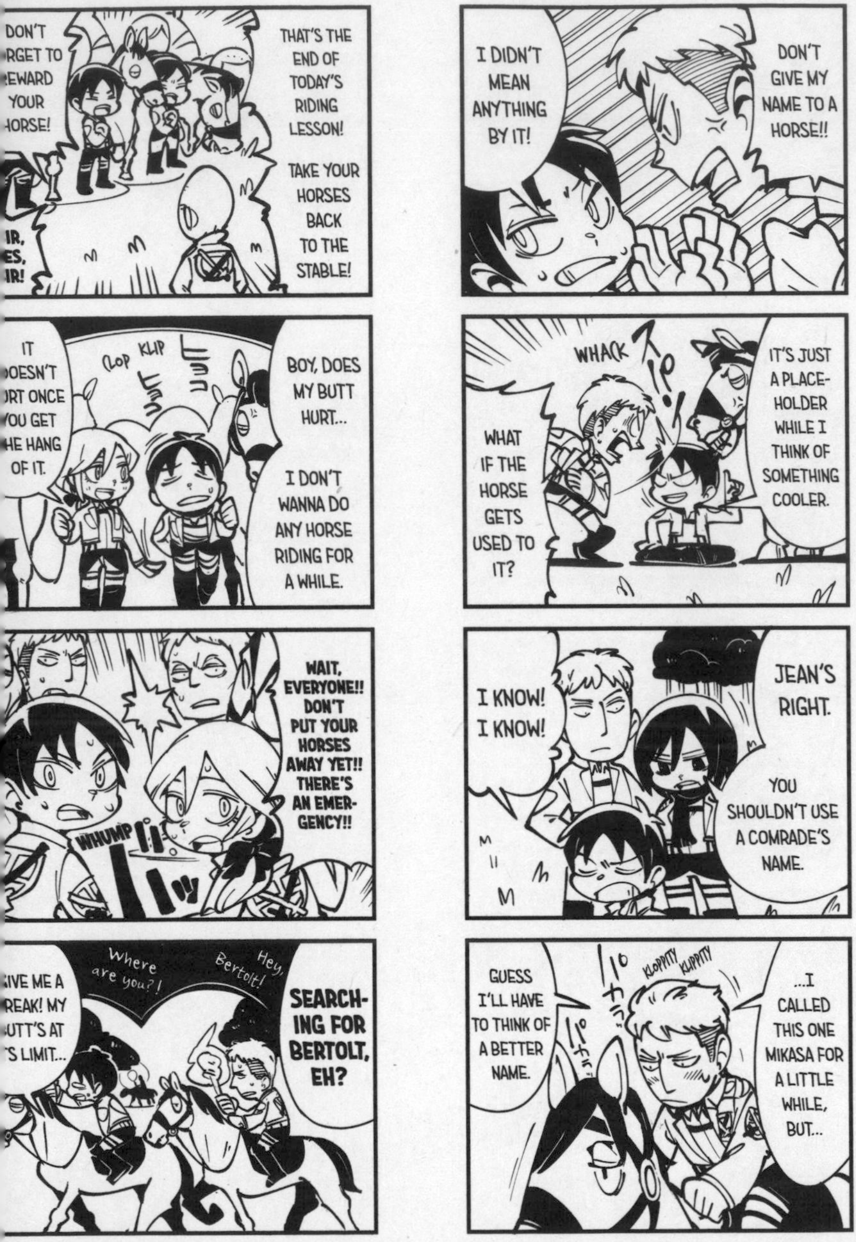
DON'T GIVE MY NAME TO A HORSE!!
I DIDN'T MEAN ANYTHING BY IT!
IT'S JUST A PLACE-HOLDER WHILE I THINK OF SOMETHING COOLER.
WHACK
WHAT IF THE HORSE GETS USED TO IT?
JEAN'S RIGHT.
YOU SHOULDN'T USE A COMRADE'S NAME.
I KNOW! I KNOW!
...I CALLED THIS ONE MIKASA FOR A LITTLE WHILE, BUT...
KLOPPITY KLIPPITY
GUESS I'LL HAVE TO THINK OF A BETTER NAME.
THAT'S THE END OF TODAY'S RIDING LESSON!
TAKE YOUR HORSES BACK TO THE STABLE!
DON'T RGET TO EWARD YOUR ORSE!
IR, ES, IR!
BOY, DOES MY BUTT HURT...
I DON'T WANNA DO ANY HORSE RIDING FOR A WHILE.
KLIP CLOP
IT OESN'T RT ONCE OU GET HE HANG OF IT.
WAIT, EVERYONE!! DON'T PUT YOUR HORSES AWAY YET!! THERE'S AN EMER-GENCY!!
WHUMP
SEARCH-ING FOR BERTOLT, EH?
Hey, Bertolt!
Where are you?!
IVE ME A REAK! MY UTT'S AT S LIMIT...

SPOOF on TITAN

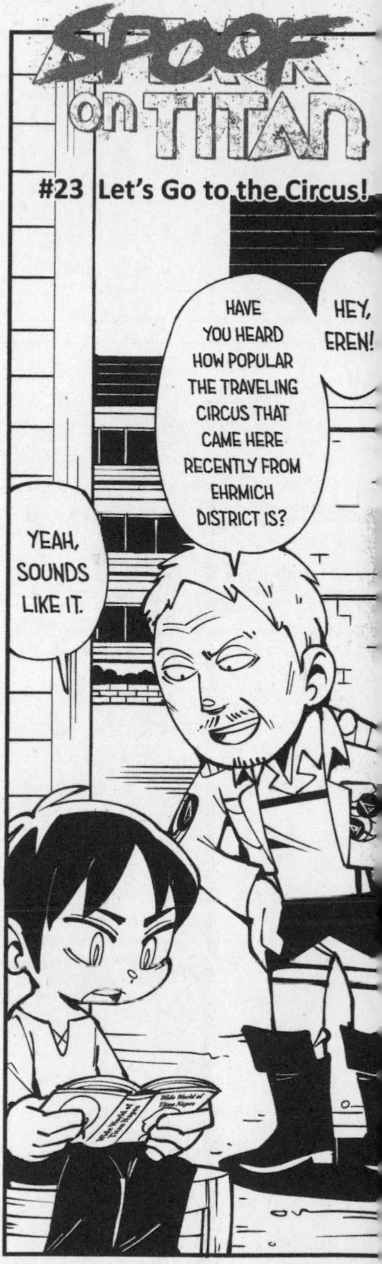
SPOOF on TITAN
#23 Let's Go to the Circus!
HEY, EREN!
HAVE YOU HEARD HOW POPULAR THE TRAVELING CIRCUS THAT CAME HERE RECENTLY FROM EHRMICH DISTRICT IS?
YEAH, SOUNDS LIKE IT.

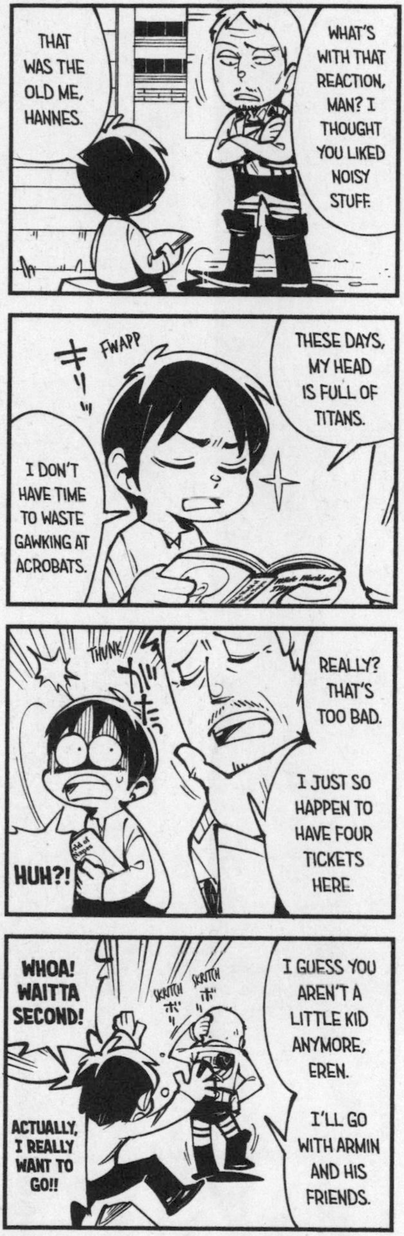
WHAT'S WITH THAT REACTION, MAN? I THOUGHT YOU LIKED NOISY STUFF.
THAT WAS THE OLD ME, HANNES.
THESE DAYS, MY HEAD IS FULL OF TITANS.
FWAPP
I DON'T HAVE TIME TO WASTE GAWKING AT ACROBATS.
REALLY? THAT'S TOO BAD.
I JUST SO HAPPEN TO HAVE FOUR TICKETS HERE.
THUNK
HUH?!
I GUESS YOU AREN'T A LITTLE KID ANYMORE, EREN.
I'LL GO WITH ARMIN AND HIS FRIENDS.
SKRITCH
SKRITCH
WHOA! WAITTA SECOND!
ACTUALLY, I REALLY WANT TO GO!!

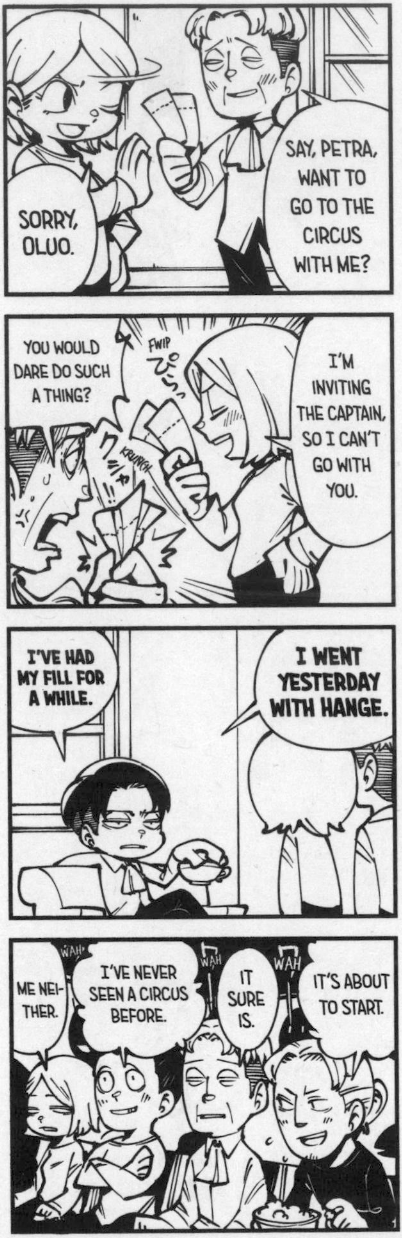
SAY, PETRA, WANT TO GO TO THE CIRCUS WITH ME?
SORRY, OLUO.
I'M INVITING THE CAPTAIN, SO I CAN'T GO WITH YOU.
FWIP
YOU WOULD DARE DO SUCH A THING?
KRUNCH
I WENT YESTERDAY WITH HANGE.
I'VE HAD MY FILL FOR A WHILE.
IT'S ABOUT TO START.
WAH
IT SURE IS.
WAH
I'VE NEVER SEEN A CIRCUS BEFORE.
WAH
ME NEI-THER.

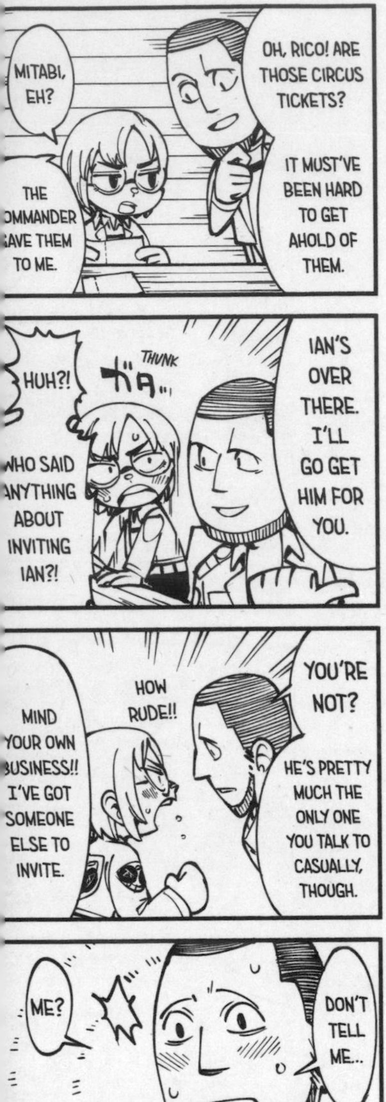
OH, RICO! ARE THOSE CIRCUS TICKETS?
IT MUST'VE BEEN HARD TO GET AHOLD OF THEM.
MITABI, EH?
THE OMMANDER AVE THEM TO ME.
IAN'S OVER THERE. I'LL GO GET HIM FOR YOU.
THUNK
HUH?!
WHO SAID ANYTHING ABOUT INVITING IAN?!
YOU'RE NOT?
HE'S PRETTY MUCH THE ONLY ONE YOU TALK TO CASUALLY, THOUGH.
HOW RUDE!!
MIND YOUR OWN BUSINESS!! I'VE GOT SOMEONE ELSE TO INVITE.
DON'T TELL ME...
ME?
NOT ON YOUR LIFE!!
THUMP

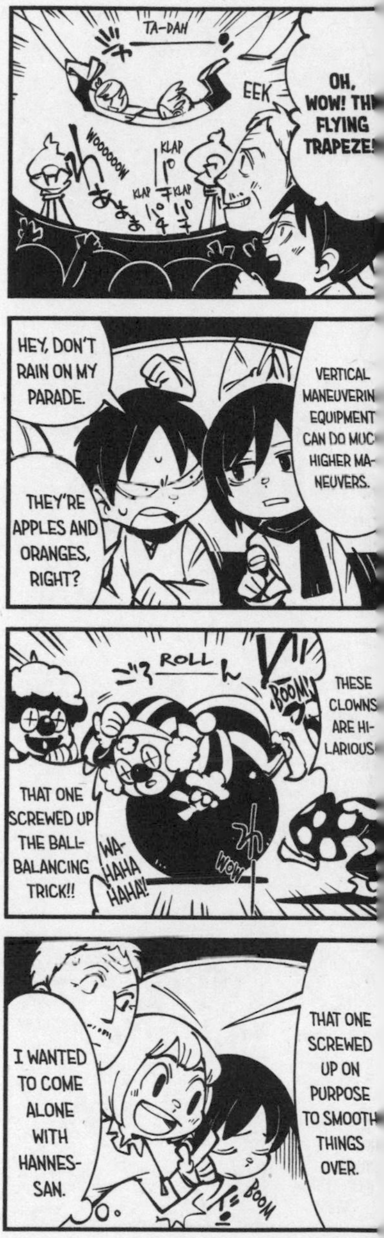
TA-DAH
EEK
OH, WOW! TH FLYING TRAPEZE!
WOOOOOOW
KLAP
KLAP
KLAP
VERTICAL MANEUVERIN EQUIPMENT CAN DO MUC HIGHER MA-NEUVERS.
HEY, DON'T RAIN ON MY PARADE.
THEY'RE APPLES AND ORANGES, RIGHT?
ROLL
BOOM!
THESE CLOWNS ARE HI-LARIOUS
THAT ONE SCREWED UP THE BALL-BALANCING TRICK!!
WA-HAHA HAHA!
WOW
THAT ONE SCREWED UP ON PURPOSE TO SMOOTH THINGS OVER.
I WANTED TO COME ALONE WITH HANNES-SAN.
BOOM

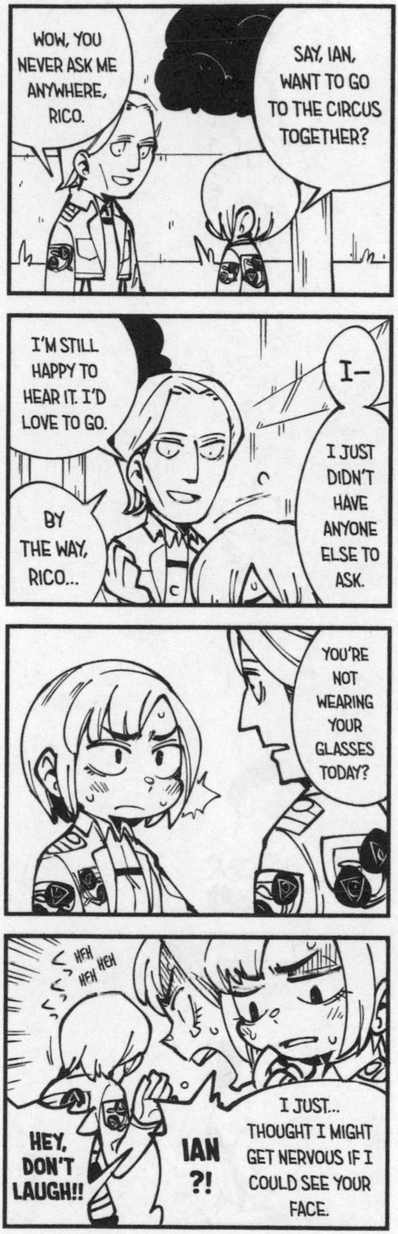
SAY, IAN, WANT TO GO TO THE CIRCUS TOGETHER?
WOW, YOU NEVER ASK ME ANYWHERE, RICO.
I—
I JUST DIDN'T HAVE ANYONE ELSE TO ASK.
I'M STILL HAPPY TO HEAR IT. I'D LOVE TO GO.
BY THE WAY, RICO...
YOU'RE NOT WEARING YOUR GLASSES TODAY?
HEH HEH HEH
I JUST... THOUGHT I MIGHT GET NERVOUS IF I COULD SEE YOUR FACE.
IAN ?!
HEY, DON'T LAUGH!!

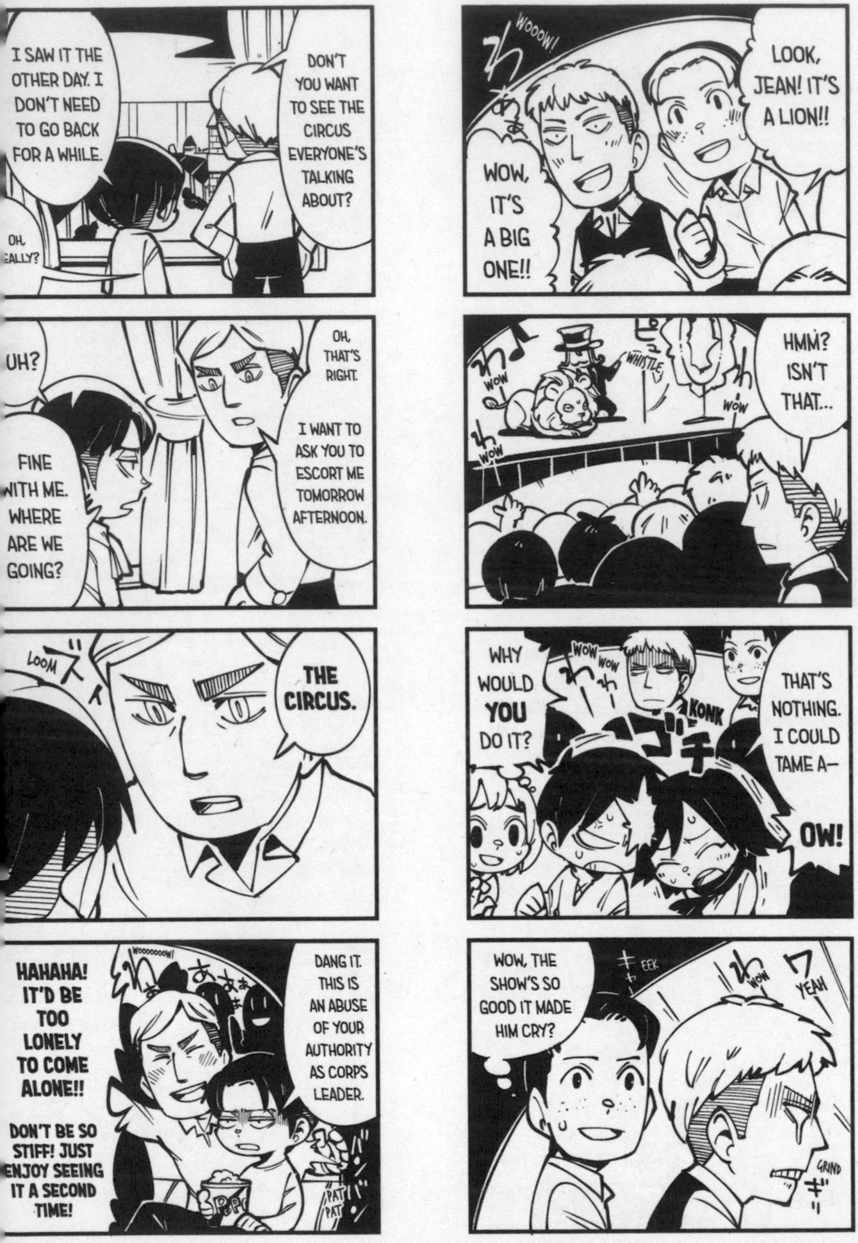
LOOK, JEAN! IT'S A LION!!
WOOOW!
WOW, IT'S A BIG ONE!!
HMM? ISN'T THAT...
WOW
WHISTLE
WOW
WOW
THAT'S NOTHING. I COULD TAME A—
KONK
WOW WOW
WHY WOULD YOU DO IT?
OW!
YEAH
WOW
EEK
WOW, THE SHOW'S SO GOOD IT MADE HIM CRY?
GRIND
DON'T YOU WANT TO SEE THE CIRCUS EVERYONE'S TALKING ABOUT?
I SAW IT THE OTHER DAY. I DON'T NEED TO GO BACK FOR A WHILE.
OH, EALLY?
OH, THAT'S RIGHT.
I WANT TO ASK YOU TO ESCORT ME TOMORROW AFTERNOON.
UH?
FINE WITH ME. WHERE ARE WE GOING?
THE CIRCUS.
LOOM
DANG IT. THIS IS AN ABUSE OF YOUR AUTHORITY AS CORPS LEADER.
WOOOOOOOW!
HAHAHA! IT'D BE TOO LONELY TO COME ALONE!!
DON'T BE SO STIFF! JUST ENJOY SEEING IT A SECOND TIME!
PAT PAT

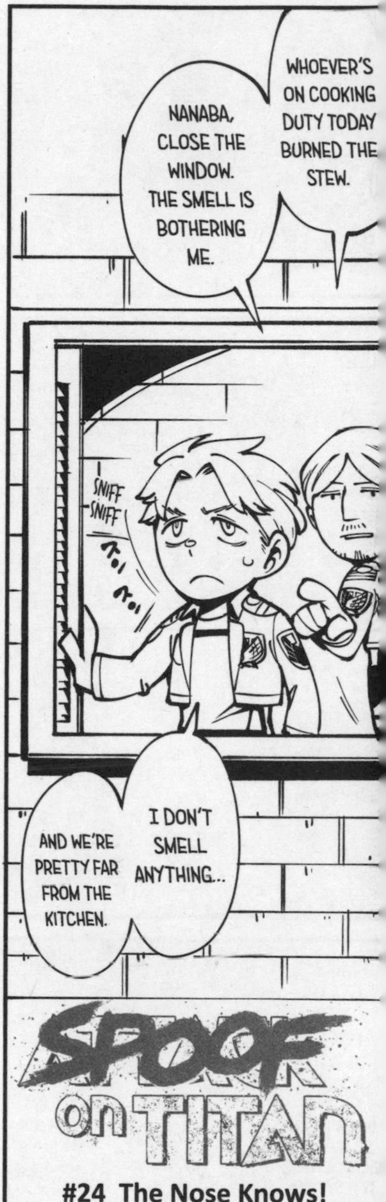
WHOEVER'S ON COOKING DUTY TODAY BURNED THE STEW.
NANABA, CLOSE THE WINDOW. THE SMELL IS BOTHERING ME.
SNIFF SNIFF
I DON'T SMELL ANYTHING...
AND WE'RE PRETTY FAR FROM THE KITCHEN.
SPOOF on TITAN
#24 The Nose Knows!

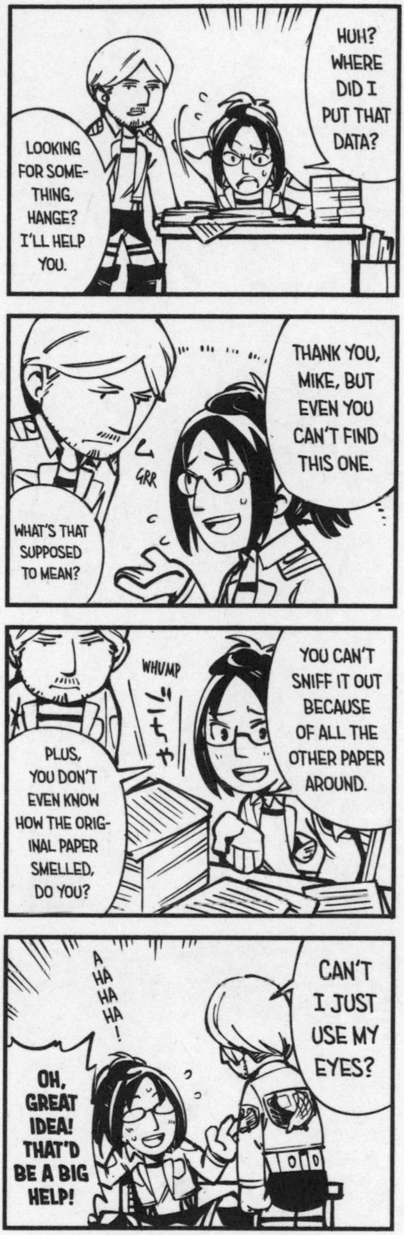
HUH? WHERE DID I PUT THAT DATA?
LOOKING FOR SOME-THING, HANGE? I'LL HELP YOU.
THANK YOU, MIKE, BUT EVEN YOU CAN'T FIND THIS ONE.
GRR
WHAT'S THAT SUPPOSED TO MEAN?
YOU CAN'T SNIFF IT OUT BECAUSE OF ALL THE OTHER PAPER AROUND.
WHUMP
PLUS, YOU DON'T EVEN KNOW HOW THE ORIG-INAL PAPER SMELLED, DO YOU?
CAN'T I JUST USE MY EYES?
A HA HA HA!
OH, GREAT IDEA! THAT'D BE A BIG HELP!

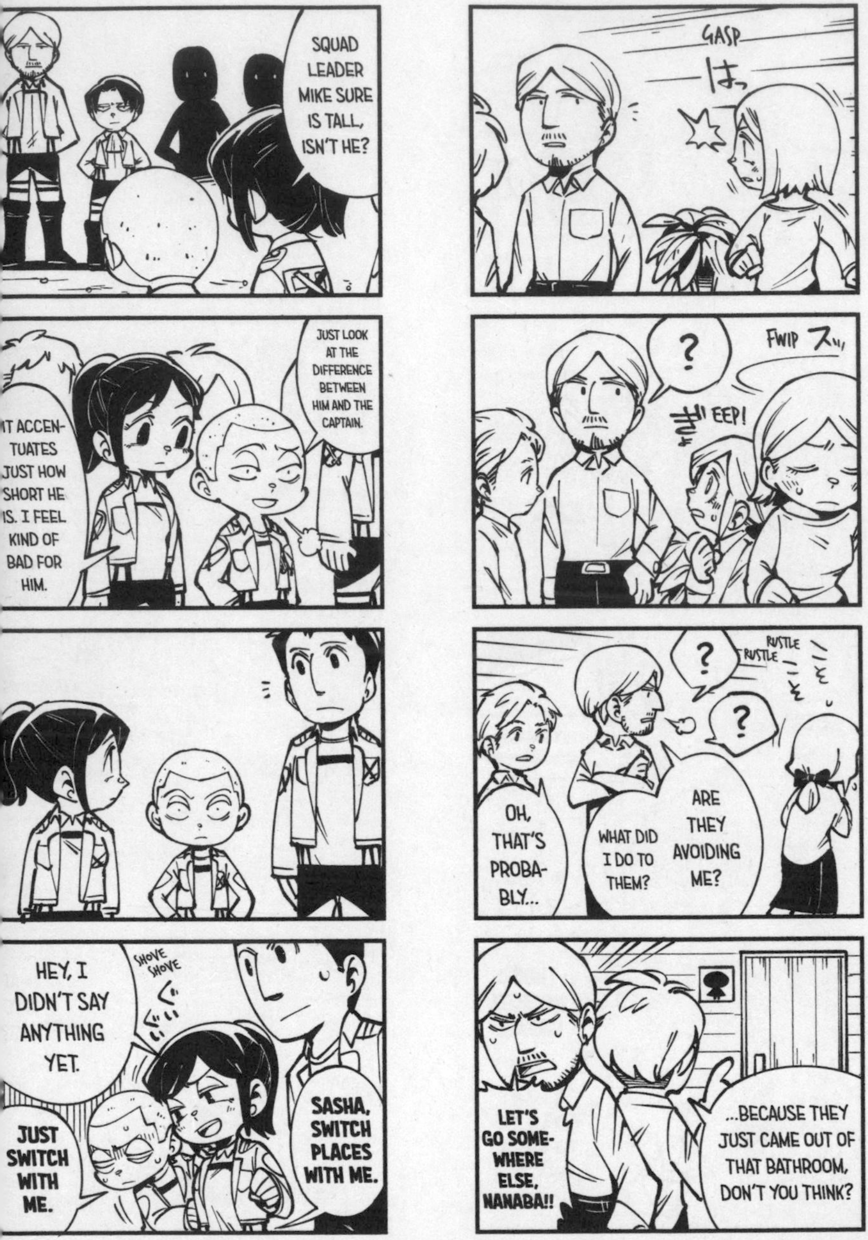
GASP
はっ
?
FWIP スッ
ぎょ EEP!
RUSTLE RUSTLE
?
?
ARE THEY AVOIDING ME?
WHAT DID I DO TO THEM?
OH, THAT'S PROBABLY...
...BECAUSE THEY JUST CAME OUT OF THAT BATHROOM, DON'T YOU THINK?
LET'S GO SOMEWHERE ELSE, NANABA!!
SQUAD LEADER MIKE SURE IS TALL, ISN'T HE?
JUST LOOK AT THE DIFFERENCE BETWEEN HIM AND THE CAPTAIN.
IT ACCENTUATES JUST HOW SHORT HE IS. I FEEL KIND OF BAD FOR HIM.
SASHA, SWITCH PLACES WITH ME.
SHOVE SHOVE
ぐいぐい
HEY, I DIDN'T SAY ANYTHING YET.
JUST SWITCH WITH ME.

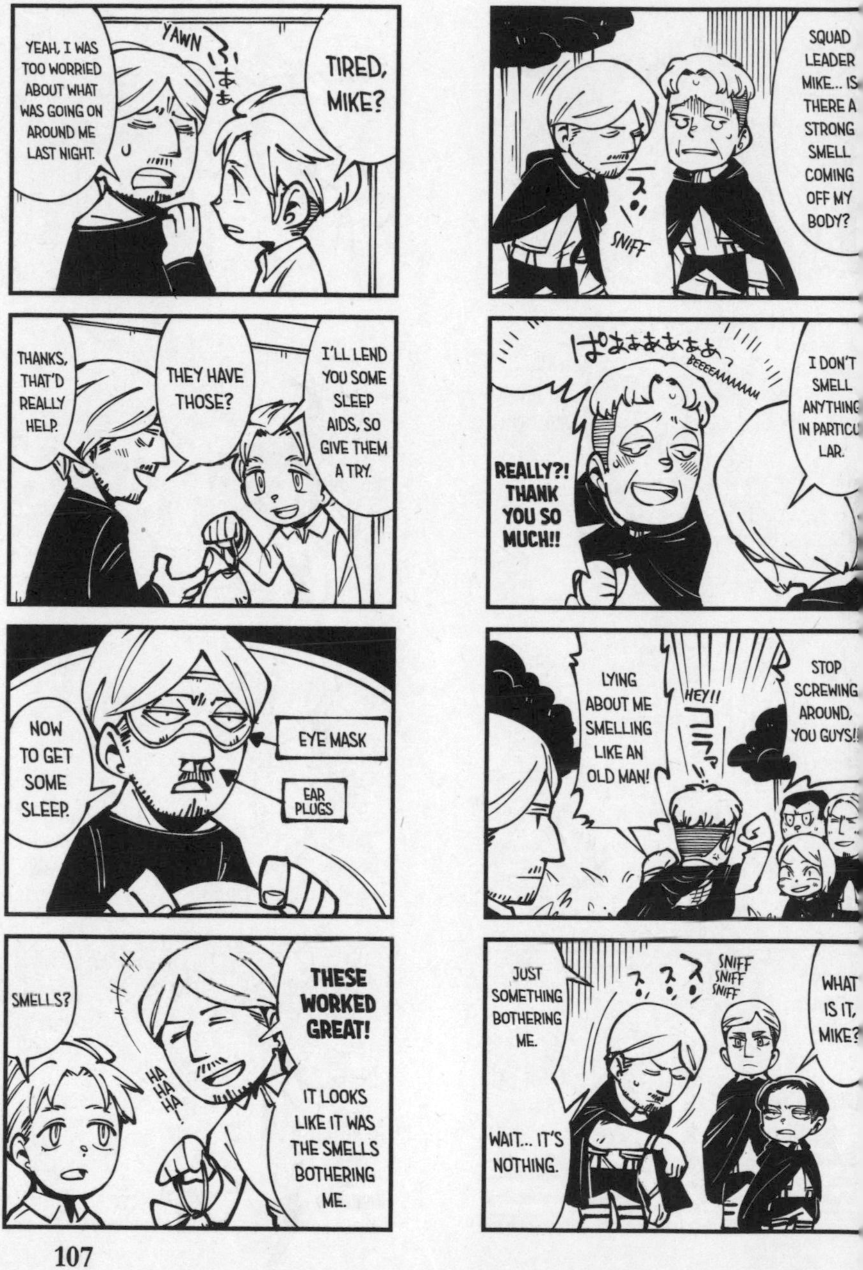
SQUAD LEADER MIKE... IS THERE A STRONG SMELL COMING OFF MY BODY?
スッ
SNIFF
I DON'T SMELL ANYTHING IN PARTICULAR.
ぱあああああああっ
BEEEEAAAAAAM
REALLY?! THANK YOU SO MUCH!!
STOP SCREWING AROUND, YOU GUYS!!
HEY!!
コラァ
LYING ABOUT ME SMELLING LIKE AN OLD MAN!
WHAT IS IT, MIKE?
SNIFF SNIFF SNIFF
スッ スッ スッ
JUST SOMETHING BOTHERING ME.
WAIT... IT'S NOTHING.
TIRED, MIKE?
YAWN
ふあぁ
YEAH, I WAS TOO WORRIED ABOUT WHAT WAS GOING ON AROUND ME LAST NIGHT.
I'LL LEND YOU SOME SLEEP AIDS, SO GIVE THEM A TRY.
THEY HAVE THOSE?
THANKS, THAT'D REALLY HELP.
EYE MASK
EAR PLUGS
NOW TO GET SOME SLEEP.
THESE WORKED GREAT!
IT LOOKS LIKE IT WAS THE SMELLS BOTHERING ME.
HA HA HA!
SMELLS?

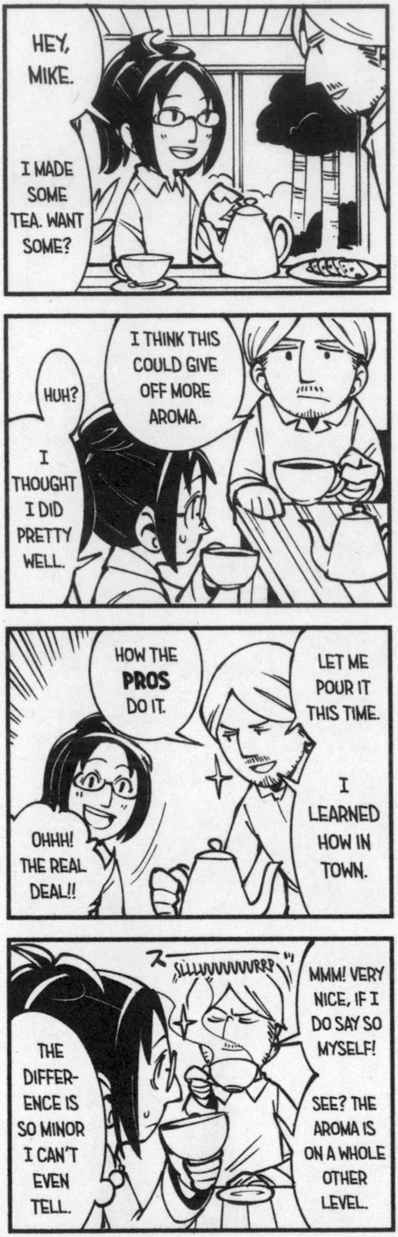
HEY, MIKE.
I MADE SOME TEA. WANT SOME?
I THINK THIS COULD GIVE OFF MORE AROMA.
HUH?
I THOUGHT I DID PRETTY WELL.
LET ME POUR IT THIS TIME.
HOW THE **PROS** DO IT.
I LEARNED HOW IN TOWN.
OHHH! THE REAL DEAL!!
SLLLUUUUUUUURRP
MMM! VERY NICE, IF I DO SAY SO MYSELF!
SEE? THE AROMA IS ON A WHOLE OTHER LEVEL.
THE DIFFERENCE IS SO MINOR I CAN'T EVEN TELL.

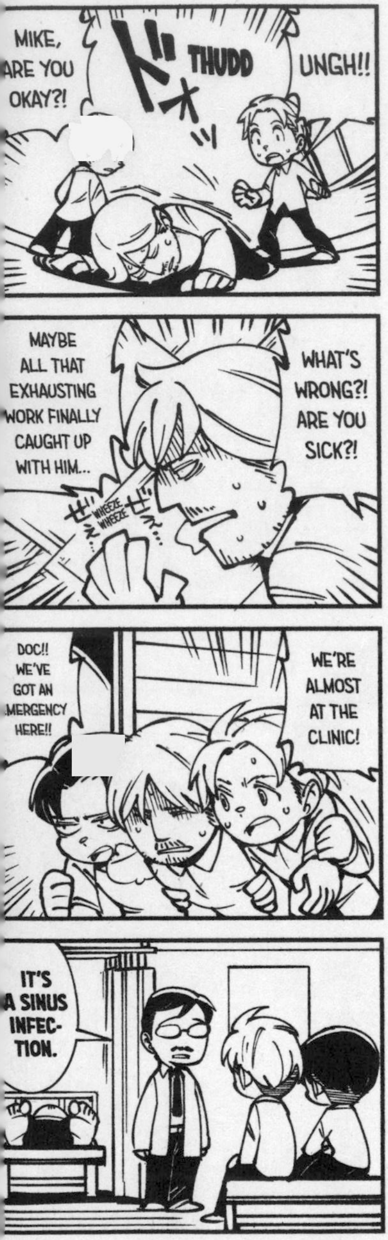
UNGH!!
THUDD
MIKE, ARE YOU OKAY?!
WHAT'S WRONG?! ARE YOU SICK?!
MAYBE ALL THAT EXHAUSTING WORK FINALLY CAUGHT UP WITH HIM...
WHEEZE WHEEZE
WE'RE ALMOST AT THE CLINIC!
DOC!! WE'VE GOT AN MERGENCY HERE!!
IT'S A SINUS INFECTION.

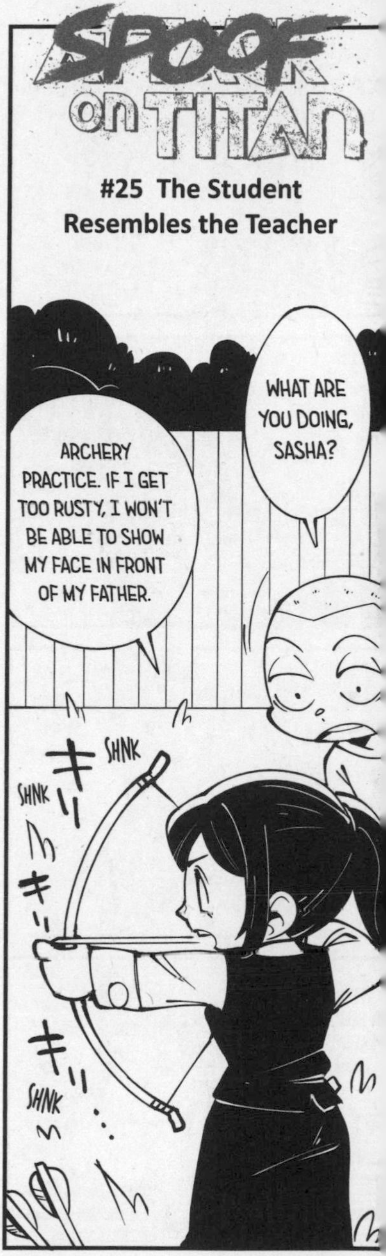
SPOOF on TITAN
#25 The Student Resembles the Teacher
WHAT ARE YOU DOING, SASHA?
ARCHERY PRACTICE. IF I GET TOO RUSTY, I WON'T BE ABLE TO SHOW MY FACE IN FRONT OF MY FATHER.
SHNK
SHNK
SHNK

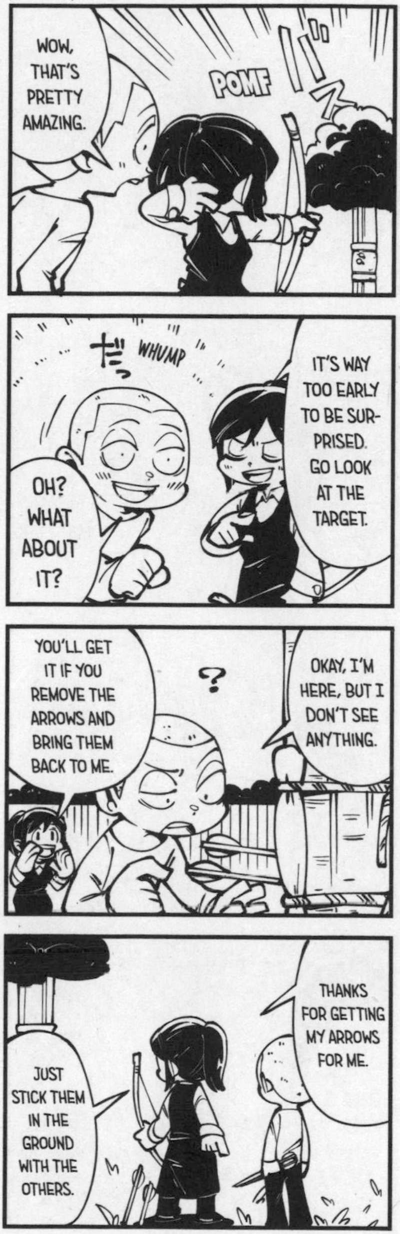
POMF
WOW, THAT'S PRETTY AMAZING.
IT'S WAY TOO EARLY TO BE SURPRISED. GO LOOK AT THE TARGET.
WHUMP
OH? WHAT ABOUT IT?
OKAY, I'M HERE, BUT I DON'T SEE ANYTHING.
?
YOU'LL GET IT IF YOU REMOVE THE ARROWS AND BRING THEM BACK TO ME.
THANKS FOR GETTING MY ARROWS FOR ME.
JUST STICK THEM IN THE GROUND WITH THE OTHERS.

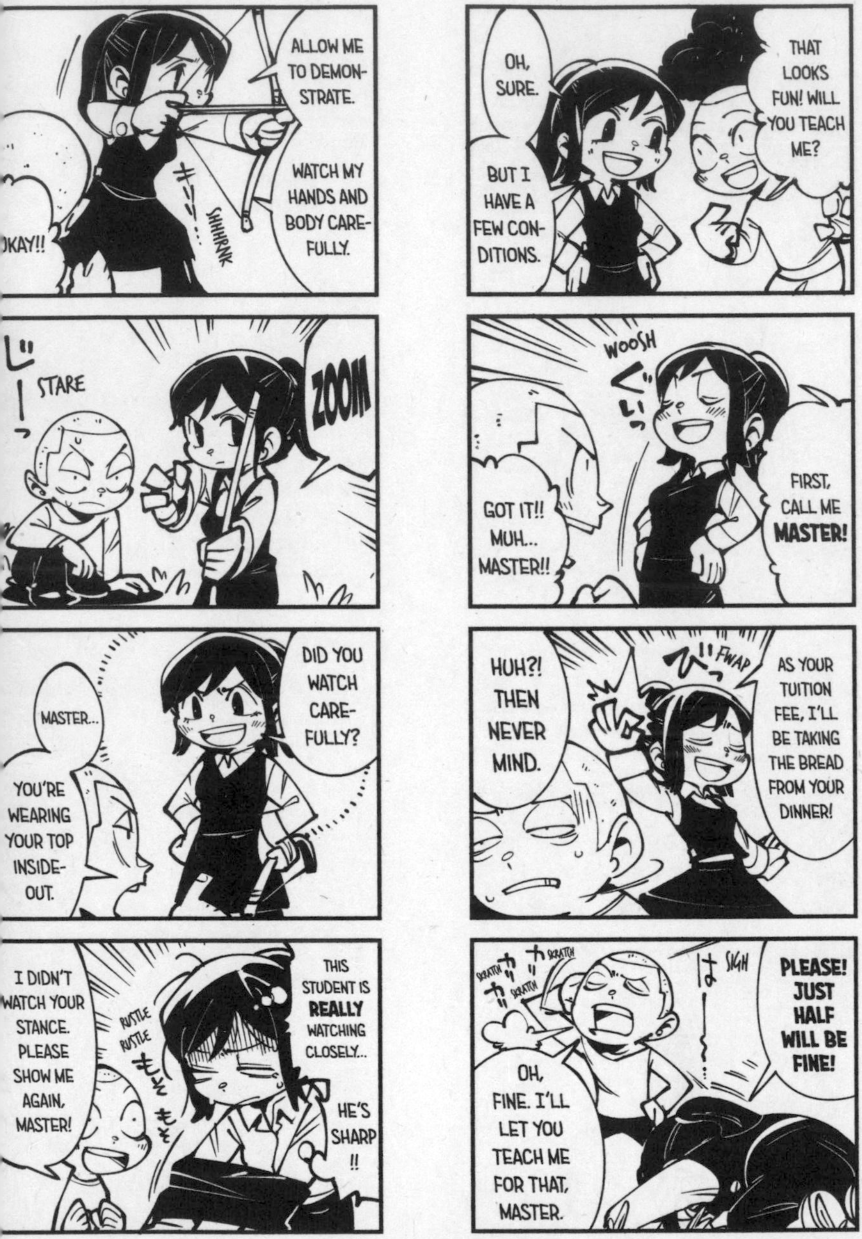
THAT LOOKS FUN! WILL YOU TEACH ME?
OH, SURE.
BUT I HAVE A FEW CONDITIONS.
WOOSH
FIRST, CALL ME **MASTER!**
GOT IT!! MUH... MASTER!!
AS YOUR TUITION FEE, I'LL BE TAKING THE BREAD FROM YOUR DINNER!
FWAP
HUH?! THEN NEVER MIND.
PLEASE! JUST HALF WILL BE FINE!
SIGH
SKRATCH
SKRATCH
SKRATCH
OH, FINE. I'LL LET YOU TEACH ME FOR THAT, MASTER.
ALLOW ME TO DEMONSTRATE.
WATCH MY HANDS AND BODY CAREFULLY.
SHHHRNK
KAY!!
ZOOM
STARE
DID YOU WATCH CAREFULLY?
MASTER...
YOU'RE WEARING YOUR TOP INSIDE-OUT.
THIS STUDENT IS **REALLY** WATCHING CLOSELY...
HE'S SHARP!!
RUSTLE RUSTLE
I DIDN'T WATCH YOUR STANCE. PLEASE SHOW ME AGAIN, MASTER!

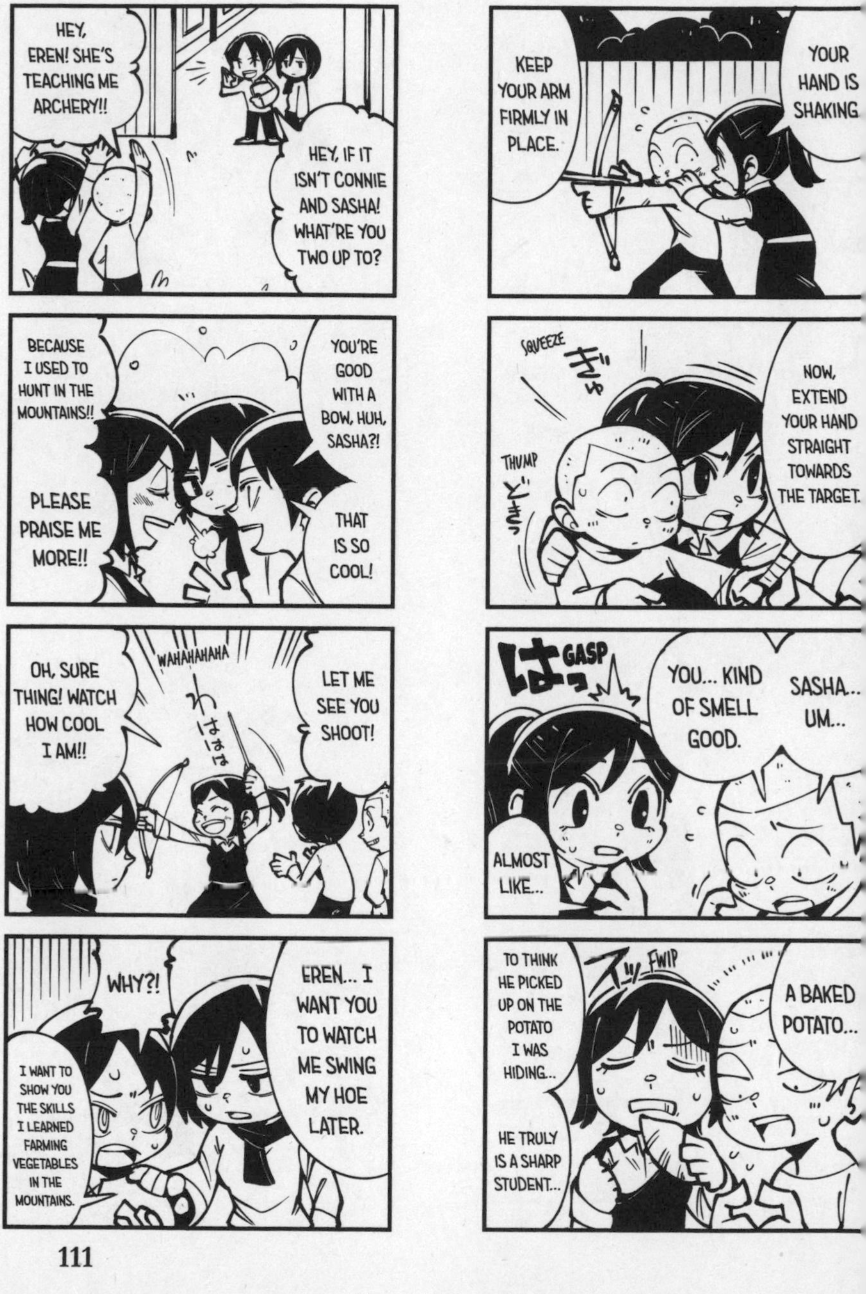
YOUR HAND IS SHAKING
KEEP YOUR ARM FIRMLY IN PLACE.
NOW, EXTEND YOUR HAND STRAIGHT TOWARDS THE TARGET.
ぎゅ SQUEEZE
どきっ THUMP
はっ GASP
SASHA... UM...
YOU... KIND OF SMELL GOOD.
ALMOST LIKE...
A BAKED POTATO...
スッ FWIP
TO THINK HE PICKED UP ON THE POTATO I WAS HIDING...
HE TRULY IS A SHARP STUDENT...
HEY, IF IT ISN'T CONNIE AND SASHA! WHAT'RE YOU TWO UP TO?
HEY, EREN! SHE'S TEACHING ME ARCHERY!!
YOU'RE GOOD WITH A BOW, HUH, SASHA?!
BECAUSE I USED TO HUNT IN THE MOUNTAINS!!
THAT IS SO COOL!
PLEASE PRAISE ME MORE!!
LET ME SEE YOU SHOOT!
わははは WAHAHAHAHA
OH, SURE THING! WATCH HOW COOL I AM!!
EREN... I WANT YOU TO WATCH ME SWING MY HOE LATER.
WHY?!
I WANT TO SHOW YOU THE SKILLS I LEARNED FARMING VEGETABLES IN THE MOUNTAINS.

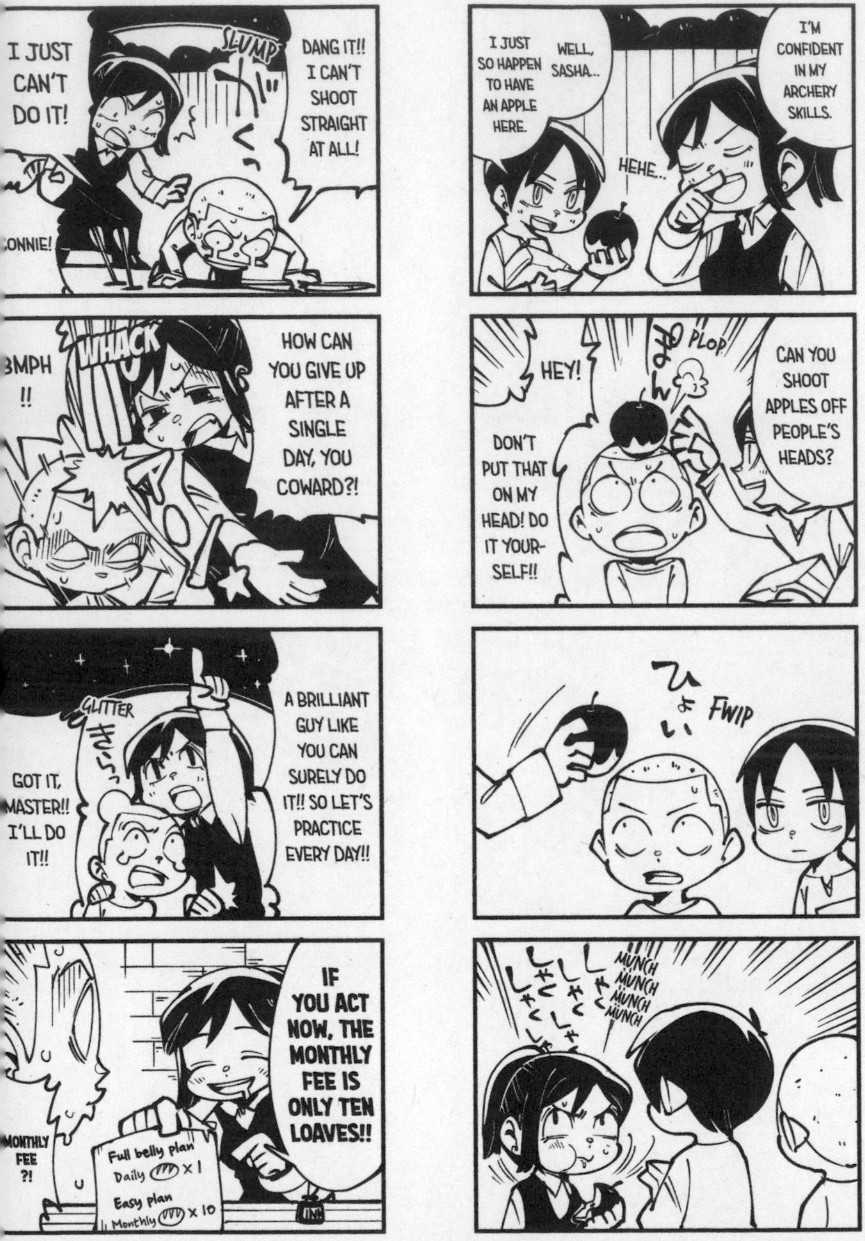
I'M CONFIDENT IN MY ARCHERY SKILLS.
HEHE...
WELL, SASHA...
I JUST SO HAPPEN TO HAVE AN APPLE HERE.
CAN YOU SHOOT APPLES OFF PEOPLE'S HEADS?
PLOP
HEY!
DON'T PUT THAT ON MY HEAD! DO IT YOURSELF!!
ひょい
FWIP
MUNCH MUNCH MUNCH MUNCH
DANG IT!! I CAN'T SHOOT STRAIGHT AT ALL!
SLUMP
I JUST CAN'T DO IT!
ONNIE!
HOW CAN YOU GIVE UP AFTER A SINGLE DAY, YOU COWARD?!
WHACK
MPH !!
A BRILLIANT GUY LIKE YOU CAN SURELY DO IT!! SO LET'S PRACTICE EVERY DAY!!
GLITTER
きらっ
GOT IT, MASTER!! I'LL DO IT!!
IF YOU ACT NOW, THE MONTHLY FEE IS ONLY TEN LOAVES!!
MONTHLY FEE ?!
Full belly plan
Daily x 1
Easy plan
Monthly x 10
INK

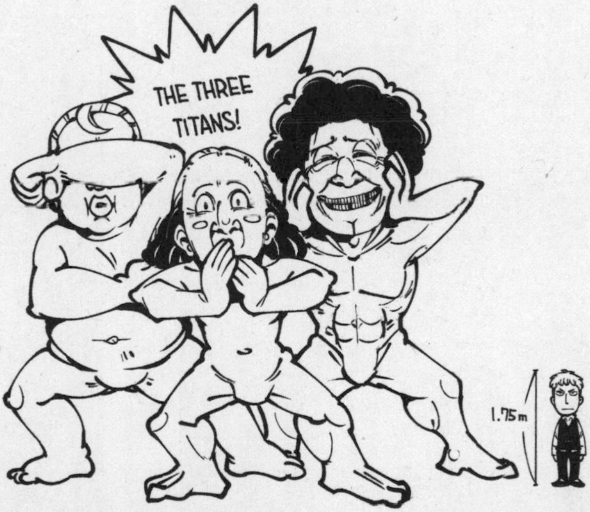
THE THREE TITANS!
1.75m

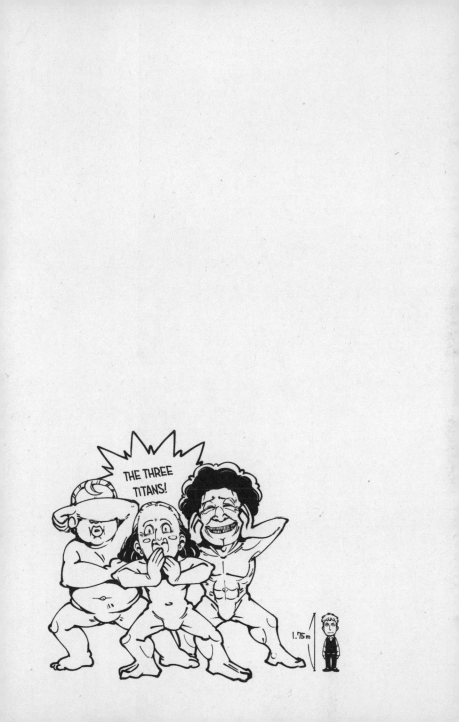

SPOOF on TITAN

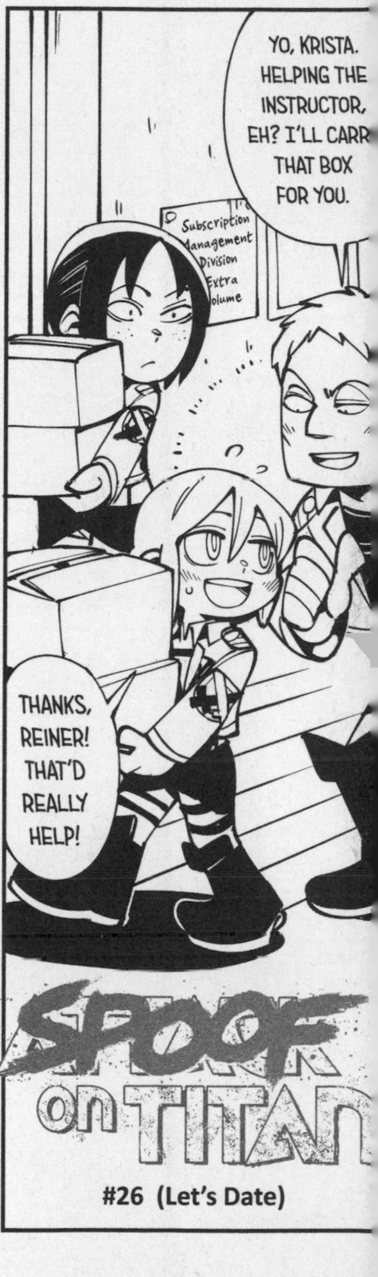
YO, KRISTA. HELPING THE INSTRUCTOR, EH? I'LL CARR THAT BOX FOR YOU.
Subscription
anagement
Division
Extra
olume
THANKS, REINER! THAT'D REALLY HELP!
SPOOF on TITAN
#26 (Let's Date)

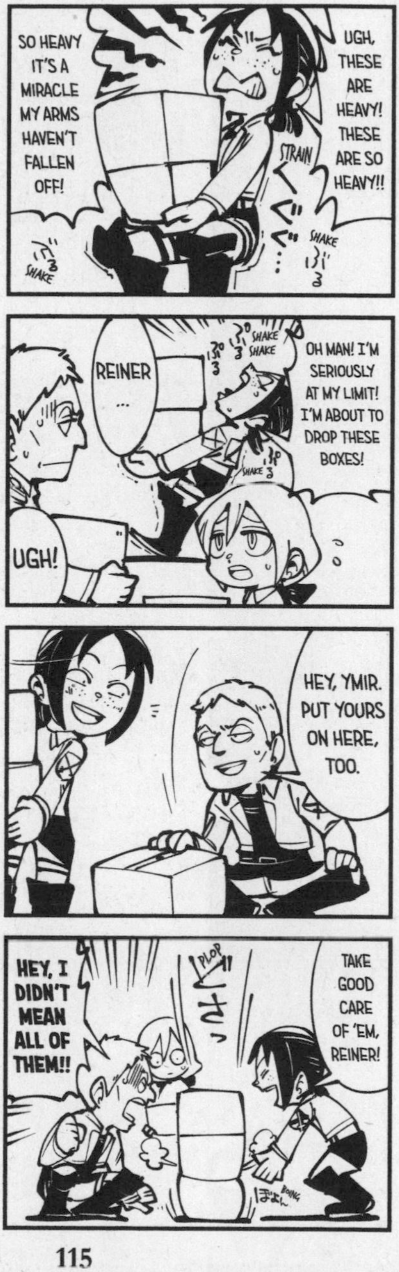
UGH, THESE ARE HEAVY! THESE ARE SO HEAVY!!
STRAIN
SHAKE
SO HEAVY IT'S A MIRACLE MY ARMS HAVEN'T FALLEN OFF!
SHAKE
OH MAN! I'M SERIOUSLY AT MY LIMIT! I'M ABOUT TO DROP THESE BOXES!
SHAKE SHAKE
REINER ...
SHAKE
UGH!
HEY, YMIR. PUT YOURS ON HERE, TOO.
TAKE GOOD CARE OF 'EM, REINER!
PLOP
HEY, I DIDN'T MEAN ALL OF THEM!!
BOING

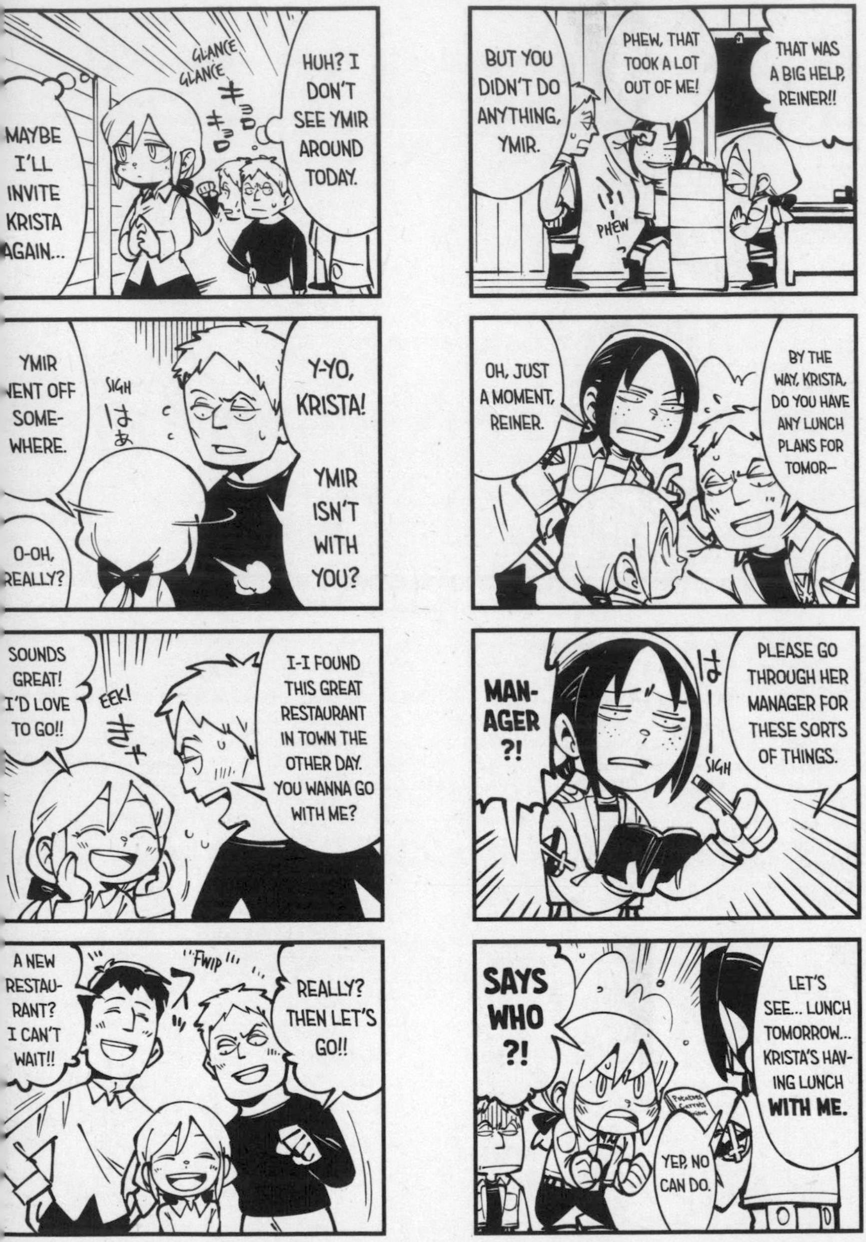
THAT WAS A BIG HELP, REINER!!
PHEW, THAT TOOK A LOT OUT OF ME!
BUT YOU DIDN'T DO ANYTHING, YMIR.
PHEW
BY THE WAY, KRISTA, DO YOU HAVE ANY LUNCH PLANS FOR TOMOR—
OH, JUST A MOMENT, REINER.
PLEASE GO THROUGH HER MANAGER FOR THESE SORTS OF THINGS.
は一
SIGH
MAN-AGER ?!
LET'S SEE... LUNCH TOMORROW... KRISTA'S HAVING LUNCH **WITH ME.**
YEP, NO CAN DO.
SAYS WHO ?!
HUH? I DON'T SEE YMIR AROUND TODAY.
GLANCE GLANCE
キョロキョロ
MAYBE I'LL INVITE KRISTA AGAIN...
Y-YO, KRISTA!
YMIR ISN'T WITH YOU?
SIGH
はぁ
YMIR WENT OFF SOME-WHERE.
O-OH, REALLY?
I-I FOUND THIS GREAT RESTAURANT IN TOWN THE OTHER DAY. YOU WANNA GO WITH ME?
EEK!
きゃ
SOUNDS GREAT! I'D LOVE TO GO!!
REALLY? THEN LET'S GO!!
FWIP
A NEW RESTAU-RANT? I CAN'T WAIT!!

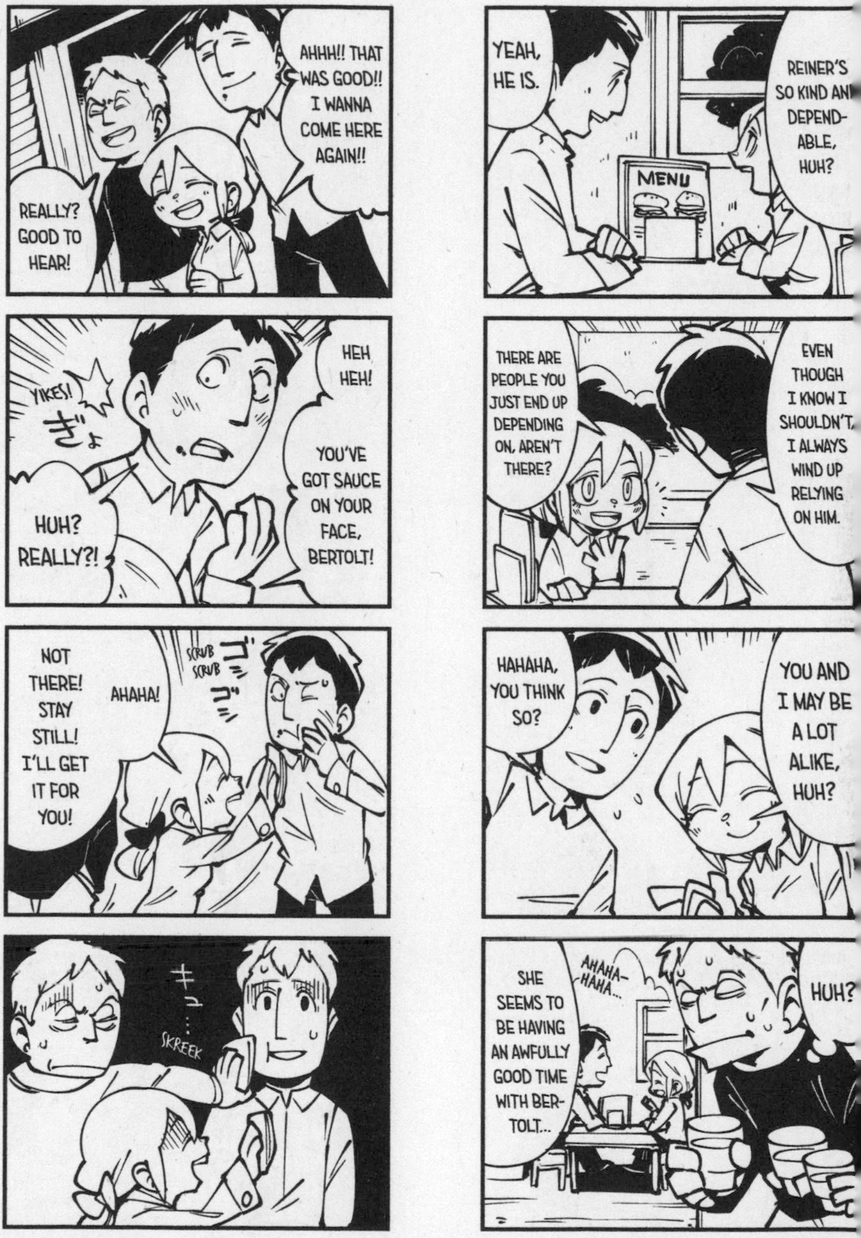
REINER'S SO KIND AN DEPEND-ABLE, HUH?
YEAH, HE IS.
EVEN THOUGH I KNOW I SHOULDN'T, I ALWAYS WIND UP RELYING ON HIM.
THERE ARE PEOPLE YOU JUST END UP DEPENDING ON, AREN'T THERE?
YOU AND I MAY BE A LOT ALIKE, HUH?
HAHAHA, YOU THINK SO?
HUH?
AHAHA-HAHA...
SHE SEEMS TO BE HAVING AN AWFULLY GOOD TIME WITH BER-TOLT...
AHHH!! THAT WAS GOOD!! I WANNA COME HERE AGAIN!!
REALLY? GOOD TO HEAR!
HEH HEH!
YOU'VE GOT SAUCE ON YOUR FACE, BERTOLT!
YIKES!
ぎょ
HUH? REALLY?!
SCRUB SCRUB
AHAHA!
NOT THERE! STAY STILL! I'LL GET IT FOR YOU!
SKREEK

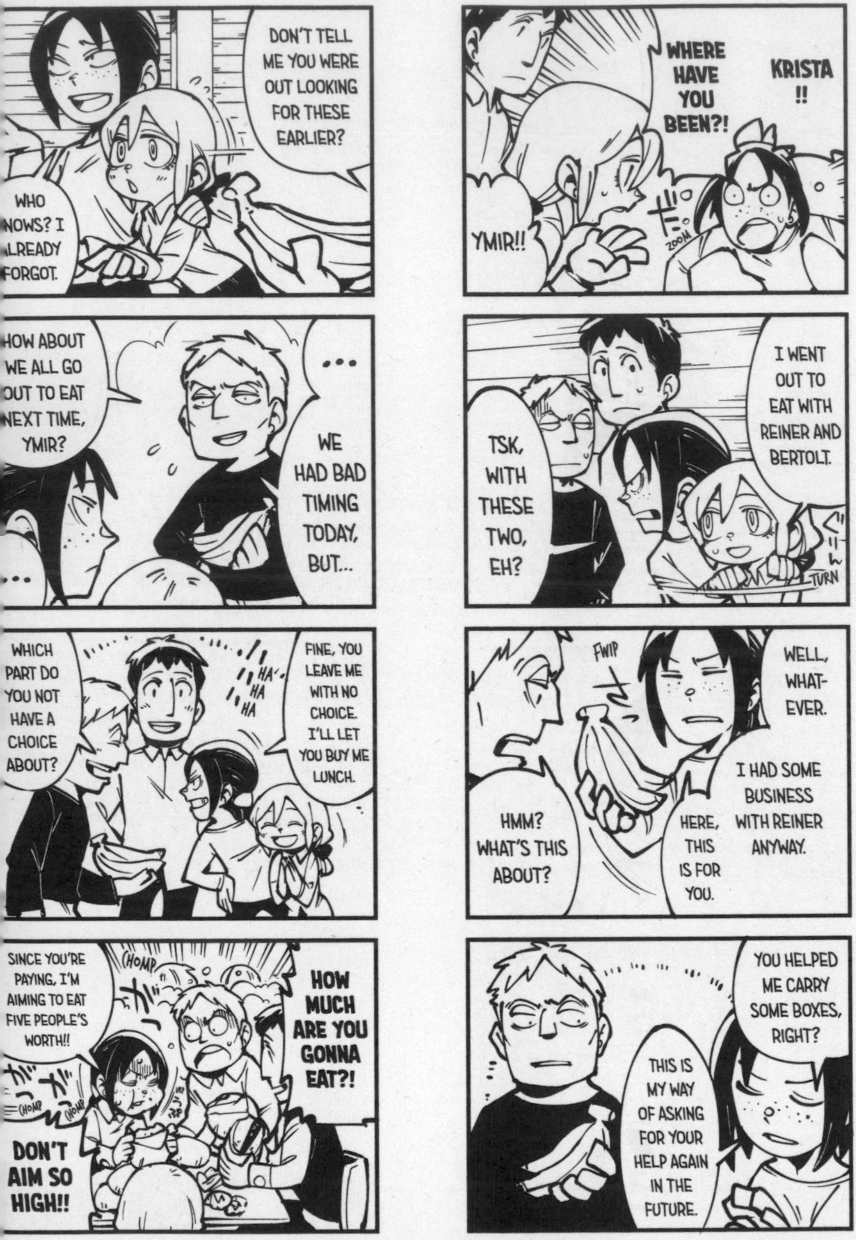
KRISTA !!
WHERE HAVE YOU BEEN?!
ZOOM
YMIR!!
I WENT OUT TO EAT WITH REINER AND BERTOLT.
TURN
TSK, WITH THESE TWO, EH?
WELL, WHAT-EVER.
FWIP
I HAD SOME BUSINESS WITH REINER ANYWAY.
HERE, THIS IS FOR YOU.
HMM? WHAT'S THIS ABOUT?
YOU HELPED ME CARRY SOME BOXES, RIGHT?
THIS IS MY WAY OF ASKING FOR YOUR HELP AGAIN IN THE FUTURE.
DON'T TELL ME YOU WERE OUT LOOKING FOR THESE EARLIER?
WHO NOWS? I LREADY FORGOT.
...
WE HAD BAD TIMING TODAY, BUT...
HOW ABOUT WE ALL GO OUT TO EAT NEXT TIME, YMIR?
...
FINE, YOU LEAVE ME WITH NO CHOICE. I'LL LET YOU BUY ME LUNCH.
HA HA HA HA
WHICH PART DO YOU NOT HAVE A CHOICE ABOUT?
HOW MUCH ARE YOU GONNA EAT?!
(CHOMP
SINCE YOU'RE PAYING, I'M AIMING TO EAT FIVE PEOPLE'S WORTH!!
(CHOMP (CHOMP
DON'T AIM SO HIGH!!

#27 Believe It, Eren!!

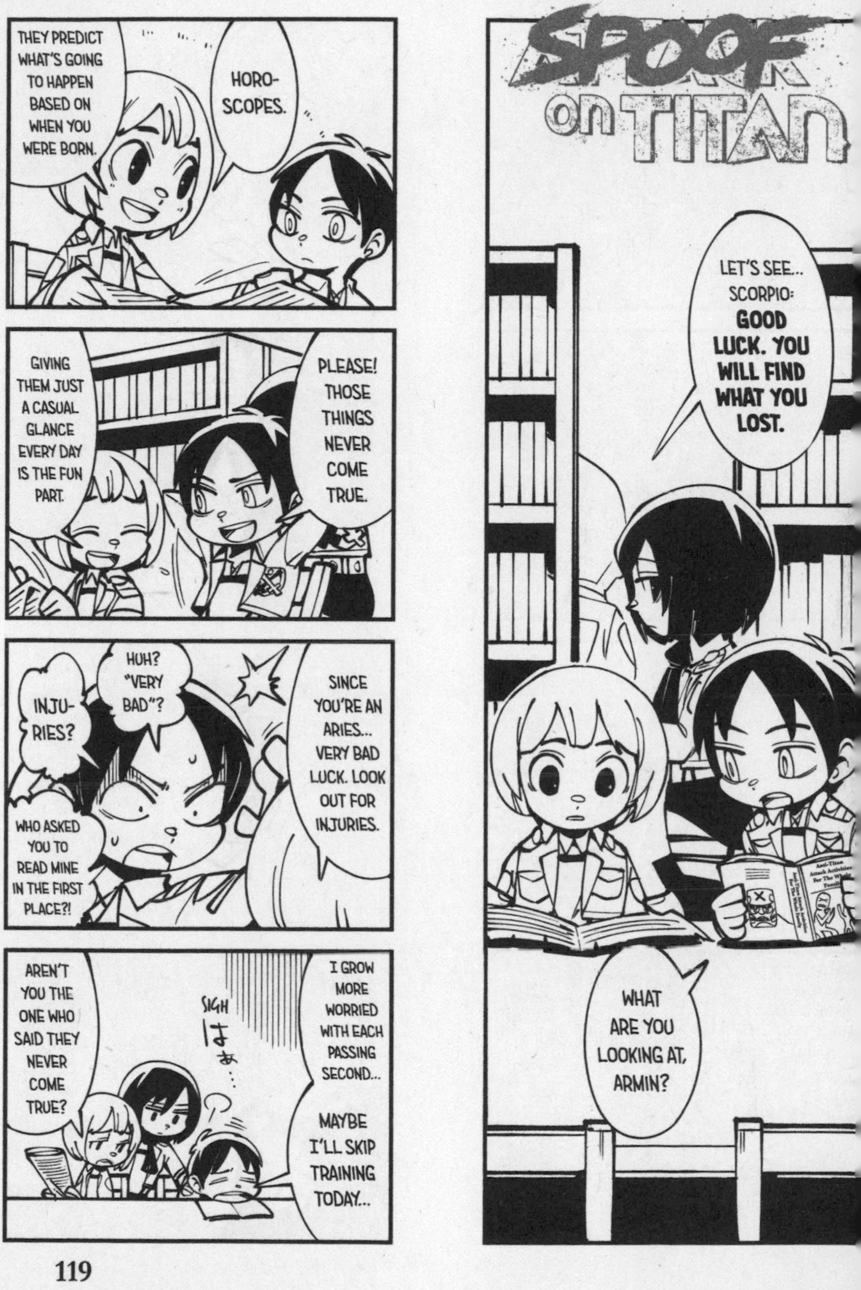
SPOOF on TITAN
LET'S SEE... SCORPIO: **GOOD LUCK. YOU WILL FIND WHAT YOU LOST.**
WHAT ARE YOU LOOKING AT, ARMIN?
HORO-SCOPES.
THEY PREDICT WHAT'S GOING TO HAPPEN BASED ON WHEN YOU WERE BORN.
PLEASE! THOSE THINGS NEVER COME TRUE.
GIVING THEM JUST A CASUAL GLANCE EVERY DAY IS THE FUN PART.
SINCE YOU'RE AN ARIES... VERY BAD LUCK. LOOK OUT FOR INJURIES.
HUH? "VERY BAD"?
INJU-RIES?
WHO ASKED YOU TO READ MINE IN THE FIRST PLACE?!
I GROW MORE WORRIED WITH EACH PASSING SECOND...
MAYBE I'LL SKIP TRAINING TODAY...
SIGH はぁ…
AREN'T YOU THE ONE WHO SAID THEY NEVER COME TRUE?

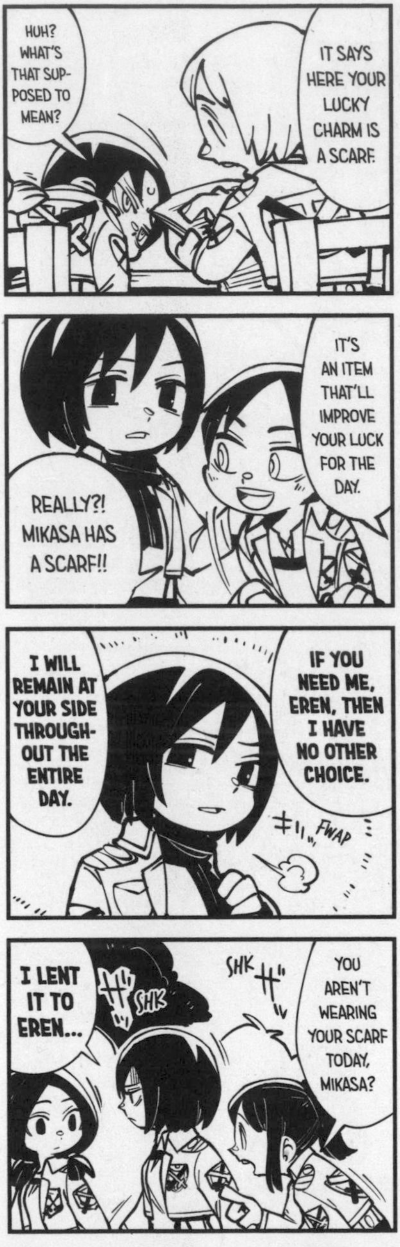
IT SAYS HERE YOUR LUCKY CHARM IS A SCARF.
HUH? WHAT'S THAT SUP-POSED TO MEAN?
IT'S AN ITEM THAT'LL IMPROVE YOUR LUCK FOR THE DAY.
REALLY?! MIKASA HAS A SCARF!!
IF YOU NEED ME, EREN, THEN I HAVE NO OTHER CHOICE.
FWAP
I WILL REMAIN AT YOUR SIDE THROUGH-OUT THE ENTIRE DAY.
YOU AREN'T WEARING YOUR SCARF TODAY, MIKASA?
SHK
SHK
I LENT IT TO EREN...

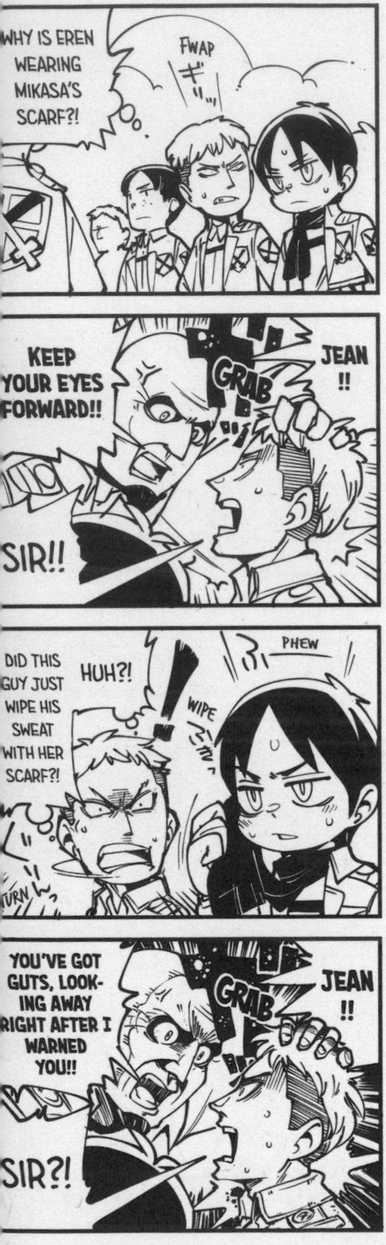
FWAP
WHY IS EREN WEARING MIKASA'S SCARF?!
JEAN !!
GRAB
KEEP YOUR EYES FORWARD!!
SIR!!
PHEW
WIPE
HUH?!
DID THIS GUY JUST WIPE HIS SWEAT WITH HER SCARF?!
TURN
JEAN !!
GRAB
YOU'VE GOT GUTS, LOOK-ING AWAY RIGHT AFTER I WARNED YOU!!
SIR?!

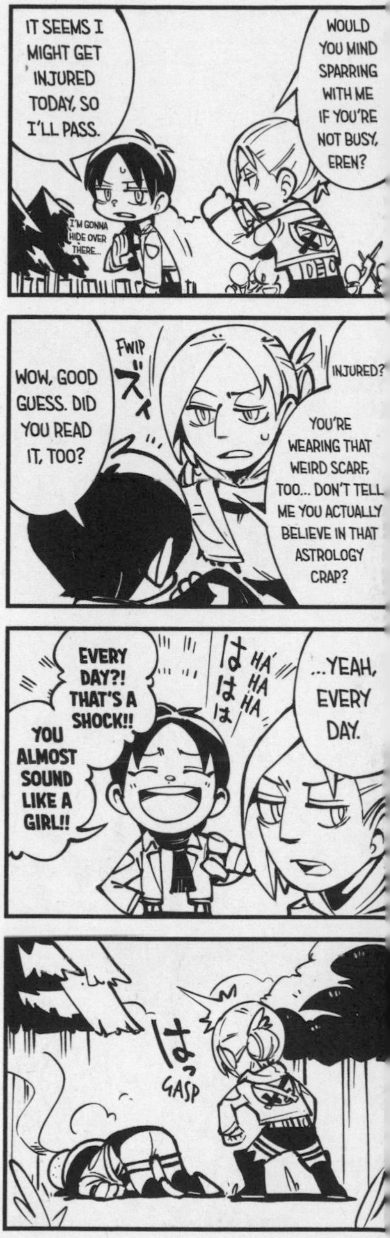
WOULD YOU MIND SPARRING WITH ME IF YOU'RE NOT BUSY, EREN?
IT SEEMS I MIGHT GET INJURED TODAY, SO I'LL PASS.
I'M GONNA HIDE OVER THERE...
INJURED?
YOU'RE WEARING THAT WEIRD SCARF, TOO... DON'T TELL ME YOU ACTUALLY BELIEVE IN THAT ASTROLOGY CRAP?
FWIP ズイ
WOW, GOOD GUESS. DID YOU READ IT, TOO?
...YEAH, EVERY DAY.
HA HA HA はは
EVERY DAY?! THAT'S A SHOCK!!
YOU ALMOST SOUND LIKE A GIRL!!
はっ GASP

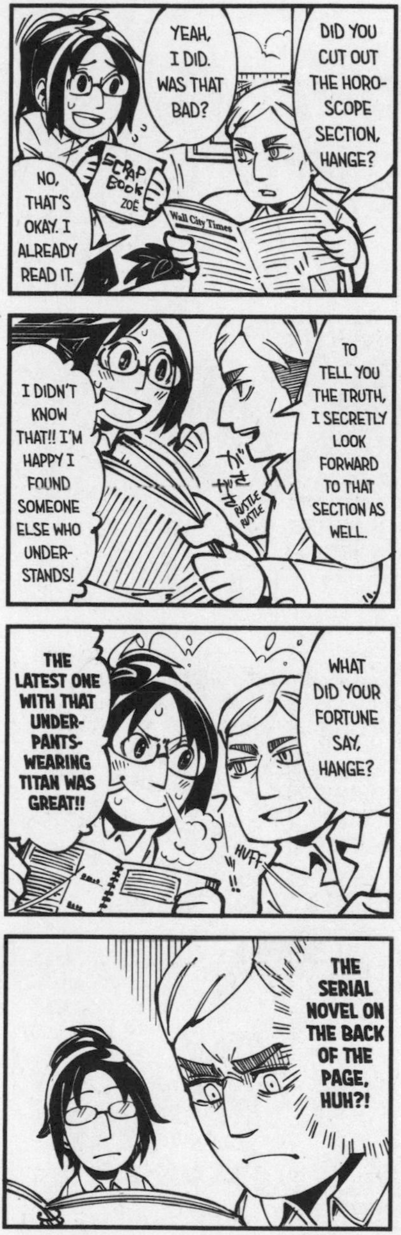
DID YOU CUT OUT THE HORO-SCOPE SECTION, HANGE?
YEAH, I DID. WAS THAT BAD?
SCRAP BOOK ZOË
Wall City Times
NO, THAT'S OKAY. I ALREADY READ IT.
TO TELL YOU THE TRUTH, I SECRETLY LOOK FORWARD TO THAT SECTION AS WELL.
がさがさ RUSTLE RUSTLE
I DIDN'T KNOW THAT!! I'M HAPPY I FOUND SOMEONE ELSE WHO UNDER-STANDS!
WHAT DID YOUR FORTUNE SAY, HANGE?
THE LATEST ONE WITH THAT UNDER-PANTS-WEARING TITAN WAS GREAT!!
HUFF!!
THE SERIAL NOVEL ON THE BACK OF THE PAGE, HUH?!

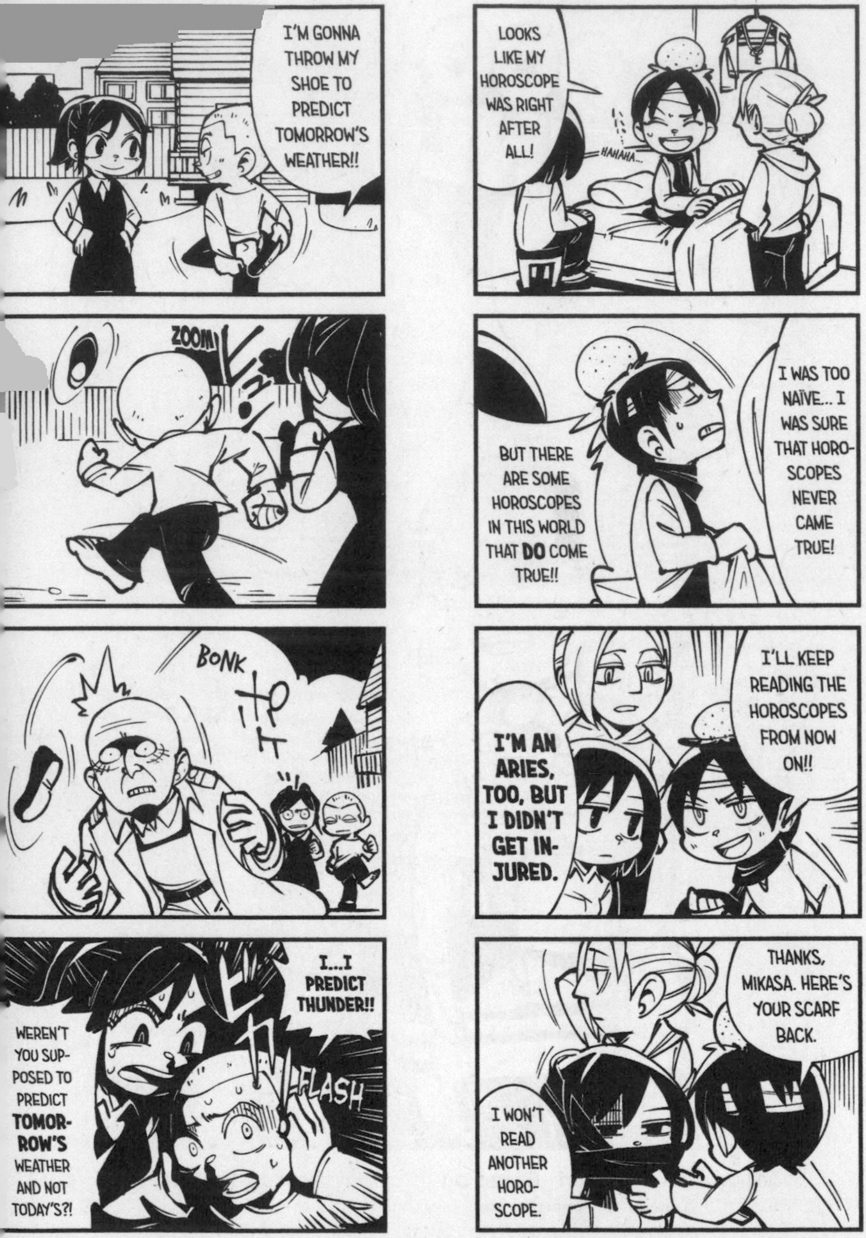
LOOKS LIKE MY HOROSCOPE WAS RIGHT AFTER ALL!
HAHAHA...
I WAS TOO NAÏVE... I WAS SURE THAT HORO-SCOPES NEVER CAME TRUE!
BUT THERE ARE SOME HOROSCOPES IN THIS WORLD THAT **DO** COME TRUE!!
I'LL KEEP READING THE HOROSCOPES FROM NOW ON!!
I'M AN ARIES, TOO, BUT I DIDN'T GET IN-JURED.
THANKS, MIKASA. HERE'S YOUR SCARF BACK.
I WON'T READ ANOTHER HORO-SCOPE.
I'M GONNA THROW MY SHOE TO PREDICT TOMORROW'S WEATHER!!
ZOOM
BONK
I...I PREDICT THUNDER!!
FLASH
WEREN'T YOU SUP-POSED TO PREDICT **TOMOR-ROW'S** WEATHER AND NOT TODAY'S?!

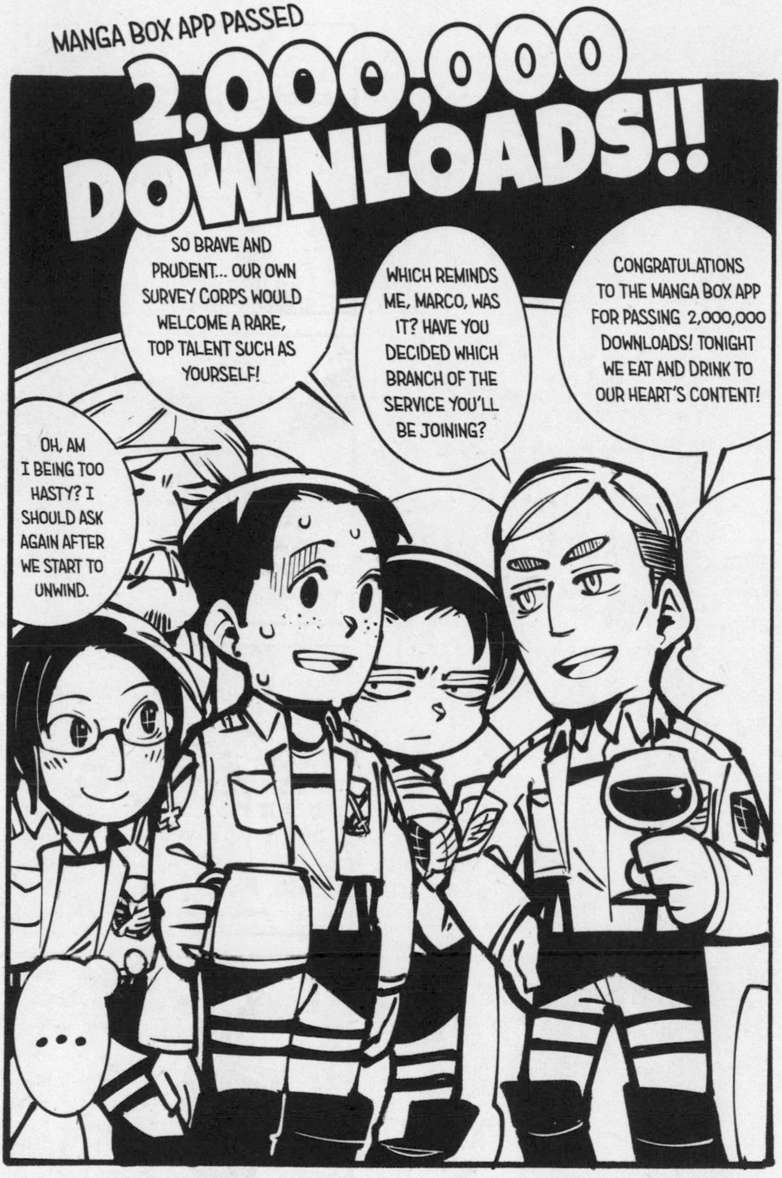
MANGA BOX APP PASSED
2,000,000 DOWNLOADS!!
CONGRATULATIONS TO THE MANGA BOX APP FOR PASSING 2,000,000 DOWNLOADS! TONIGHT WE EAT AND DRINK TO OUR HEART'S CONTENT!
WHICH REMINDS ME, MARCO, WAS IT? HAVE YOU DECIDED WHICH BRANCH OF THE SERVICE YOU'LL BE JOINING?
SO BRAVE AND PRUDENT... OUR OWN SURVEY CORPS WOULD WELCOME A RARE, TOP TALENT SUCH AS YOURSELF!
OH, AM I BEING TOO HASTY? I SHOULD ASK AGAIN AFTER WE START TO UNWIND.
...

Spoof on Titan: **hounori** **Based on *Attack on Titan* by Hajime Isayama**

This illustration was to commemorate 2,000,000 downloads of the Manga Box app. It originally appeared in color, but here it is in black and white.

FREE PAGE: EREN

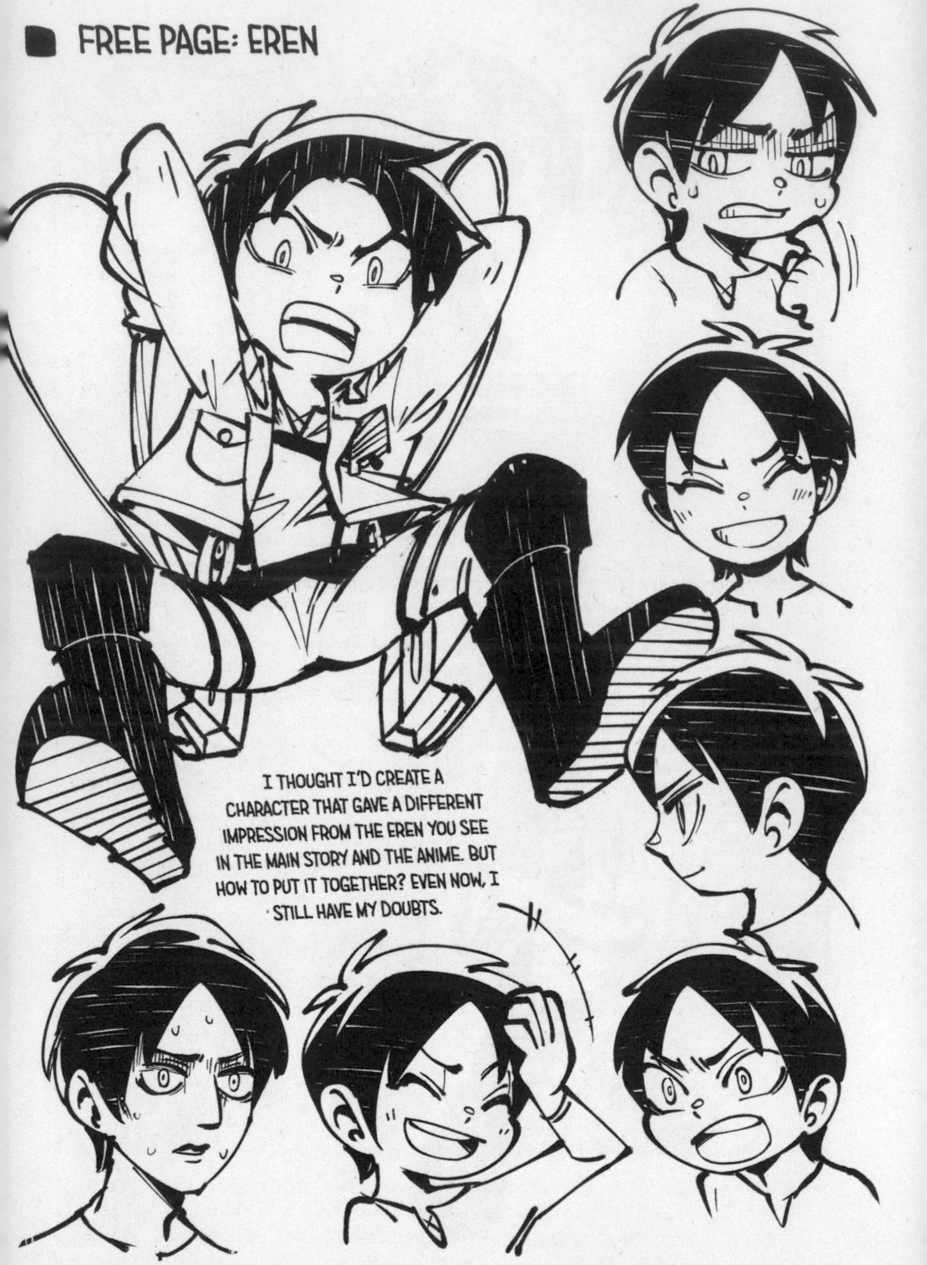

I THOUGHT I'D CREATE A CHARACTER THAT GAVE A DIFFERENT IMPRESSION FROM THE EREN YOU SEE IN THE MAIN STORY AND THE ANIME. BUT HOW TO PUT IT TOGETHER? EVEN NOW, I STILL HAVE MY DOUBTS.

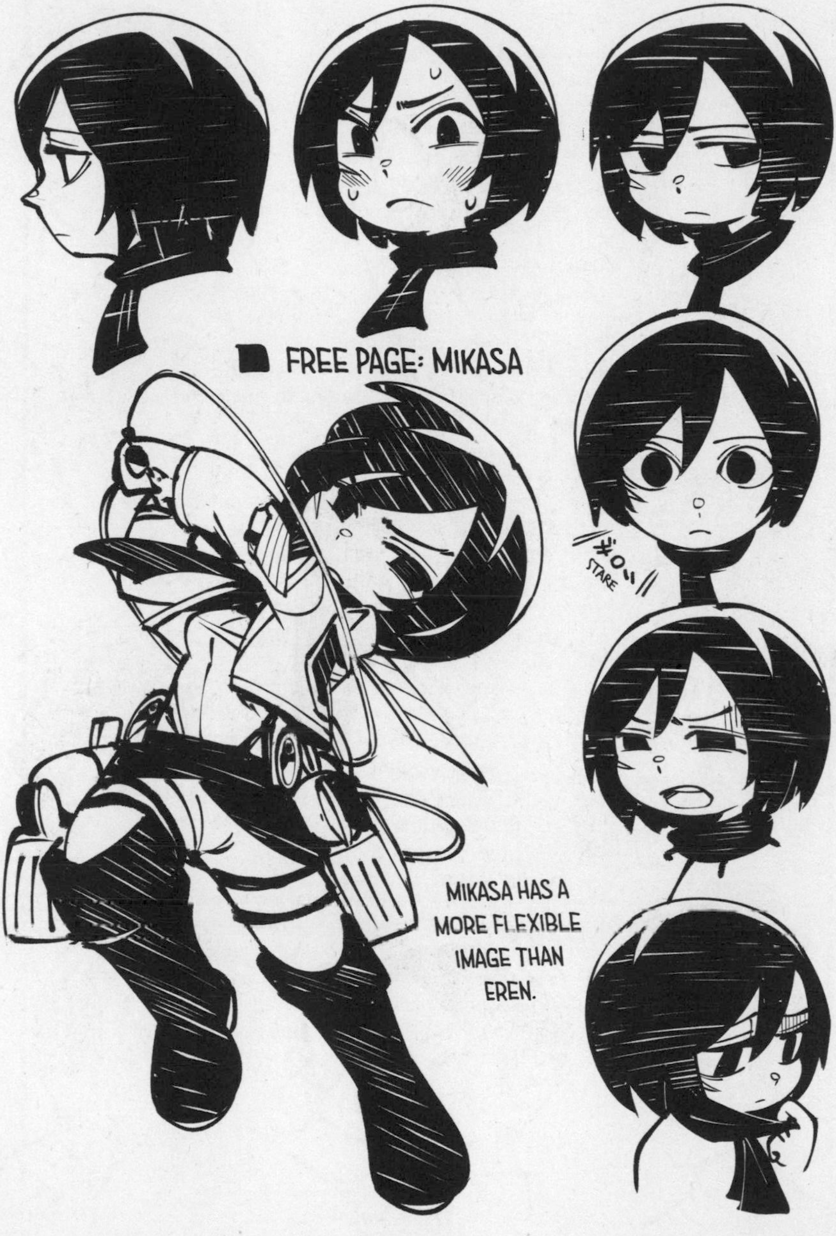
FREE PAGE: MIKASA
STARE
MIKASA HAS A MORE FLEXIBLE IMAGE THAN EREN.

TRANSLATION NOTES

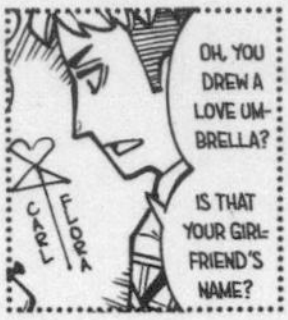
OH, YOU DREW A LOVE UM-BRELLA?
IS THAT YOUR GIRL-FRIEND'S NAME?

Love Umbrellas, page 33

In Japanese, the phrase *ai ai gasa* can mean either "sharing an umbrella" or "lovey-dovey umbrella," and the image of two people sharing an umbrella is a common trope in romantic stories. The custom of writing your name and your crush's name under an umbrella is common in Japan, like writing initials in a heart in the U.S.

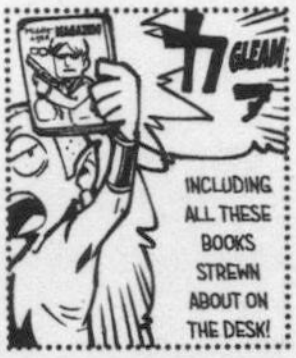
GLEAM
INCLUDING ALL THESE BOOKS STREWN ABOUT ON THE DESK!

***Middle-aged Magazine*, page 39**

The magazine the original *Attack on Titan* and spinoff manga *Attack on Titan: Lost Girls* run in is called *Bessatsu Shōnen Magazine*, with the *shōnen* referring to young men (it is also referenced on page 79). Here, the author titled the magazine *Chūnen Magazine*, with *chūnen* referring to middle-aged men.

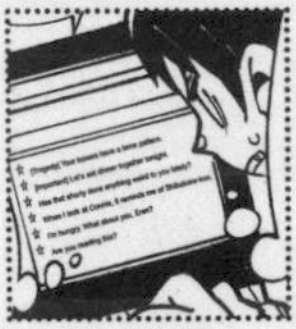

Shibakare-kun, page 78

It's unclear if there is a specific "Shibakare-kun" Mikasa is referencing here. One possibility is that she's alluding to *shibakiri* (lawn mowing) – in that Connie's head reminds her of freshly cut grass. Another possibility is *shibaku*, or "someone who is (often) scolded."

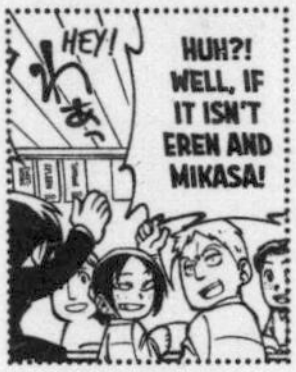
HUH?! WELL, IF IT ISN'T EREN AND MIKASA!
HEY!

Going out with the gang, page 80

In Japan, colleagues will often go out for food and a beer after work, to strengthen bonds and build camaraderie. It seems the favorite haunt of the Survey Corporation crew is either a *yakiniku* (grilled meat) restaurant or *izakaya* (Japanese-style pub) that serves *horumon-yaki*, or grilled intestines and other often-discarded parts of beef or pork.

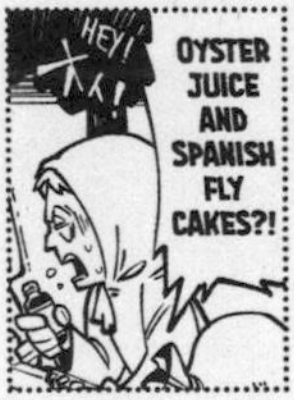
OYSTER JUICE AND SPANISH FLY CAKES?!
HEY!

Oyster juice and Spanish fly cakes, page 86

While these two are well-known aphrodisiacs in the Western world, the items Hitch originally picked up were *Aka-mamushipai* (an alcoholic drink with a red viper inside) and *suppon-dorinku* (a drink for vitality made with turtle extract), which are both supposed to have, ahem, invigorating effects on men when consumed. Oh, Hitch.

Spoof on Titan volume 1 is a work of fiction. Names, characters, places, and incidents are the products of the author's imagination or are used fictitiously. Any resemblance to actual events, locales, or persons, living or dead, is entirely coincidental.

A Kodansha Comics Trade Paperback Original

Published in the United States by Kodansha Comics, an imprint of Kodansha USA Publishing, LLC, New York.

Publication rights for this English edition arranged through Kodansha Ltd, Tokyo.

First published in Japan in 2014 by Kodansha Ltd., Tokyo as *Sungeki no kyojin*, volume 1.

ISBN 978-1-63236-408-1

Printed in the United States of America.

www.kodanshacomics.com

9 8 7 6 5 4 3 2 1
Translation: Steven LeCroy
Lettering: Sara Linsley
Editing: Tania Fukuda/Lauren Scanlan
Kodansha Comics edition cover design by Phil Balsman

STOP!

You are going the *wrong way!*

Manga is a *completely* different type of reading experience.

To start at the *BEGINNING,* go to the *END!*

That's right! Authentic manga is read the traditional Japanese way-from right to left, exactly the opposite of how American books are read. It's easy to follow: just go to the other end of the book, and read each page-and each panel-from the right side to the left side, starting at the top right. Now you're experiencing manga as it was meant to be.